THE LIVE CLASSROOM

AN ESALEN BOOK

THE LIVE CLASSROOM

*Innovation through
Confluent Education
and Gestalt*

Edited by GEORGE ISAAC BROWN
with Thomas Yeomans and Liles Grizzard

The Viking Press New York

An Esalen Book
First published in 1975 by The Viking Press, Inc.
625 Madison Avenue, New York, N.Y. 10022
Published simultaneously in Canada by
The Macmillan Company of Canada Limited

LIBRARY OF CONGRESS CATALOGING IN PUBLICATION DATA
Brown, George Isaac.
  The live classroom.

  (An Esalen book)
  Bibliography: p.
    1. Educational psychology.   2. Gestalt psychology.
  I. Yeomans, Thomas, 1940–   joint author.
  II. Grizzard, Liles, joint author.   III. Title.
  LB1051.B68   370.15   74-5806
  ISBN 0-670-43439-6

Printed in U.S.A.

ACKNOWLEDGMENTS
National Council of Teachers of English: "Beetlewolf" by John Duffin.
Copyright © 1972 by the National Council of Teachers of English.
Reprinted by permission of the publisher.
Random House, Inc.: From *Future Shock* by Alvin Toffler. Copyright
© 1970 by Alvin Toffler. Reprinted by permission.

*Dedicated to the Ford Foundation,
and especially to Mario Fantini
and Ed Meade, Jr., who helped make
all this possible.*

PREFACE

This book is directed toward bringing more life and better learning into classrooms through confluent education, which, in simple terms, means putting feeling and thinking together in the learning process. In it we place a heavy stress on the contributions that Gestalt therapy, transmuted into an educational context, can make to education. As you read you will notice how principles of Gestalt can be applied to teaching and learning and how valuable these contributions can be.

Our book is a gestalt. Gestalt means a whole, a functional unit. The book contains theory illustrated by practice, and practice underlined by theory or explanation. In a sense, just as in confluent education, we are weaving emotional and intellectual components together.

This book is not for all teachers, all parents, or all readers. Some may find the practices described here offensive, ridiculous, or threatening. Others will find them exciting, practical, and stimulating. A prerequisite to using this book as a teacher, a parent, or interested reader, is that the user be somewhat "up front," at least with himself and, it is hoped, with some others, in terms of his own feelings and values. Of course, it is not a prerequisite that one do this in order to be considered a good teacher. There are many good teachers who consider their private thoughts and feelings sacrosanct and they are absolutely entitled to their privacy. The confluent teacher, however, tends to be more sharing of himself. (I doubt if anyone shares himself completely. I am speaking of relative willingness to share.)

We have often been asked how many teachers we believe are, or could be, confluent teachers. We have no way of verifying this, but we would say as a rule of thumb that about twenty-five per cent of teachers are already intuitively teaching confluent education, approximating the methods described herein. We would say another fifty per cent are capable of learning these approaches, their degree of acceptance and capacity to learn varying from high to low. The remaining teachers will assuredly continue to teach in ways or styles to which they have become accustomed.

The implications of this variance calls for a pluralistic approach to education. One of the great stranglers of change and growth in American education has been the emphasis on consensus. This emphasis on consensus is an illusion never realized. Consensus is touted as establishment window dressing, but significant actual variance remains. Feelings of frustration and guilt and resentment permeate the educational establishment because this implicit demand for consensus cannot be met by many teachers. It would be equally as wrong to impose — if such were at all possible — a consensus of confluent education for all. A practical solution is the pluralistic one. School districts should allow opportunities for teachers, students, and parents of students who want particular approaches to learning. Give them the opportunity and the freedom and the responsibility to demonstrate that what they do makes good educational sense.

Confluent education is not a panacea. It does, however, provide nourishment for those who struggle to make their teaching more authentic, who know perhaps intuitively what they want to do, or who are dissatisfied with the way things are.

The authors of these articles are nearly all experienced teachers. They write from a context of reality. We hope you find your browsing of this book to be a rewarding experience. We intentionally use the word "browse" because although our book is a mosaic, it should be digested slowly. We had our own gestalt in putting it together. We hope you will create your own gestalt as you read it.

GEORGE ISAAC BROWN

University of California,
Santa Barbara

CONTENTS

THE LIVE CLASSROOM

INTRODUCTION

— George Isaac Brown

Are all classrooms dead?

No, not all. But too damned many are. And, if nothing else, this is a pervasive, stupid waste of our most important resource — our children.

We point no fingers of accusation. Instead, we believe that through this book we extend a helping hand. With those who already have live classrooms we share our ideas and experiences to reinforce the excitement and challenge of such a learning environment. For those who are dissatisfied with education — as teachers, parents, or interested parties — we hope to provide stimulation, concepts, and practical suggestions, which individual teachers can use to modify their own teaching strategies, and which schools and school districts can uniquely utilize as guidelines for their own innovations. To those who are turned off to life, who have psychically deadened themselves as professionals or as private persons, we can only say that despite all life's frustrations you are missing a good and grand experience.

What is the difference between a dead and a live classroom? The real way to tell is to experience both of them. In the dead classroom learning is mechanistic, routine, over-ritualized, dull, and boring. The teacher is robotized, and the children are conceived of as containers or receptacles whose primary function is to receive and hold subject matter. This is essentially the consequence of the misuse of an industrial model. The efficiency of the process, when there is such concern, is usually also based on technological or business constructs.

The live classroom, on the other hand, is full of learning activities in which students are enthusiastically and authentically involved. Students take on as much responsibility for their learning as their capabilities allow. Each student is genuinely respected and treated as a human being by his teacher. He, in turn, participates in the learning-teaching process as one who structures strategies for learning, as individualized as possible, while focusing on process as well as subject matter. Therefore, he is always ready to modify a teaching strategy as a consequence of his intelligent continuing appraisal of what emerges in terms of need and opportunity in his classroom. It is not just fun here. There is frustration in the live classroom, but at a level which is perceived by the learner as a challenge rather than as an overwhelming obstacle.

In the live classroom, the learning involves living. In the dead classroom, the learning turns destructively on itself and on the learner. To survive this, the student must numb himself, his real self, for he is caught between the pressures of socialization and the grim irrelevance and inertia of his lessons. He may drop out. At best, he plays the learning game wherein he creates a role or subpersonality called "me as student" that has little or no relation to the rest of himself.

A following article on awareness training and creativity based on Gestalt therapy provides a beginning description of some of the principles of Gestalt and how these relate to the creative process, which is connected to living a fuller and more alive existence. One of the problems we all have is how to break set from the "programs" which we have adapted and adopted for our existence. This is not to negate programs per se. What is more important is whether we are using the programs or we are being used by them. Have we given up responsibility for making choices in our lives? Have we become overwhelmed by the need for conformity and security to the extent that, though they may be ostensibly warm and comforting, we use these thick blankets to smother our sparks of life? Or, instead, do we have these blankets available for those times when we want them, out of some temporary need to be warm, while at other times we are able to run free and naked through the forest?

So this all seems to boil down to whether we want to be biophiles or necrophiles, favoring life or death. And it is no simple decision. Psychic death can be very attractive. Imagine having to make no decisions or choices and taking no responsibility for what you do or for what happens to you. Life means responsibility, along with excitement and change. There will be more about this is in some of the articles that follow.

Here, of course, we are talking about a continuum and the extremes of this continuum. It is our hope that confluent education, as a concept and a methodology, can become more available for those who want to move education in the direction of life.

Simply stated, confluent education means combining thinking with feelings so that both benefit. Thinking is sometimes called the cognitive domain. Feelings and emotion fall in the affective domain. Confluent education seeks to integrate these two domains so they emerge to the extent that they both lose their boundaries and result in more holistic or "together" behavior on the part of the student. Instead of having emotions clash or conflict with intellectual activity, we try to have both work in a harmonious relationship for the ultimate welfare and productivity of the learner. One of the major thrusts of this book will be to elaborate the meaning and process of confluent education.

Essentially we are attempting, through the development of confluent approaches to education, to pour back some juice into dehydrated educational practices. As a result, the dried-up prunes of classroom process become plums of learning — plump, sweet, and nourishing. We want to help change those schools in which teachers and students are bored with routine and ritual into exciting, challenging places where content and learning come alive, generating the curiosity and excitement we all once had as young children discovering a world full of wonder and marvels. The world can still be a wondrous place, even though some of us may not now be seeing it as such.

The live classroom could be considered one or two steps beyond the open classroom. The first difference in emphasis between the two approaches is that confluent education requires an open teacher for the open classroom. Structure alone will not necessarily accomplish the goals of the open classroom. If you have an open classroom with a closed teacher, you might as well have a closed classroom. Witness the copious research indicating that class size seems to make no difference in students' learning achievement. Usually the factor responsible for this is that the teachers involved teach a class of fifteen the same way they teach a class of thirty-five. This is like the truck driver who becomes so accustomed to driving fully loaded trucks at forty miles an hour because of the limitation the load puts on his engine's power that he continues to drive at forty whether his truck is loaded or not. It is so easy to be trapped within patterns of the status quo. This book is concerned with breaking a set of conventional wisdom about learning and teaching without sacrificing the stated goals of an educational system serving a democracy.

We are even beginning to change the structures of our schools as well as our classrooms. Witness the growth in the "Alternative School" concept. Increasingly, in schools all over the country, programs are being developed to fit the particular needs of students, in the form of elective course systems and in the form of complete schools within a school, which are devoted to a particular concern, orientation, or discipline. These alternative schools have greatly increased the vitality of educational experience and they give hope for more pluralistic approaches to education.

Confluent education provides substance for both the open classroom and the alternative-school structure. It could be thought of as new meat for those new bones.

It is time for a renaissance in education, with change coming not from gimmicks, panaceas, and naïve enthusiasms, but from careful study and examined practice. We cannot expect utopias but we can use utopian models to provide direction. We can do research into questions that may not be neatly and precisely manageable, and in so doing, perfect our instruments for measuring and determining the utility of our research design. To be careful does not mean staying on the conventional carousels of research. How long have we known that emotions have much to do with learning? Look at the research literature in educational psychology and see how proportionally little energy has been spent exploring this problem. Yet, what problem is more basic? Fortunately, certain undaunted workers are beginning such investigations, and certain courageous teachers and administrators are examining and modifying their curricula and teaching strategies with this problem in mind.

The Jencks report, *Inequality: A Reassessment of the Effect of*

Family and Schooling in America,[1] has stimulated considerable controversy over whether schools make any difference in terms of the students' eventual economic or social quality. The criticism of the report up to this point has been directed largely at statistical issues and the research methods used by Jencks and his colleagues, or at the authors' value biases. Most of the professional response to the report reflects little attention given to the question of the effectiveness of schools.

Why Jencks' finding of the ineffectiveness of schools should come as a surprise is in itself surprising. Anyone who has been around schools knows how wretchedly ineffective they can be. For example, it is a kind of in-joke among graduate faculty that the best way to create an excellent graduate program is to accept only excellent students. This does not mean that schools *have to be* ineffective. We might look at what is commonly left out of the educational process as a possible highly significant factor in creating more effective education. One such factor is the intelligent use of feeling or emotional components in learning. That's what this book is about.

Perhaps I can provide illustrations of what I mean about the place of emotions in education from some early personal history.

I suppose everyone has at least one tale to tell about certain teachers he has had in school. I want to tell of three of my teachers — two elementary and one high-school — because what happened between them and me is central to this book.

First, my fifth-grade teacher, Miss Gwendolyn Voight, was a snappy, gray-haired little terrier of a woman who I suspect had dedicated her life and virtue to her teaching. During the first day or two of school, we had some kind of achievement test. About three weeks later, after the flag salute and other nondiscursive morning rituals, Miss Voight in her clear, no-nonsense, high voice announced, "Well, children, I have corrected the tests we had at the beginning of the year and Georgie Brown got the highest score." My classmates clapped. Somewhat embarrassed, I shyly beamed. Miss Voight quickly interrupted, "No, children, you mustn't applaud, for we all know Georgie is lazy."

How true. How true. And I became even lazier. My parents told me I was lazy. Nearly all my teachers reiterated that message. Who was I to question these authorities? In my small-town high school I never took home a book, except for biology. When I graduated sixtieth in a class of seventy-two, I was still able to enter the state university, for in the early 1940s this was possible. I majored in chemical engineering for the simple reason that my father had been a chemical engineer, and I had sense enough to hover around a C average. After two years of this, World War II exploded. I enlisted in the infantry and soon found myself in combat, where I swiftly ceased to be lazy. When peace came, I returned to the university, changed my major to English, which at the time was what I really wanted, and with a new concept of myself as not necessarily lazy, had little difficulty achieving good grades and, in fact, began to enjoy scholarly pursuits.

The incident with Miss Voight highlights one dimension of confluent education. This has to do with certain preconditions to a learning experience. These are called concerns and blockages. We are indebted to the work of Mario Fantini and Gerald Weinstein for having defined certain fundamental human concerns for identity, connectedness, and potency or power. Blockages to learning include inadequate self-concepts. How we perceive ourselves, how we feel about ourselves — influenced so tremendously as children by the messages, silent as well as spoken, we received from the adults in our lives — firmly fixes us into the collective programs of our existence.

These factors of concerns and blockages are threaded together in a convoluted way in this first illustration. My concern for identity (who am I?) was related to my concept of myself as being lazy, and I certainly recall feeling different from others because I was the lazy one — everyone else did his work. This, in turn, interfered to some extent with my sense of connectedness with my classmates and with the community as represented by my teachers and parents, and with the world as they represented it. As for feelings of potency or power, I didn't have many because I was lacking in motivation and drive — or at least that was the message I was receiving from others.

This fabric certainly interfered with my formal learning and it was not until the reality of combat thrust new self-perceptions upon me, stimulated by an obvious need to survive, that I could find a new concept for myself.

A confluently oriented teacher is sensitive to his students' concerns, uniquely evident in each student's action and behavior. Such a teacher is also concerned with what may be interfering with a normal desire to learn and a healthy curiosity about the universe. The teacher wants to know what may be inhibiting these processes.

My sixth-grade teacher, Mrs. Hortense Rauch, was an overly large woman with a violin. At times she played for us, sans vibrato. I am sure we all must have been ambivalent as to whether it was worth getting out of classwork to have to listen. Mrs. Rauch was committed to the Finer Things in Life, always pronounced as if in capital letters. The finer things in life included specimens of music, art, literature, Greece and Rome, and other elements which had as their source what approximated, in an elementary way, the liberal arts. Somehow she fastened on me as her one shining hope among the rag, tag, and bob-tail crew of barbarians who made up her class. I'm not sure how this came about. I have been told I had a deep and soulful look in my brown eyes during that period of my life. I do remember a class assignment in writing musical notation in which I randomly placed notes on a five-line staff. She played mine. It sounded awful to me, but she went into raptures about my genius — all this in front of the class. From then on my classmates made my last year at the Bank Street Elementary School a disaster.

The illustration concerning Mrs. Rauch's emphasis on a liberal arts orientation has to do with the fundamental goal of confluent education as we see it. This involves having available one's intellectual processes so that these may be used both to survive and to enhance one's self in a real world. Her stress on a liberal arts context for intellectual endeavor precipitates an examination of the hallowed halls of liberal arts. Colleges of liberal arts within institutions of higher education have goals often stated in terms of participating in the richness of life. The experience at the institution is to prepare one to continue this liberating and intellectually ameliorative pursuit. The College of Letters and Science in my own institution, the University of California at Santa Barbara, defines the educated person as "one who is able to fulfill his potentialities and deal effectively with his environment." Of available statements in college bulletins, this seems to me more grounded in common sense and reality than most.

The problem, however, is that the methodology and implicit sets of values of institutions of higher education in general, which underlie the accomplishment of these goals, are to a large degree not realistically related to these goals. Much confidence is placed on rational processes. Great faith is placed in objectivity and critical processes of the mind. Emotions are considered as an interference with a process that the institutions define as "scholarly rigor." There is some small room for aesthetic appreciation. The implication remains, however, that emotions must usually be tempered with Apollonian judgment.

There is an unfortunate confusion here between those emotions which interfere with reality-connected intellectual processes and those which are an essential part of these processes. This confusion has lead to great waste, inefficiency, and ineffectiveness at many formal educational institutions. Facts such as these exist: college graduates tend not to read many books; it's not the A students who are the creative producers of the world, but rather those with B's and under.

Here are two conspicuous examples of the way emotions contribute to intellectual processes and productive activity. The first example is the creative process itself, which relies not only on hard work in many cases, but also relies on an essentially intuitive process in all cases. Intuition is a subtle thing and, in contrast to rational thinking, is strongly rooted in emotions. The second example is how emotional components motivate and sustain the pursuit of knowledge and truth. Although sometimes subtle, there is always present the passion of the scholar, the passion of the inventor, the passion of the explorer. All who move into the unknown in order to make it known have a passion, whether this be to grow, or to make, or even to become. Whatever the roots or manifestations of this passion, there it is.

Returning to Mrs. Rauch. An appreciation of the finer things in life is rooted in the act of appreciating, which has obvious emotional components. Very seldom in formal educational processes is attention paid to these emotional components. In fact, they are denied, repressed, or distorted, and sometimes even treated as a kind of disease to be stamped out or to be inoculated against. Appreciation is taught as a rational process. In essence this is almost like providing a manual or cookbook of appreciation, to be followed without deviation.

One other point that Mrs. Rauch missed was that I was not special in terms of the finer things in life. These should be made available to all people. I am sure that not only were my classmates turned off to me as teacher's pet, but they were also turned off to the very things that Mrs. Rauch was trying to teach them. Part of the problem is that educators tend to respond to small groups who usually, because of family background, already fit into the "elite" who are born to appreciate these finer things. The failure of American education to communicate the finer things to the mass of its citizens is clearly demonstrated by the television programming preferences of the populace. These people were in school at one time or another, but the schools left them with a very limited potential for appreciation of great literature, great art, and great scholarship. And if, as you read this, you too are saying to yourself, "Oh, yes, but . . ." — don't kid yourself. Every human being manifests only a very small percentage of his potential — perhaps five to ten per cent — geniuses, perhaps fifteen to twenty-five per cent. We all have our moments — perhaps a moment of crisis or emergency, perhaps a special moment in time — when we surprise ourselves with our strength and insight and capacity to appreciate. We may even experience once or twice in our lives a sense of exaltation from a spiritual or mystical experience that deeply touches or moves us. Western civilization is slowly coming around to an awareness of the ecstatic experience as being something in addition to sexual orgasm.

I often wonder if we perceive only what we can conceive. Generally, I believe this is so; however, we apparently have moments when, below the conscious level, processes somehow emerge to startle us with intensity, vision, and overwhelming wonder. These may occur only seldom in a person's lifetime, and at such times we may be so overwhelmed that we run away from these experiences, only now and then allowing ourselves a wistful recollection of each incident. Then reluctantly, being "practical" people, we turn back to our humdrum existence. It is as if each of us contains within him an immense ocean of affect and yet, most of the time, conceive there only a mud puddle.

Donald Brewster was the only science teacher in my high school. He taught physics and chemistry. In my junior year the state education department had decreed that biology should also be taught. To make this tale a short one, Paul Cattabriga, my best friend, and I became involved in helping Mr. Brewster, who knew nothing about biology and had to learn it along with us. Biology became a living experience. We related it to ourselves and to all the teeming life around us. We planned field trips with Mr. Brewster, set up exhibits, helped in class, cleaned up, arranged the stock room, did all kinds of "neat" things. I lived and learned so much biology that later in college, even as an engineering student, I was able to help some of my friends with their college-level biology.

This last illustration concerning my biology teacher shows what can happen in learning when the student is personally involved. Biology at that point seemed directly related to my existence. At least I obtained great personal satisfaction from my involvement in learning about biology and how it was directly connected with my life, my living processes, and all living things in my world. I not only thought biology, I felt it as well, for I experienced it as a total living human being directly connected to a living universe. And, most important, I had much responsibility for my own learning.

Much has happened since the publication of our first work on confluent education entitled *Human Teaching for Human Learning: An Introduction to Confluent Education.* That book was a report of the work done with a grant of $25,000 from the Ford Foundation. As a partial consequence of this initial work we were able to develop an academic program on the graduate level at the University of California, Santa Barbara, providing both master's and Ph.D. degrees in confluent education. This program was later assisted by another grant from the Ford Foundation, this time for a three-year period. The purpose of the second grant was both to strengthen the academic program in confluent education through developing a critical mass of faculty and students, and to provide funds for further research and development in confluent education. As a consequence of the latter objective, DRICE (Development and Research in Confluent Education), a center toward achieving this end, was established and a number of projects were initiated.

These projects included research in teacher training, the development of a reading curriculum, an early-childhood social-studies curriculum, secondary-school curriculum in English, social studies, and related areas, and work at the community-college level in the teaching of English. One of the unique features of all these projects is that the teachers who participated were encouraged to move more and more into roles of leadership and decision-making, so that by the end of the project the teachers were truly taking responsibility for their own projects. Many of the articles contained in this book resulted from the activities of DRICE.

In addition to the work at the University of California, Santa Barbara, there has been increasing national and international interest in confluent education. Besides many schools and study groups throughout the United States, there is a large project in the province of Manitoba, Canada, and a school built around concepts and practices of confluent education has been established in Mexico City. An increasing variety of applications in confluent education have emerged. These, too, seem to have extraordinary range. Examples extend from the combining of groups of adolescents with groups of old people as mutual support systems under the leadership of Muriel Shapiro, to the department of pathology at the School of Medicine, University of Rotterdam, where, through the initiative of Dr. Marco DeVries, attempts are being made to design an international course in pathology, using confluent approaches — the thrust being to focus on health rather than sickness, and life rather than death.

For those who demand a more rigorous and systematic development of theory and practice for confluent education, this book is but a second step toward that end. *Human Teaching for Human Learning* was described as an introduction to confluent education and, although it is still a most worthwhile document in our own eyes and one in which we maintain some pride, we are more aware now than at the time of its writing that our formulations were simplistic. In essence, we saw confluent education as the integration of the affective-domain (emotions, attitudes, values) with the cognitive-domain (intellectual functioning). This remains as the core of our work. We have, however, become somewhat more sophisticated in describing the nature of this integration, its components, and the various matrices contained within the ostensibly simple formulation.

We present in the first and second parts of this book a mosaic for the use of the reader. A complete and all-encompassing theory remains to be developed. I doubt if this ever will come to pass, because in confluent education we are dealing with what is essential to education per se, an enormous complexity. All education, whether we like it or not, whether we admit it or not, has, as part of its process, thinking (cognitive) and feeling (affective) components. These components interact, influencing one another, and although one or the other may be ignored consciously by the teacher and spitefully or pathologically by the student, or consciously by the student and spitefully or pathologically by the teacher, they exist and cannot be denied. They will not be denied, even though this may mean tearing down the thick brick walls of intellectual rationality we in education have so carefully constructed around ourselves and our students. Actually, our walls have brick so porous and so full of holes, in spite of our careful construction, that though the walls hold us in they cannot keep feelings and emotions out or in, so deviously do these affective elements filter through. The necessity for filtration, however, does destroy spontaneity and often authenticity.

We have said it a thousand times, and will probably say it a thousand times more: Instead of trying to deny or distort the existence of our emotions let us make good use of them in learning and teaching.

For those impatient for a more sophisticated theoretical treatment of confluent education, we recommend two doctoral dissertations: "Toward a Confluent Theory of the Teaching of English" by Thomas Yeomans, and "Confluent Education: A Descriptive Analysis of the Concepts and Elements, Goals and Objectives, Basic Philosophy and the Relationships Between Them" by Aaron Hillman, both of the University of California, Santa Barbara.

And for those interested in empirical research, we can provide a monograph, *Confluent Education: Attitudinal and Behavioral Consequences of Confluent Teacher Training* by John M. Shiflett and George I. Brown.[2] This monograph also contains a description of a year-long experiment with a confluent teacher-training procedure based primarily on Gestalt. (A variety of other research is in process.)

We have included in the first part of this book some articles explaining Gestalt therapy, or Gestalt Awareness Training as we tend to call it, and how these principles and practices are used directly in various ways. The purpose is to give the reader a general introduction to Gestalt, one of the theories and methodologies we have found to be of major use when transmuted in the context of confluent education.

Gestalt therapy is a relatively new theory. It is existentially based; i.e., the focus is on what is happening *now* with the client or patient rather than on analyzing or interpreting an individual's history. As a therapy it has had rapid growth and increasing influence in the psychiatric establishment. For those who are not familiar with this growth, the following is presented not as propaganda but as illustrative information only.

For example, in the eight years I have been doing Gestalt Awareness Training, leading approximately twenty workshops or seminars a year, I have had at least one psychiatrist, and sometimes as many as five, in a workshop. Thus I could say I am responsible for introducing over one hundred psychiatrists to this approach. There are many other workshop leaders who I am sure have had a similar record.

The popularity of Fritz Perls' books, which sold in the thousands when originally published by Real People Press, have been widely expanded through their publication by Bantam Books. An extensive literature is now available. There are now Gestalt training institutes in many cities, including Los Angeles, San Francisco, Chicago, Cleveland, and New York.

Aside from its potential as a therapeutic theory, I believe Gestalt has even greater implications for educational practice, and I think many parts of this book will be illustrative of this point.

The second part of the book presents an elaboration of confluent education. Carrying on from *Human Teaching for Human Learning*, here may be found a more sophisticated and extensive development of the theory of confluent education and the educational process of confluence, which, though related, are two somewhat different operations.

The third and fourth parts are the meat and potatoes of this book and are directed toward practices that illustrate how Gestalt as part of confluent education, and confluent education in toto, are actually used in various educational settings. These range from kindergarten through high school and cover a variety of subject matter including science, social studies, mathematics, English, art, physical education, and foreign language teaching. These articles, lessons, units, and course plans are written by teachers in the field. In other words, they have all been field-tested and are not just what someone thinks could be done. Which does not imply that everyone else should carry them out exactly as described, or even duplicate them roughly. In fact, we shudder at the thought. The third part includes descriptions of practices of confluent education ranging from the first grade through high school. The articles cover a variety of situations and problems in curriculum areas. The last part is concerned exclusively with the teaching of English, beginning with the teaching of reading in the early grades on up through more formal concerns such as *Beowulf* and *The Canterbury Tales*, and ends with a total course for the teaching of drama.

The articles in Part III are provided primarily as examples of how confluent education can be used in a variety of situations. They are only models. The lessons, units, and course outlines in Part IV are presented also as models. We earnestly hope that teachers who read these and want to use them will modify and adapt them to their own teaching style and their own unique classroom context. We *urge* all teachers not to use them as cookbooks or manuals, but rather as models to be adapted to their own separate educational realities.

This book can be read in the sequence in which it is presented, or it can be browsed or used as a sourcebook. However the reader may use it, we hope that he will find it both provocative and nourishing. Confluent education is plain good common sense. The authors' collective wish is that this book demonstrate that fact.

REFERENCE NOTES /

1. Christopher Jencks *et al.*, *Inequality: A Reassessment of the Effect of Family and Schooling in America* (New York: Basic Books, 1972).
2. John M. Shiflett and George I. Brown, *Confluent Education: Attitudinal and Behavioral Consequences of Confluent Teacher Training* University Center Monograph Series (University Center, Mich.: Saginaw Valley State College, 1972).

ONE

Gestalt: Theory with Practice

We begin the book with a section on Gestalt theory and some of its applications to the field of education. Gestalt is central to work in confluent education, and though at first it may strike the reader as strange that we are combining therapeutic practice with pedagogy, a second look will reveal that in fact the two are closely related, though educators (and therapists, for that matter) seldom make the connection explicit.

Children in classrooms are growing — physically, emotionally, intellectually, spiritually — as they would anywhere else. Traditionally, teachers have focused primarily on intellectual growth, and have left the other kinds of growth to the playground, corridors, neighborhoods, and homes, and, in some cases, to counselors, ministers, psychologists, and psychiatrists. Recently, however, some educators have begun to point out the need for attention to emotional growth within the context of the classroom, and so, naturally, have turned to the various therapeutic practices available to examine their usefulness, specifically, for this pedagogic purpose. The writers in this section have done just that with Gestalt theory and practice. Each, basically, is asking, how emotional growth can best be related to cognitive process so that both are enhanced and their confluence facilitated in learners.

The first article, "Gestalt and the Transformation," by Geri Metz, is an enthusiastic appeal for the use of Gestalt in education to foster the process of transformation which George Leonard in his book The Transformation suggests Western civilization is experiencing. Although perhaps a bit proselytizing in tone, the article does present a strong argument for the use of Gestalt in schools in response to the special conditions described by Leonard.

The second article, by George Isaac Brown, on awareness training and creativity based on Gestalt therapy, provides a beginning description of some of the principles of Gestalt and how these relate to the creative process, which, in turn, is connected to a fuller and more alive existence.

The third article presents a more extensive theoretical introduction to Gestalt therapy by Dr. James Simkin, who worked closely with Frederick Perls, the founder of Gestalt therapy, throughout Dr. Perls' life and was perhaps as responsible as anyone in this country for introducing Dr. Perls and his theories into the American scene.

David McCarthy and Bert Pearlman present articles that relate Gestalt to explanations of learning. McCarthy compares objectivity and subjectivity; Pearlman posits a fascinating critique of conventional educational theory which uses scientific premises for its model construction.

In the sixth article Liles Grizzard describes the use of a videotape recorder for working by oneself on Gestalt awareness techniques. This is followed by two articles directly relating the use of Gestalt to teaching. "Gestalt and the First-Year Teacher," by Melinda Rogers, describes how she used some of her training in Gestalt in that difficult first year of teaching. Victoria Grizzard relates how the principles of Gestalt can be used in the classroom, this time by the substitute teacher, the oft-forgotten, nonperson to whom little attention is paid within the educational scene.

In the ninth article Tom Yeomans presents a highly stimulating description of fresh new approaches to the teaching of literature which do not detract from the conventional content of literature courses.

The last article, entitled "Beyond Gestalt Therapy," again by George Isaac Brown, expands concepts of Gestalt to those analogous to Martin Buber's formulation of the I-thou concept.

The articles are selected both to give the reader a working understanding of Gestalt and to provide the reader with a sense of some of the underpinnings on which confluent education rests.

1

GESTALT AND THE TRANSFORMATION
— Geri Metz

George Leonard speaks in *The Transformation* [1] of the gift we give our children, the NDD: neurosis, disease, discontent. Many members of the medical profession acknowledge that up to ninety per cent of all their patients' complaints stem from psychological causes and are not biologically induced. Leonard also cites the work of biologist René Dubos showing that the presence of germs is not the only cause of illness: ". . . the microorganisms of our most common diseases are with us always and . . . they cause obvious harm only when the conditions of living create some sort of stress." [2]

The mental illness in civilized societies is so generalized and widespread that it goes unnoticed in all but its most extreme manifestations. The allergies, the headaches, the "common" colds, the acid indigestions, the constipations, the bodies pulled out of shape by muscular tension — all these are considered "normal" and not serious. Somewhat more advanced symptoms such as ulcers, early heart attacks, moderate alcoholism, moderate drug abuse (and this definitely includes the tranquilized housewife and business executive) — these are unfortunate, but still within the acceptable. Further along is the occasional individual whose symptoms, perhaps very controlled for the most part, one day explode into an orgy of anger resulting in the murder of innocent victims; or the schizophrenic, withdrawn into his own world. And we don't even mention the general unhappiness and discontent etched into the faces of civilized man, or the suicide, the broken homes, the ceaseless drive for more, the lack of satisfaction.

The saddest part of this sad picture is that we accept most of it as the norm and that we allow our society to perpetuate the sickness.

Perls states that we educate to fit people into the society; but with the rapid changes that confront modern man, it becomes more diffi- cult, and he adds, "I consider that the basic personality in our time is a neurotic personality." [3] "Neurosis is growth disorder. The question shifts from the medical to the educational field." [4] If neurosis is in- deed a matter of poor education, then we educators must be con- cerned. The average citizen spends six to seven hours, five days a week, for nine months of the year during a period of ten to sixteen years in school. That represents a lot of time, a lot of influence. And while it is true that education is not therapy and teachers are not psychologists, it should be evident from the condition of our NDD society that we do need an educational process that is therapeutic and that is designed to lessen the NDD rather than to contribute to it.

I am proposing Gestalt therapy as a necessity for our age. Western man needs a new awareness of his wholeness, of his complex union of body, mind, and emotions. We are accustomed to thinking of ourselves as separate from our feelings, or as being unrelated to, and in control of, our emotions — as being divided beings. Gestalt therapy speaks to this split. If an epidemic of a disease such as typhoid broke out in our country and millions of our citizens were afflicted with it and dying from it, a massive educational effort would be launched in the schools to acquaint the public with the causes, symp- toms, and treatment of the illness. I submit that a disease of giant proportions is running virtually unchecked through our society, and that the teacher in school can have a broad influence on its detection, prevention, and possibly even its cure. This disease is the split be- tween thought and feeling within the personality.

And further, I feel that along with any diffusion of Gestalt therapy into the arena of public education must go a serious re-evaluation of existing systems, of existing values, of where we are and of where we are going. Any significant application of therapeutic principles to public education would seriously affect the current system and the minds and attitudes of the students touched. I think that those who opt for these principles should be sure they are prepared for the con- sequences. For example, one problem that strikes me immediately is the emphasis in the present system (societal, not just educational) on competition. A capitalistic society has competition, personal aggressiveness, pushing ahead, producing, at its center. The Gestalt therapist helps us accept ourselves as we are, as growing and changing, but not by comparison to others. The Gestalt "prayer" has become a cliché, which is unfortunate, because it contains profound truths:

> I am not in this world to live up to your expectations
> And you are not in this world to live up to mine.
> You are you, and I am I. . . .

This belief is inconsistent with education as we know it, where the student is very definitely directed to live up to someone else's expectations, and where his individuality is rarely accepted, much less encouraged. This Gestalt principle might upset the whole concept of grades, of competition, of academic standards. And if this principle does not cause enough trouble within the school family, add to it the pressure from parents who are eager to endow their children with their own NDD!

An application of Gestalt therapy principles would force us to question our personal values, our social values, and the goals that we set for education. A statement on goals from a confluent-education viewpoint is given by Tom Yeomans: Education "becomes a 'leading out' of an individual's capacities, talents, uniqueness, person, into his whole possibilities, and its aim becomes the balanced development of the personality toward intellectual, emotional, social and moral maturity." [5] With this as a goal, what changes might have to take place in teachers, in the curriculum, in the standards of a school system, in the parents' attitudes?

In terms of changing society, of encouraging "The Transformation," what should we teach? We are all a part of a past, of a heritage. Is it of value to us now? Does it make us more alive or does it deaden us and tend to keep us hung up on outmoded ways of thinking and perceiving? Does it tie us to old models and goals for ourselves and for our children that are passé and counterproductive to a society without NDD? I feel that these questions must be looked at, thought about, dealt with. Can we overlay Gestalt principles onto the old system, or do the two tend to cancel out each other? Our current system, based on progress and limited by what can be proved scientifically, has brought mankind perhaps to the brink of worldwide ecological and mental disaster. I cannot help feeling that to continue in that same direction, and to judge ourselves according to the traditional viewpoint of Western civilization is to remain part of another age, another concept, no longer applicable to present and future needs. If we are indeed heading toward "The Transformation" as George Leonard maintains, then we are in a state of transition, and all previous values must be questioned and re-evaluated in the light of new goals for a new age.

I believe that we are indeed in a period of transition, and that American society, while very conservative in many respects, is slipping almost imperceptibly into the dawning of a new consciousness. There are some signs of opening up into other expressions and other perceptions. A few examples will illustrate: Acupuncture has made news recently in popular publications and is being considered seriously by even ultraconservatives in the medical profession. A number of television programs on extrasensory or psychic perceptions have been broadcast of late. Encounter groups and other group-oriented activities are springing up rapidly. A class in Transcendental Meditation is planned for a local high school. Books on astrology and the occult traditions form a large part of the titles in book shops. In one recent week the television viewer could watch a special on LSD, featuring realistic simulations of "acid trips" and a discussion among psychiatrists of the importance of LSD in psychotherapy and research, and another program based on the claims made by Eric Von Daniken in his book, *Chariots of the Gods*, in which he offers very provocative evidence for the intervention of highly developed beings from other planets at various stages in the evolution of earth-man. The educator is now in a position to capitalize on the public exposure to these phenomena. If we can admit the possibility of the new and bizarre, we are in a better position to know ourselves and accept new concepts and ways of thinking and feeling that were strange and unacceptable to us previously.

And so we come back to the educator. We must begin by reaching the teachers with Gestalt therapy principles. My personal contact as a teacher with Gestalt experiential exercises has not only shown me their usefulness, but has helped me to become more aware and to realize much personal growth. The emphasis on noncompetition, on no right or wrong, combined with the development of personal responsibility, have helped me to allow myself more expression. I have become freer in artistic activities and in movement and sharing exercises. I am convinced that these affective techniques that put us in touch with our feelings and our creativity are vitally important to every teacher, and must be a part of every teacher's training: first for himself as a human being, and then as a means of helping his students grow and realize their full human potential.

At this point I feel that Gestalt therapy principles — openness, uniqueness, awareness, personal responsibility — are essential to human growth and to the realization of human potential, and it is through these that we can begin to confront the NDD's. And eventually we can help quicken the necessary transformation we are undergoing at the present time.

REFERENCE NOTES /

1. George Leonard, *The Transformation* (New York: Delacorte, 1972), p. 70.
2. Ibid., p. 93.
3. Frederick S. Perls, *Gestalt Therapy Verbatim* (Lafayette, Calif.: Real People Press, 1969), p. 32.
4. Ibid., p. 30.
5. See Chapter 14, below.

2

AWARENESS TRAINING AND CREATIVITY BASED ON GESTALT THERAPY

— George Isaac Brown

Gestalt therapy, to quote its founder, Frederick Perls, "is one of the rebellious, humanistic, existential forces in psychology which seeks to stem the avalanche of self-defeating, self-destructive forces among some members of our society." The therapist or trainer does not interpret but instead is directed toward helping an individual to be aware of his Here and Now in feeling and sensory terms; not in terms of *why* he is behaving so, but rather toward *what* he is doing and how he is experiencing it. Central to Gestalt therapy is the goal of helping the individual move from moment to moment, experiencing the freshness of each.

Gestalt therapy has consequently sometimes been defined as awareness training. The definition is based on the existential nature of Gestalt therapy, the concern for experiencing a Here and Now state, of experiencing the reality of the instant and avoiding any involvement in the past or future which would replace or distort the awareness of the present. There exists what may seem to be a paradox in Gestalt therapy, in that as one works either as patient or therapist the only way to allow for change to occur is through the absence of a desire to change. A desire to change is directed toward some goal or ideal created or "computed" in fantasy form by the intellect. To the degree the individual is caught up in his fantasized idea of "should" or "ought to," he cannot attend to, or be aware of, reality as it is. The theory of Gestalt therapy affirms that natural and healthy growth can only occur as the individual is aware of, and lives, each

This article first appeared in the *Journal of Contemporary Psychotherapy*, vol. 2, no. 1 (Summer 1969). Reprinted by permission of the editor.

instant in its most real sense, a Here and Now existence. The condition of avoiding feeling, of anaesthetizing affect, of retreating to a fantasy existence in order to avoid altering the status quo of one's life is directly related to the lack of realization of the creative potential of each individual. Gestalt therapy offers a philosophy *and* a methodology for moving from the maintenance of the status quo and deadness toward creativity and life.

Change through flexibility is both an implicit and an explicit quality of creativity; this is true whether creativity is thought of as a value or a process. As might be expected, what is explicit in change as a quality of creativity is the more obvious. The creative act requires an overt search and its consequences produce change. What is implicit in the relationship between change and creativity is a prerequisite to overt creative behavior. Once an individual takes the responsibility for accepting the consequence of living fully in each moment, which Gestalt therapy can help bring about, he will experience each moment as fresh experience. One thereby accepts the implicit value that alternatives to what is may exist, that by being open to experience one might experience one of these alternatives. The condition of being open to new experience, to being flexible, is essential if one is to energetically engage in innovation.

Barron [1] describes the creative person as one who seeks out complexity and chaos. The creative person is willing to experience the tension or frustration or pain of temporarily unresolved chaotic condition in that part of the universe in which he intentionally places himself. According to Barron, he does this in anticipation of the satisfaction he experiences when, through the creative process, he makes order out of chaos, simplicity out of complexity, or meaning out of confusion. While Barron's description is intriguing as far as it goes, there are dimensions in the work of Perls that may be added profitably to Barron's description. The creative person is first *aware* that chaos exists. He is then willing to confront this chaos and to "stay with it." The person who is busily engaged in maintaining his status quo is unwilling to move into new experience, chaotic or otherwise, for he never knows — the experience being new — whether it will be chaotic or not. He is not only unwilling to move into new experience, chaotic or otherwise, but he cannot perceive the reality of new possibilities even when they are directly in front of his nose. He is so actively engaged in defending his fantasies that he must substitute fantasies for real perception and genuine experience. He thus rides a merry-go-round, remaining as he is, not even experiencing the deadness of his existence, but instead combining the thinking about his pseudo-feelings with thoughts (fantasies) about his pseudo-reality.

This cardboard person replaces the reality of the world with cliché posters of washed-out colors all painted by himself. The posters are not creative because they do not meet the ultimate criterion of creativity: How does that which is created compare with what already exists and is experienced? This criterion holds whether the form be personal creativity, that which has primary meaning only to the individual, or social creativity, a creativity with which more than one person may be involved. Though the comparative judgment may be purely subjective, as in the case of personal creativity, or pragmatic, empirical, aesthetic, ethical, etc., as in the case of social creativity, the criterion requires the existence of alternatives with which to compare what has been created. The cardboard person "knows" no alternatives; he is even afraid to admit their existence and thus is stuck on his merry-go-round, seeing only his posters.

His potentialities for the creative process continue to be unrealized, because the cardboard person, through living in his computed fantasies, persists in maintaining his separation from the real world. "Out of this world," he cannot experience, with either mind or feelings, what is real. As a consequence, both his so-called conscious or cognitive knowledge and his intuitive and affective resources are shut off from enrichment through real and total experience. One draws upon both cognitive and affective dimensions of the self for the creative act. Furthermore, in the healthy, alive, creative individual, the affective and cognitive domains are integrated. What one *thinks* coincides with what one *feels*. Not so in the case of those who deny change through living primarily in the past or in the future or both. In the latter case, the non-real individual either anaesthetizes his feelings when they conflict with his thought-produced, substituted-for-the-real-world fantasies, or else is caught in a conflict between feelings and thoughts that can produce the impasse, the deadness and emptiness or, at best, the despair of being stuck. When there is no integration of the affective and cognitive domains, not only is there no new data to enrich either conscious or intuitive processes, but there is also no energy for the individual to spare for the creative process. This energy is instead committed by the cardboard person to preserving his anaesthetization so that feeling will not emerge, or it may be dissipated in maintaining or intensifying the conflict between emotion and thought at the source of his impasse.

The meaning of "integration" between the affective domain and the cognitive domain can perhaps be made more clear by the following examples of three common relationships between affective and cognitive functioning.

(a) The cognitive domain functions, but affect or feeling is anaesthetized: A child sits on the floor playing with an Erector set, perhaps because his mother has told him to. He reads the directions and carefully, step by step, puts the pieces together. There is little joy in the process. He then takes the pieces apart with the same lack of enthusiasm.

(b) The affective domain is predominant and in conflict with the cognitive domain. In one case the child throws pieces of the Erector set at his baby brother. In another, he jams pieces together so hard that they break. There are a number of behaviors that could be described here.

(c) The affective domain and the cognitive domain are harmoniously integrated: The child, sometimes experiencing excitement and pleasure, sometimes frustration, puts the pieces together making his own design or invention. He stays with his process of construction — personal creativity — until he feels and knows he is finished. As he constructs he uses both his feelings about the pieces he is putting together in their new patterned relationships, and his knowledge about characteristics such as the length, diameter, and function of each piece. The child's energy is directed toward a personally *satisfying* process of independent creativity. He feels alert, excited, substantial, worthwhile, and capable of experiencing temporary frustration in the confidence of his strength and ability; in short, he feels alive. The only "cardboard" here is in the toy.

What then can Gestalt therapy do for the cardboard person, or to help bring life to those parts of ourselves that are dry, stiff, weak, and like cardboard?

First, Gestalt therapy can help the individual be aware of what is obvious, of those parts of himself that are cardboard. This is done by helping him experience what "being cardboard" is like. Included here would be the experiencing of one's resistance to change — without falling into the trap of wanting to change. Wanting to change implies goals or ideals toward which the change is to be directed. To the degree one actively focuses on these goals or ideals which are actually fantasies not presently in existence, one cannot be in touch with the only reality available, the reality of the moment. Growth and change occur only through the experience of reality. Thus growth occurs in the growing, not in the wanting to grow. Paradoxically, wanting to grow can get in the way of growing. Gestalt therapy can provide methods and techniques to help facilitate change and growth through enabling the individual to experience himself as he actually is. As he more openly experiences the reality of himself, he will at the same time experience himself within reality, that is, himself partaking of the universe. For as he more fully experiences himself, he will experience himself in some place — probably with other people. At each moment he will become more aware of both himself and the world in which he finds himself. "Himself" will include both his intuitive reservoir and his conscious knowledge. He can draw upon these to merge "himself" with what is new and fresh in his experience of the external world and thus create new patterns, relationships, ideas, and things.

There are four stages of the creative act as conventionally described. Although I have reservations about this four-stage structure because it implies a sequential time character which belies certain creative acts,[2] and also because it does not correspond to an existential understanding of behavior, there is some convenience in examining how training in awareness through Gestalt therapy can improve creative functioning at each stage.

The first stage, the preparation stage, involves the selection or differentiation of data available in the universe which can be used in the process of creating. Usually these data are described as that which exists in the external environment. It is likely, however, that once differentiated, they would be combined at conscious or below-conscious levels with other meanings, understandings, or knowledge, remaining both in memory as experienced and in these new combined forms until utilized in the act of creation. What then seems involved in the preparation stage are three substages: (a) the experiencing of the data, (b) the storing of the data in pure or combined states at either conscious or below-conscious levels, and (c) the retrieval of the data for use in the creative act.

Gestalt therapy can have direct relevance to substages a and c. A greater awareness of reality as fresh experience from moment to moment, which is the consequence of successful Gestalt therapy, not only allows for richer perceptual and affective experience as one becomes aware of the universe, but can also help the individual become more in touch with himself including those below-conscious parts of his existence, thereby making available the content existing there. Perhaps most important, however, is that the gestalt of the "person-universe" can be better experienced or sensed, as a consequence of Gestalt therapy, so that the meaning of each personal experience fits into this rich and more unified context and is therefore much richer itself. The accumulation of these richer experiences (richer because of the broader and deeper meanings inherent in a person-universe unity as opposed to a dichotomous, person vs. universe context) should lead to a more creative act, there being richer data and experience to draw upon for creative activity.

The potential contributions of Gestalt therapy as described above apply also to the second stage of the creative process, the incubation stage. Here the "data" in the broadest sense of the word, mill, stew, and percolate about, combining and recombining into new patterns and relationships. Especially crucial here can be the insight which work in Gestalt therapy can teach, the importance of "letting be" — in this case, letting oneself be, staying with one's own life flow without straining to change direction, speed, or content, including immersion in painful experience. Descriptions by creative persons of their own creative processes often show the need to get away from their work through sleep, recreation, or in Poincaré's case, riding streetcars.

Whether this nonpressuring situation allows the incubation stage to flourish or permits the next stage to emerge is a moot question. In either case, the ability to let oneself be seems essential.

The next stage is called the illumination stage. It is here that the new concept, idea, invention, etc., emerges into consciousness, usually accompanied by expressions of "A-ha!" "Eureka!" "I've got it!" or in comic strips by an electric bulb shining over a character's head. The willingness to tune into one's feelings that can be experienced through Gestalt therapy is especially important here. A phenomenon, called the "hedonic impulse," is sometimes described as a vague, pleasurable feeling occurring just before illumination takes place. It is not the same joyful burst or glow of feeling which occurs at illumination, but precedes this more obvious sensation. Creative individuals, having learned to trust this feeling, apparently are able to allow illumination to take place more readily and to know when it is coming. Most people have repressed the hedonic impulse and thus do not have it available. Because there has been little attention paid the hedonic impulse in research, there is little published evidence to support the following thesis, but it is quite possible that repression of the feelings involved in the hedonic impulse could also tend to repress the emergence of the illumination stage. The acceptance of one's feelings as a general mode of existence for the individual who has achieved some increased health through Gestalt therapy should directly facilitate the phenomena of the hedonic impulse and the illumination stage.

The hedonic impulse has also been described by Brown and Melchior [3] as a precursor to synchronicity, beyond so-called meaningful chance or coincidence. Synchronicity occurs in a condition or situation where things just seem to fit together, the right people in the right place at the right time, without planning. The spontaneous quality of these occurrences often seems mysterious in its beyond-random-chance nature. I believe that the relationship between synchronicity and creativity will one day be more clearly delineated, and the common quality touching both will be the ability of the experiencer, through extreme flexibility, to move into the flow of the universe at that moment. From what has been said about Gestalt therapy helping the individual to tune into his own flow, which includes the flow of others and the flow of the world around him, it seems evident that Gestalt therapy can play a significant role in helping persons to become more creative and more synchronistic.

There is one final stage in the creative process. This is called the verification or elaboration stage. Here, whatever has been brought into consciousness in the illumination stage has to be given form in reality — the painting is painted, the music written and played, the invention constructed, the idea written, spoken, or elaborated — and in this form tested or compared with what has previously been in existence to see if it is more desirable, beautiful, elegant, worthwhile, etc. Training in Gestalt therapy can obviously be helpful here, in that what is real can thereby more likely be perceived and experienced, making the testing or comparison a more valid one. This is in contrast to the blindness to reality in part or whole, or the distortion of reality that can occur in those who prefer fantasy to reality as the foundation of their existence. Getting in touch with what is and staying with what is, brings one closer to the only reality one can experience, the reality of the moment. Gestalt therapy can teach this.

There is another kind of teaching that Gestalt therapy can provide to help the individual become more creative. This has to do with his feelings about himself as capable of change, as being flexible. In order to experience himself as possessing the possibility of selecting alternatives or new experiences for himself, he must as an individual (1) assimilate, digest, and integrate this possibility of change or selecting alternative ways of behaving, of altering his status quo, and (2) take responsibility for himself and his behavior.

If he can take responsibility for his behavior, including the possibility of growth through new experiences, he moves closer to the state of being creative. I said earlier that I was dissatisfied with the four-stage construct of the creative process. At the risk of seeming simplistic, I feel that to be creative is to be aware of, to discover, what already exists in the universe. Polanyi[4] states that research is successful and original only if the problem is good and original. The point is to see the problem. The problem is hidden. "To see a problem that will lead to a great discovery is not just to see something hidden, but to see something of which the rest of humanity cannot have even an inkling." Polanyi goes on to say that it is through tacit knowing, including "intimations of something hidden, which we may yet discover," that we discover the problem.

It is possible then to hold that nothing is ever created. Rather, it is discovered in the moment of experience. And it is discovered through the individual's awareness of the universe, an awareness which includes intuitions, intimations, and tacit sensings as well as conscious and explicit perceivings and knowings. When I imply that everything to be discovered or created already exists, this does not mean that what is discovered may necessarily exist in a concrete form. It may exist only in terms of an idea or an essence, or even derive its meaning from previously undetected relationships between concrete things that already exist.

Furthermore, this theory does not negate the existence of the conventional four stages of the creative process. They may well be involved all together at the same time or in different proportions at the moment of discovery. They could singly or in combination be descriptions of what might be going on in the individual as he becomes aware of this new thing that is already in existence.

The awareness trainer, by using principles of Gestalt therapy and by skillfully giving feedback to the student or teacher, can help him to experience himself at the moment — including perhaps his avoidance of experiencing himself at the moment — and can help him to become more in touch with the Now, especially that part of the Now that is himself. As he becomes more aware of himself, he becomes increasingly aware of the universe as a part of a special gestalt, the "person-universe." Of course, the increased awareness of the universe would include that of other humans with whom he lives.

Sometimes an impediment to awareness and creativity is a major split of the individual self into two selves. One is an authoritarian, intellectual self that insists on perfection, ideals, all the "shoulds." The other self is primarily hedonistic and emotional, and through clever and cunning ways attempts to avoid all the demands of the first self. The two selves thus can be in desperate conflict. The first self bullies, threatening all sorts of dire consequences if the person doesn't shape up. The second self professes weakness, promises to try harder, but always tomorrow, meanwhile slyly sabotaging the bully's demands. The individual remains in an unproductive bind. Until the two can be integrated into a whole person, another gestalt, much energy will be worthlessly and stupidly expended in the conflict. This energy then cannot be directed at experiencing reality.

The awareness trainer, again using principles and techniques of Gestalt therapy, can help the individual become aware of the split in himself and the nature, strengths, and weaknesses of these polarities. He can then help the polarized selves to become conscious of each other and, hopefully, bring about some integration of the two selves into an individual person — self. An example would be the integration of a bullying topdog with a weak underdog into a quiet firmness.

There are many dimensions to the characteristics and qualities which keep individuals from living in the present, from experiencing the Now, from being aware of the universe as it is, and thus from realizing their creative potential. Unfortunately, these obstacles and the various techniques and approaches used to help the individual reduce or eliminate these obstructions to awareness and reality can only be touched upon here. The reader is directed to the references cited below for a more adequate and detailed description.

Awareness training based on Gestalt therapy not only can increase the creativity and flexibility of one's life style, it can also be invaluable in many ways for teachers and others who work with human beings. Awareness training teaches one to really listen to, and to really see, who is there. Too often teachers see and hear a *concept* of an individual child, one they have "computed" for themselves, rather than the child as he actually is *at the moment*. The learning experiences they provide as a consequence of this concept often have little relevance to the child as he is. Being aware of a child as he really is at the moment is half the battle toward effective and creative teaching, especially in terms of relevant curriculum content and teacher behavior.

We have only one relevant reality available to us. Through an increasing awareness of this reality we can become more creative. As we become more aware, more creative, more in touch with reality, it consequently follows that we become more flexible, and thus we become more alive.

Fra Giovanni in A.D. 1513 said: "The gloom of the world is but a shadow. Behind it, yet within reach, is joy. There is a radiance and glory in the darkness, could we but see, and to see we have only to look. I beseech you to look!"

REFERENCE NOTES /

1. F. Barron, *Creativity and Psychological Health* (Princeton, N.J.: D. Van Nostrand, 1963).
2. G. Brown and D. Gaynor, "Athletic Action as Creativity," *Journal of Creative Behavior*, vol. 1, no. 2 (1967), pp. 155–162.
3. G. Brown and P. Melchior, informal discussion at Esalen Institute, April 1967.
4. M. Polanyi, *The Tacit Dimension* (New York: Doubleday, 1966), pp. 21–22.

3

AN INTRODUCTION TO GESTALT THERAPY

— James S. Simkin

Gestalt is a German word meaning whole or configuration. As one dictionary of psychology puts it, Gestalt is "an *integration* of members as contrasted with a summation of parts." [1] The term also implies a unique kind of patterning. Gestalt therapy is a term applied to a unique kind of psychotherapy as formulated by Frederick S. Perls and his followers.

Dr. Perls began, as did many of his colleagues, as a psychoanalyst, having first been trained as a physician in post–World War I Germany. In 1926 he worked under Professor Kurt Goldstein at the Frankfurt Neurological Institute, where he was first exposed to the tenets of Gestalt psychology, but, as he puts it, ". . . was still too preoccupied with the orthodox psychoanalytical approach to assimilate more than a fraction of what was offered [to me]." [2] Later Dr. Perls was exposed to the theories and practice of Wilhelm Reich and incorporated some of the concepts and techniques of Character Analysis into his work.

While serving as a captain in the South African Medical Corps, Perls wrote his first manuscript in 1941 and 1942, outlining his emerging theory and technique of personality integration that later appeared as a book, *Ego, Hunger and Aggression*, subtitled *A Revision of Freud's Theory and Method*. The term "Gestalt therapy" was first used as the title of a book on Perls' methods written by him with two co-authors, Professor Ralph Hefferline of Columbia University and Dr. Paul Goodman of New York City.

A thumbnail sketch of the aim of psychoanalysis has sometimes been given as Freud's dictum: "Where Id was shall Ego be." The instinctual striving is replaced with self-control as mediated by the ego. A capsule comment describing Gestalt therapy might be Perls' "I and Thou, Here and Now." In Gestalt therapy the emphasis is on the present, ongoing situation — which, in individual therapy, involves the interaction of at least two people, the patient and the therapist.

According to the theory underlying Gestalt therapy, man is a total organism functioning as a whole, rather than an entity split into dichotomies such as mind and body. With the philosophical backing of humanism à la Otto Rank, the organism is born with the capacity to cope with life, rather than what I call "the original-sin theory of human development," which holds that the organism must learn to repress or suppress its instinctual strivings in order to become "civilized." Recently the emergence of existential philosophy appears to be so compatible with the development of Gestalt therapy that Dr. Wilson Van Dusen in his article "Existential Analytic Psychotherapy" makes the claim that there is only one psychotherapeutic approach which unites the phenomenological approach with existential theory, and that is Gestalt therapy.[3]

Before examining some of the main concepts of Gestalt therapy and describing actual situations which will give the experiential flavor necessary to an understanding of the approach, I need to do a little more "talking about" (which is really a taboo approach to Gestalt therapy) to supply an adequate context or background.

The theoretical model of the psychodynamic schools of personality — chiefly the Freudian school — envisions the personality like an onion consisting of layers. Each time a layer is peeled away, there is still another layer until you finally come to the core. (Incidentally, in the process of "analysis" of the onion, you may have very little or nothing left by the time you come to the core.) I envision the personality more like a large rubber ball which has only a thick outer layer and is empty inside. The ball floats or swims in an environment so that at any given moment, only a certain portion is exposed to the outside while the rest is submerged in the water. Thus, rather than inventing an unconscious or preconscious to account for behavior that we are unaware of, I would suggest that the unaware behavior is a result of the organism not being in touch with — not sensing — what is out there because of being submerged in its own background (environment), or of being in contact with fantasies and usually preoccupied by them.

In his paper "A Review of the Practice of Gestalt Therapy," [4] Yontef summarizes the theory of Gestalt therapy. Organismic needs lead to sensory motor behavior. Once a configuration is formed that has the qualities of a good Gestalt, the organismic need that has become foreground is met and a balance of state of satiation or no-need is achieved. "When a need is met, the Gestalt it organized becomes complete, and it no longer exerts an influence — the organism is free to form new gestalten. When this Gestalt formation and destruction are blocked or rigidified at any stage, when needs are not recognized and expressed, the flexible harmony and flow of the organism/environment field is disturbed. Unmet needs form incomplete gestalten that clamor for attention and, therefore, interfere with the formation of new gestalten." [5] Perls states, "The most important fact about the figure-background formation is that if a need is genuinely satisfied, the situation changes." [6]

Thus, in order to bring about change, patients are taught to focus their *awareness* which is the primary tool for effecting change in Gestalt therapy. Frequently, undirected awareness alone is sufficient to insure change. At other times, a person needs to experiment with *directing* awareness, as in some of the exercises found in the Perls, Hefferline, and Goodman book.[7]

Gestalt therapy emphasizes organismic self-regulation. The organism, in order to survive, needs to mobilize itself and/or its environment for support. The means whereby the organism contacts its environment is through the mobilization of aggression. If we successfully survive the attempts of others to civilize or enslave us, we pick and choose what we need from our environment to support ourselves. Picking and choosing, however, is not enough; we need also to chew up and swallow those parts of what is out there that we find edible and to our liking and thus make it (food or idea or whatever) part of ourselves. What we do not need, we discard as waste products, garbage, etc. Thus, if we are able to mobilize sufficient aggression not only to pick and choose but also to chew up and swallow, we are able to get the support necessary for our survival. It is important to note that it is the organism itself which picks and chooses, chews and swallows, and *not* the significant "other" out there who determines for us what is palatable or nourishing.

In Gestalt therapy the therapist is frequently "active" in attempting to have the patient learn once again to use his sensory-motor equipment. At one time Dr. Perls described the process as a sort of "losing your mind to come to your senses" activity. This means that the patient is taught how to direct his awareness via the resensitization of his primary sensory modalities. To look rather than stare, to listen rather than overhear, to play deaf and dumb, and the like. Directed awareness experiments help the patient get off what I call the "why merry-go-round." Many patients trust only their capacity to intellectualize, think, have fantasies. Thus, when they become aware of a bit of their own behavior which is incongruous, which doesn't fit their ideal self-image or role, they jump on the "why merry-go-round," only to repeat the same unacceptable behavior and then again go chasing after reasons and explanations. Frequently, learning *how*, by directing his awareness, the patient is able to undo the unacceptable behavior. At least, the patient does not remain an intellectual cripple.

In working with my patients in the "here and now," using the techniques of directed awareness, "Where are you now?" or "What are you aware of now?", I have discovered that verbal communication is usually misleading or misdirecting while body language is not. Thus both the patient and I take his symptoms seriously because these symptoms — I call them "truth buttons" or "truth signals" — communicate *how* a patient really feels. If he is in conflict, experimenting first with taking one side of the conflict in fantasy and then the other, he will usually bring on the body language — the "truth signals" — when he takes sides with that aspect of the conflict which is anti-self. Here is an example. Recently a patient was describing a conflict between continuing a project on his own, which he had begun with a partner, or dropping the project. His "truth button" was a hard, rocklike feeling in the pit of his stomach. He worked through his conflict by imagining first that he would continue the project without his partner and would see it through to the acquisition of property, erecting a building, and manufacturing the article in the new plant. As he fantasized these various steps he experienced increasing discomfort in his stomach — his "rock" was getting more and more unbearable. He then proceeded to fantasize about dropping the project — abandoning the plans which had already been made plus his investment of time and money — and reported feeling more and more relaxed and comfortable, especially in the pit of his stomach. Experimenting several times (reversing, so that at times he fantasized giving up the project first and at other times continuing the project first) brought the same results. The patient became convinced that he knew, via his "truth button," which was the appropriate decision for him.

Being able to self-validate what is the correct solution through one's own body language is a tremendous help in the economy of psychotherapy. Many of the transference and countertransference difficulties can be avoided, as well as the pitfalls of interpretation, through teaching oneself and one's patients how to use their symptoms — how to listen to their own body language.

One of man's most basic experiences is excitement. If you become aware of your excitement and attempt to suppress its overt expression, inevitably you will wind up squeezing or tensing yourself. In addition, you will stop breathing. Perls formulated the idea that excitement minus sufficient support of oxygen equals anxiety and, as we know, anxiety is the experience least tolerated by the human organism.

In all cases that I have seen thus far, people seeking psychotherapy show an imbalance among their three primary modes of experiencing. Most patients I see, and this seems to be also true of the bulk of the patients seen by my colleagues, are very dependent on, and have overstressed their development of, the intellectual or the "thinking-about" mode of experience. Most of the time, these people are in touch with their thought processes and their experience only by a fantasy (memory) of the past or a fantasy (wish, prediction) of the future. They are able to make contact with their feelings only infrequently and many are also sensory cripples — not seeing or hearing or tasting, etc.

In the organismically balanced person, there is the capacity to experience intellectually and emotionally and sensorially. So the therapeutic task is to help the patient regain the use of his own equipment, which has been desensitized at some earlier time and is no longer at his disposal.

Contrary to the approaches of some schools which stress "insight" or "learning why we behave the way we do," Gestalt therapy stresses learning *how* and *what* we do. Gestalt therapists are convinced that the only possibility for changing behavior is through an awareness of what we are doing — using our sensory and motor equipment, as well as our intellectual equipment — and how we are doing whatever it is we are engaged in.

In Gestalt therapy, we begin with the obvious, with what is ongoing at the moment, recognizing that patients quickly learn to tell us dreams if we stress dreams as the "royal road to the unconscious." Or, they will spend session after session telling us stories about their previous experiences if we are convinced that cures are dependent on the recall of genetic material. Thus my questions to the patient — "Where are you now?" or "What are you experiencing now?" — may lead to the past or a dream. But the patient may just as likely not be in fantasy — he may be experiencing in the "here and now" feelings of expectancy or joy or anger. He may be concentrating his awareness on sensory experiences — seeing the room we are in, or listening to sounds, or experiencing his body against the chair he is sitting in.

Many patients are quite startled to discover that they filter every experience through their "thinking machine"; that it is almost impossible for them to trust their feelings or senses without first getting approval, so to speak, from their intellect. Frequently, when a patient becomes aware that he is overly dependent on his intellectual equipment, he will try to manipulate me into telling him that he should not be. He is very fearful of exploring other modes of experience without some support — approval from me — if he cannot experience support within himself. All people need support from within and from without. Each person finds a suitable balance of self-support and environmental supports. Many patients have very inadequate self-supports and tend to lean heavily on environmental supports.

They become very hurt or disappointed or shattered when the other person to whom they give this power — the shifting of self-support to someone out there — fails to live up to their expectations.

During Freud's time, repression appeared to be the most frequently used defense. My own clinical experience leads me to conjecture that projection is now by far the most commonly encountered defense. We project onto another person those attributes or traits that we find unacceptable in ourselves. Then, we point our finger at the other person and castigate him for being whatever it is we don't like in ourselves. This permits us to maintain a fantasy or fiction of how we imagine we are, rather than being in touch with and accepting how we are. The problem here is the problem of the introject — swallowing something whole without first adequately chewing it and then swallowing the idea (or food, etc.) if it is nourishing, or spitting it out if it is toxic.

My primary psychotherapeutic task, as I see it, is to help the person I am working with accept himself. My patients say to me in effect, "I want to change how I am," or "I don't like myself when I act this way," or "I'm so stupid," and the like. Yet, they expect to change how they are, not by fully *experiencing* their behavior as discomfort, embarrassment, joy, humiliation, excitement, pleasure, shame, but by *judging* their behavior as "bad," "stupid," or "unacceptable," thus talking about rather than fully coming in contact with what they do and how they do it. And, paradoxically, these people will be the first to claim the organismic truism that "we learn from experience." They confuse "thinking about" with "experiencing."

I trust that if I fully experience what I do and how I behave, I will successfully complete a particular bit of behavior and learn from this experience. The crux of the matter is *how* I learn. Do I learn by fully experiencing organismically (sensing and feeling as well as judging), or must I restrict my experience to "thinking about"? When my patient says, "I did it again. I got angry at my wife and beat her," my patient is telling me a story, a memory of an event which has already taken place. I may ask, "What are you aware of now?" If his response is, "See how stupid I am — I never learn. I repeat the same idiotic behavior!" I may ask, "In telling me stories?" Once he understands what he is doing now, telling me a story, and thereby keeping two situations unfinished — the beating of his wife by recalling the event, and the using of this memory with me *now* while playing the "good patient" in telling me how "bad" or "stupid" he is — he has the possibility of learning *how* he remains stupid. He can only learn by being fully aware of what he is experiencing. The other way, he is split into the two (sometimes more) aspects of himself.

Dr. Perls referred to these two selves as the topdog and underdog who are constantly carrying on an internal (infernal, might be a better term) dialogue. "You stupid idiot, why did you beat her again?" "Gee, I'm sorry, I promise I won't do it again." Or, "How many times do I have to tell you not to repeat that silly mistake?" "I'm going to do better next time, I promise." Perls claimed that the underdog self — the promiser — usually wins, defeating the topdog through unkept promises, sabotage, etc. I believe the underdog *always* wins.

The integration of these selves — the full acceptance of how one is, rather than how one should be — leads to the possibility of change. As long as people persist in remaining split selves and not fully acknowledging (taking sides with and experiencing) what and how they are, real change, I believe, is not possible.

There has been a sharp increase in interest in, and the practice of, Gestalt therapy during the past decade (1960–1970). At the time this article is being written (early 1971) there are several Gestalt therapy institutes throughout the United States, at least three of them offering systematic training (Cleveland, San Francisco, and Los Angeles).

Several books have appeared in the last three years, ranging from a collection of ten older articles collected by Pursglove [8] and twelve original articles in Fritz Perls' *Festschrift* [9] to the excellent collection of twenty-five articles in Fagan and Shepherd's book on theory, technique, and application. [10]

Kogan, [11] unhappy with the (then) absence of a systematic bibliography of source material in Gestalt therapy, collected and published a pamphlet which lists books, articles, papers, films, tapes, and institutes, and includes the Gestalt therapist directory. He has some ninety references. Fagan and Shepherd list over sixty, and Yontef, in his paper referred to above, cites forty-five.

Perls' autobiographical book *In and Out the Garbage Pail* [12] and Simkin's interview with him in 1966 [13] give much of the historical background of the development of Gestalt therapy. Also of historical interest are the two excellent papers written by Perls' widow, Laura Perls.[14, 15]

Practically none of the Gestalt therapy literature has been channeled through conventional sources during the three decades of its existence. Major exceptions are Perls' 1948 article in the *American Journal of Psychotherapy* and Polster's more recent article in *Psychotherapy*.[16]

Until 1969 the only films depicting Gestalt therapy were those of Perls. His are still the primary sources (more than thirty varied films) with one exception: Simkin's training film.[17] An excerpt from Simkin's film follows:

JIM: What do you experience at this moment?

COLMAN: A feeling of sadness . . . I don't know why. Because I said that they were in. I said I wanted them in.

JIM: Yeah. Colman, would you be willing to say now that you are sad.

COLMAN: I am sad.

JIM: Again.

COLMAN: I'm sad. I'm sad. And I'm angry.

JIM: Yeah.

COLMAN: Crazy.

JIM: Okay, add that. "I'm sad, I'm angry, I'm crazy."

COLMAN: I'm sad, I'm angry, I'm crazy.

JIM: And now?

COLMAN: Now I feel good again.

JIM: Yeah. Now I think you're beginning to catch on. Any time that you acknowledge, really go with how you are, you finish . . . let go. You *are* sad, you *are* angry, you *are* crazy, you *are* happy, and so on. If you stay with . . . all of your me's.

COLMAN: My sad, angry, crazy, me.

JIM: Yeah. Okay, I'd like to stop at this point.

The above excerpt illustrates how, by being aware (responsible), Colman's sadness changes to anger, his anger changes to perplexity, and as he experiences the humor of his situation he feels good again. Much of the impact of this transaction, however, is not conveyed through the arid medium of the printed word. The best way to fully experience Gestalt therapy is obviously through the experiential mode. As Fagan and Shepherd say in their preface:

. . . in Gestalt therapy, much importance is attached to tone of voice, posture, gestures, facial expression, etc., with much of the import and excitement coming from work with changes in these nonverbal communications. Fortunately, the increasing availability of Gestalt films and tapes helps in making the nonverbal communications more accessible.[18]

Or, in the words of the late Fritz Perls, "To suffer one's own death and to be reborn is not easy." [19]

REFERENCE NOTES /

1. Howard C. Warren, *Dictionary of Psychology* (New York: Houghton Mifflin).
2. F. S. Perls, *Ego, Hunger and Aggression* (New York: Random House, 1969).
3. W. Van Dusen, "Existential Analytic Psychotherapy," *American Journal of Psychoanalysis*, 1960, p. 35.
4. G. M. Yontef, "A Review of the Practice of Gestalt Therapy." Trident Shop, California State College, Los Angeles, 1969.
5. Ibid., p. 3.
6. F. S. Perls, "Theory and Technique of Personality Integration," *American Journal of Psychotherapy*, vol. 2 (1948), p. 571.
7. F. S. Perls, R. F. Hefferline, and Paul Goodman, *Gestalt Therapy* (New York: Julian Press, 1951), pp. 116 ff.
8. P. D. Pursglove, *Recognitions in Gestalt Therapy* (New York: Funk & Wagnalls, 1968).
9. J. S. Simkin, ed., *Festschrift for Fritz Perls* (Los Angeles: Author, 1968).

10. J. Fagan and I. L. Shepherd, *Gestalt Therapy Now* (Palo Alto, Calif.: Science and Behavior Books, 1970).
11. J. Kogan, *Gestalt Therapy Resources* (San Francisco: Lode Star Press, 1970).
12. F. S. Perls, *In and Out the Garbage Pail* (Lafayette, Calif.: Real People Press, 1969).
13. J. S. Simkin, *Individual Gestalt Therapy: Interview with Dr. Frederick Perls.* Audio-Tape Recording. A. A. P. Tape Library, No. 31, Philadelphia, Pa.
14. Laura Perls, "Notes on the Psychology of Give and Take," *Complex,* vol. 9 (1953), pp. 24–30.
15. Laura Perls, "Two Instances of Gestalt Therapy," *Case Reports in Clinical Psychology,* Kings County Hospital, Brooklyn, New York, 1956.
16. E. Polster, "A Contemporary Psychotherapy," *Psychotherapy: Theory, Research & Practice,* vol. 3 (1966), pp. 1–6.
17. J. S. Simkin, *In the Now.* A training film. Beverly Hills, 1969.
18. Fagan and Shepherd, op. cit., p. viii.
19. F. S. Perls, *Gestalt Therapy Verbatim* (Lafayette, Calif.: Real People Press, 1969).

4

GESTALT AS LEARNING THEORY
— David N. McCarthy

Much of the work done in confluent education is based on the theory of Gestalt therapy. The interrelationships between Gestalt and education are numerous and complex. Yet these interrelationships are based largely upon the premise that the theory of Gestalt therapy is also a theory of learning. In this article I shall attempt to explain how this is so.

Fritz Perls defines Gestalt psychology as "field theory" psychology. According to this theory, the perception of a thing takes place not by itself, but within a "field" which contains its opposite. The perception of day is realizable only by the existence of night; the emergence of a clock on the wall is possible only by an awareness of the wall, or what is "non-clock." To this way of looking at the world, Perls applies the term "differential thinking," that is, thinking in terms of opposites. Such a "holistic" approach is markedly different from logical-positivism, or the analysis of a thing into its parts. According to the theory of holism, the part can be defined only in relationship to the whole.

As Wallen [1] points out, Perls applied this theory of perception to organic perceptions and feelings. Living is seen as a continual process of completing gestalten, of completing wholes. The example Perls gives is that of a person reading a book. The book is the figure, the reader's body is the background. As he reads, he becomes aware that he is thirsty. The sensation of thirst in his throat now emerges as figural, and the book becomes part of the background. Perhaps our reader now imagines a glass of water or a can of beer. He gets up, satisfies his thirst, and returns to his reading. His actions have been determined by his *need*, the need of his organism to be in a state of balance, a state of wholeness. Thus, needs organize perception and behavior. The parallel with the learning situation is obvious. If there is no need to know, learning will not take place. Gestalt learning theory deals with creating such needs; it also deals with the obstacles, such as repressions, fantasies, and other blockages which prohibit these needs from emerging naturally. Thus, Gestalt learning theory concerns itself not only with learning about the world, but with learning how we prevent ourselves from doing so.

The idea that perceptions and actions are determined by needs suggests that all knowing and learning begins and is carried out subjectively. The most basic way of knowing is a deeply felt organismic sensing. It is a process of integrating an awareness of particulars into an awareness of a whole entity. In the case of our reader, dryness in the throat was integrated into an image of the can of beer in the refrigerator. This is not a passive act, but an active shaping of experience. And when it involves the learning process, it takes place in stages. A brief example will help to clarify this theory.

I perceive for the first time, let us say, a spherical object — a rubber ball. My initial perception must involve some motoric activity. My eyes focus, trace the shape of the object and follow the play of light defining the object's three-dimensionality. In addition to this motoric activity, I am actively integrating countless experiences from my memory, such as circles, cubes, and plane surfaces, into my awareness of the figure "ball." This is the active shaping of particulars into a new whole. Thus, I attend from its features to their total meaning, just as our thirsty reader attended from an awareness of his dry throat to the meaning, "I am thirsty." The process can stop here, as it did with the reader after he had quenched his thirst. But as a theory of learning, the Gestalt formation is not destroyed — it is used for the next stage.

Perhaps I am next presented with the concept, "The Earth is a sphere." With my awareness of what a sphere (ball) is, I can now focus on this new concept. It is noted that, just as I used my awareness of shape and color to be able to focus on the idea of a ball, I can now attend from my awareness of what a ball is to an understanding of the Earth as a sphere. Thus, the process of learning involves the formation of gestalten used to form new gestalten, and moves outward from the self. But it is always subject, moving from internal awareness to external knowing. According to Gestalt learning theory, then, learning takes place in two-part stages which alternate between Gestalt formation and integration. To this process of integration Perls applies the metaphor "chewing." Just as the body cannot assimilate food without first chewing it, so the mind cannot assimilate experience without integrating it into awareness.

To define learning as integrating is to state how it takes place under ideal conditions. It does not deal with the impediments to this process. This is where that aspect of Gestalt therapy which deals with personal growth is important. As indicated earlier, we are concerned not only with how we learn, but how we keep ourselves from doing so.

Suppose I were to raise the hypothesis, "Am I angry?" Given the subjective basis of all learning and knowing, I could check my hypothesis only by referring to my internal flow of experiencing. I might experience a rapid pulse, grinding teeth, and a tight chest. My hypothesis would not be checked against the external environment, but only against my internal sensations. Rogers defines this process of internal referencing as "subjective knowing." [2]

In contradistinction to this way of knowing is what Rogers refers to as "objective knowing." [3] This process deals, not with internal sensations, but rather with measurable and definable external events. The internal is definable only in terms of the external. With this method I myself cannot answer the question, "Am I angry?" I must rely on another's objective observation. My observer will test the hypothesis in two ways. First by observation: "He's grinding his teeth, his pulse is fast, and he's breathing hard." He may even measure my pulse and the pressure between my teeth. Next he will correlate this hard data with like data from a large body of theoretical knowledge formulated by other scientists operating in identical situations. His conclusions will be based on these facts.

This empirical method is the basis for all logical-positivism, and is responsible for incalculable developments in the physical and biological sciences. But objectivity can be concerned only with objects; it must transform into an object anything it observes. It assumes that it is possible to separate the subject observer from the object he observes. As discussed earlier, perceptions (observations) are determined by needs; they involve a subjective shaping of experience. The idea of "total objectivity" is thus patently ridiculous; objective observation will *a priori* limit its conclusions by asking only questions whose solutions can fit within measurable parameters. Such scientific observation is reductionistic, directed toward analyzing the whole into its component parts. As Michael Polanyi has pointed out, analyzing a machine into its component chemical and physical parts will not tell you how it works, or indeed, even that it is a machine.[4] You've got to look at the whole picture.

Gestalt looks at the whole picture. It combines the best aspects of both subjective and objective knowing. From the empiricists it takes the idea of observation. For example, the therapist observes me grinding my teeth. However, instead of measuring, analyzing, and fitting the clenched-teeth observation into a theoretical framework, instead of abstracting and moving the observation away from the current situation, the therapist asks me to integrate the clenched teeth into my awareness. This does not mean saying, "You are clenching your teeth," but rather, "Are you aware of what your teeth are doing?" The concern is not with the therapist's awareness, but with my awareness. Yet my awareness of clenched teeth might not emerge without the therapist's observation.

From the theory of "subjective knowing" Gestalt takes the process of internal referencing as the ultimate validator of the meaning of observable behavior. That is, the meaning of my clenched teeth must emerge from my own subjective experiencing. Rather than an object, I am treated as a subject. The therapist does not overlook his own subjective "intuitions." He will allow his own awareness to play a part in what becomes an empathic, subject-subject relationship, rather than trying to be skeptical and objective. Thus, Gestalt goes beyond both the objective and the subjective to include the person and the perceptions of both the observer and the observed.

This is the process by which Gestalt develops self-awareness. I would like to indicate that the structure of this process is precisely the same as that involved in learning about the world outside the self. For it is on the basis of this parallel that learning about one's world and about oneself can be brought into confluence in the live classroom.

In order to do this, it will be necessary to make a distinction between experience, and what Gendlin [5] refers to as experienc*ing*. Experiencing is the preconceptual, ongoing feeling of having an experience. As a preconceptual feeling, it is prior to symbolization, and is first known to the individual through direct referencing and differentiation: "I am sensing tightness in my chest." Experienc*ing* becomes experience, it takes on meaning, when it interacts with symbols: "I am angry." This is a concept. Implicit chest tightness has been made explicit. The next step is to take this concept of anger and to stay with it, get in touch with it, own it — that is, internalize or integrate it into myself. In so doing, the next concept emerges: "I am angry with my sister." Again I own or internalize this new concept, perhaps by holding an imaginary conversation with my sister, and so experience the next concept. This process continues until some sense of completeness, of wholeness, has been reached. It is only through this process of moving from experienc*ing* to conceptualization or experience to experienc*ing* that growth will take place. Thus, though I can have experiencing without conceptualization, I cannot have growth without it.

This same step-by-step process is followed in my learning about the outside world. For example, I may begin by experiencing a shape in the bushes. From this subjective awareness emerges the concept, "It is a man." I now internalize this concept of a man to focus on what he is doing. I use my awareness of what he is doing to conceptualize his motives, his motives to determine his personality, etc.[6] As with the knowledge of my anger, it is noted that the experiencing began subjectively, and that with each step, the concept had to be internalized or "chewed up" in order to be of use in focusing on the next level of reality.

This process, this movement from experiencing to conceptualization to integrating and experiencing, is the cornerstone of Gestalt learning theory. It applies both to learning about the self and learning about the world. It is why we are able to substitute "student" for "patient," and "teacher" for "therapist." It is why we can teach academic subject matter and self-knowledge at the same time. The vastly complex relationship between Gestalt and education begins here, with Gestalt *as* learning theory.

REFERENCE NOTES /

1. Richard Wallen, "Gestalt Therapy and Gestalt Psychology." In Joen Fagan and Irma Lee Shepherd, eds., *Gestalt Therapy Now* (Palo Alto, Calif.: Science and Behavior Books, 1970).
2. Carl R. Rogers, "Toward a Science of the Person," *Journal of Humanistic Psychology*, Fall 1963, p. 73.
3. Ibid., p. 75.
4. Michael Polanyi, *The Tacit Dimension* (New York: Doubleday, 1966), pp. 38–39.
5. Eugene T. Gendlin, *Experiencing and Creation of Meaning* (New York: Free Press, 1962), pp. 1–29.
6. Michael Polanyi, "The Logic of Tacit Inference." In Marjorie Grene, ed., *Knowing and Being* (Chicago: University of Chicago Press, 1969), pp. 138–180.

5

SCIENTIFIC THEORY AND GESTALT: A JUXTAPOSITION

— *Bert Pearlman*

We are humans. We live. We feel. We love. We perceive the world. We think. One of the tasks to which we put our thoughts is the job of describing things we cannot immediately perceive. These thoughts give us a focus by which we view, and thus see and work with, certain phenomena. In an important sense our thoughts, and the subsequent descriptions they engender, define and give ultimate meaning to any discussions of the phenomenon called education.

In dealing with abstractions (e.g., space, sanity, personality, education) we rely on theories to bind conceptually the elements of the abstraction, to make them manageable. This conceptually binding tool, the theory, consists of an ordered set of assumptions about a complex system. It is a conceptual tool used for understanding some aspect of our enormously varied world. It is a means of getting a "handle" on an abstraction.

A brief example from science will help clarify this point. In the age of the astronomer Ptolemy, the planets, sun, and stars were thought to revolve around the earth. The universe was described in terms of this frame of reference. For example, Ptolemy might have said, "The universe consists of the heavenly bodies revolving about the earth." At that time scientific discussions involving the term "universe" were grounded and made meaningful by such frame of reference. The theory of revolving planets provided a means whereby an abstraction (the universe) was rendered manageable and useful.

To a large extent, the usefulness of scientific theory is determined by two factors. A theory should account for and explain currently known data, and the theory should provide a predictive means for generating new data. The Ptolemaic Theory was accepted as true as long as it accounted for the astronomical data available at the time, and as long as newly discovered data was subsumable under the conceptual framework of the theory. History tells us data was discovered eventually that did not fit into Ptolemy's schema. Inability to satisfactorily modify the Ptolemaic Theory gave rise to a need for a new conceptual tool: thus, the Copernican Theory of the universe was postulated. By theorizing that the earth rotates daily on its axis, and that the planets revolve around the sun, the advocates of the Copernican Theory were able to (1) account for data known as of that era, (2) account for newly discovered data, and (3) make predictions as to where and how new data could be discovered. The Copernican Theory replaced the Ptolemaic Theory as a conceptual tool, and was accepted as true for as long as it met these scientific criteria.

If theories are conceptual tools for managing abstractions, it follows that educational theories are theories for managing the abstract concepts of education. That is to say, an educational theory provides a means for conceptually binding the elements of the abstraction — education. What education is, and how it operates, draws its possible explanations, and thus its meaning, from educational theory. This is but to say that educational theory makes the concept "education" meaningful and useful.

Gestalt theory is one of the conceptual tools that can be used to give meaning to the concepts of education. As its epistemological basis, Gestalt theory holds that the discrete elements of a whole are meaningful only in relation to the whole. This is to say that the whole is not explainable in terms of any possible enumeration and conjunction of its parts, but rather, we can only know that the elements of anything are elements of that thing by having a prior conception of the whole. This is not nearly as confusing as it might initially appear to be. Returning to the example from astronomy, it is clear that the elements of the universe, the planets and stars, etc., take whatever meaning they have only in relation to the theoretical whole. Traditional scientific theories come under critical scrutiny when the elements of a theory (empirical observations of celestial bodies, in the case of astronomy) are seen as meaningless in reference to the whole theory.

When education is viewed through this epistemological perspective, several important points come immediately into focus. From the premise that the elements of education gain their meaning only in relation to a whole conception of education, it is clear that when an element is without meaning it is either not properly an element of education, *or* our whole conception, our theory, our gestalt, is faulty. By making this observation more concrete, we can see, for example, that if objective tests fail as indices of what we consider intelligence, or of what is learned, it is either because they are not good indicators or because intelligence, or what is learned, is not measurable in their terms. This leaves us with two alternatives: we can redesign our tests, or we can ask ourselves whether what we are after in education is measurable in traditional terms. By using this tool from Gestalt theory, every time we encounter loss of meaning in regard to an element of education, we have a means by which we can deal conceptually with our impasse. The Gestalt principle tells us to examine the element in the light of our whole conception of education. We learn that if we cannot disregard the element, we must change our conception.

Gestalt theory also tells us how ultimately we formulate our conceptions. "We do not look at the world as though our eyes were the lenses of a photographic camera. We select objects according to our interests, and these objects appear as prominent figures against a dim background." [1] In other terms, this means that we have a whole body of prejudices and predilections that somehow determine what we observe as the data of our experience. The pilot notices which way the wind blows because it suits his interests. The biologist notices subtle mutations. The astronomer notices the movements of heavenly bodies. The educator notices whether his pupils have grasped the subject matter; he notices whether his students pay attention; he notices the presence or absence of his pupils' enthusiasm for their subjects; he notices his own responses to the subject matter and to his class; he notices his administrator's attitudes toward him, etc. Working further with the example of the educator, if any of the data of the educator's experience are not seen as relevant, he must (if he wants to be theoretically consistent) either reject the data as being without meaning, or he must reformulate his theory to accommodate and give meaning to the data. Here we find the core of a strong *reductio* argument for confluent education. The few items listed above are representative of the type of foreground (figure) interests of educators. These interests include both cognitive and affective elements. If we wish to deny relevance to either of these elements, we have to rethink the theoretical assumptions with which we have been working. But Gestalt theory tells us that the meaning of any elements of a whole are only derived through reference to the whole. Further, if an element is noticed, it is only because it is in accord with our interests, which is to say that if we grant meaning to something (i.e., if we take note of it) it *is* relevant to our interests. Now, if we want to disregard the importance of affective elements, it necessarily entails a denial of the existence of our operative educational theory. This is so because we would never have noticed these elements if we were not operating out of a reference to a whole conception (a gestalt) which itself rendered the elements meaningful. The foolishness of choosing to deny what we actually do is inescapable. Whether or not educators realize it, their underlying operational theory of education has a confluent basis. Any denial of the relevance of the interaction of affect and cognition runs counter to their operational theory. It would seem that if an educator understood the theory from which he operated, and if he denied the importance of confluence of affect and cognition in education, he would be inconsistent and hypocritical.

Empirical research has its place in education — unfortunately, it is sometimes misplaced and subsequently misused. Remember, in order for empirical research to produce meaningful results, it must be used in conjunction with a realistic and consistent theory of education. Using our basic Gestalt principle again, if the element is not in alignment with our basic Gestalt, it is meaningless. This seems to be the problem with much of the basic research in education. In their zeal to follow the lead of the "hard sciences," social scientists, including the scientists of education, have rushed ahead in their efforts to accumulate empirical data. Good theories generate predictive means for gathering supportive evidence and new data. Areas for constructive research must come from the theory, and must not be *ad hoc* pseudo-scientific adventures. One area for sound theoretical research in education would be an empirical investigation of attitudes and interests of educators and students. The *reductio ad absurdum* argument used above is a valid reinforcement of the tenets of confluent education — the support or the downfall of the cogency of the argument rests on the empirical existence or nonexistence of affective attitudes of educators, some of which I have enumerated above. The affective elements have meaning in relation to the theory; empirical data can be meaningful only if given this theoretical framework.

What does all this mumbo jumbo amount to? Is it just more useless verbiage, more "elephant shit"? I think not. If we come to understand the theory we work with, we can come to know its assets and its limitations. Further, if we can show educators what underlies their theories, if we can make them aware of some of their misapplications of scientific procedures, if we can make the implicit explicit, we can help pave the way for constructive educational progress. "Awareness per se — by and of itself — can be curative." [2] Let us be aware of what we do. Let us also be aware of the nature of the demands we place upon ourselves. Let us not be the victims of splits between theory and practice in an attempt to satisfy our introjected scientist's topdog demands.

REFERENCE NOTES /
1. F. S. Perls, *Ego, Hunger and Aggression* (New York: Random House, 1969), p. 41.
2. F. S. Perls, *Gestalt Therapy Verbatim* (Lafayette, Calif.: Real People Press, 1969), p. 17.

6

GESTALT THERAPY: ENGAGING THE VIDEO SUBSELF

— Liles Grizzard

In the electric age, when our central nervous system is technologically extended to involve us in the whole of mankind, and to incorporate the whole of mankind in us, we necessarily participate in depth, in the consequences of our every action. . . .[1]

— MARSHALL MC LUHAN

. . . the simplicity of the Gestalt approach is that we pay attention to the obvious, to the utmost surface . . . a good therapist doesn't listen to the content of the bullshit the patient produces, but to the sound, to the music, to the hesitations . . . so don't listen to the words, just listen to what the voice tells you . . . what the movements tell you, what the image tells you . . . there is so much invaluable material here, that we don't have to do anything else except get to the obvious, to the outermost surface, and feed this back, so as to bring this into the patient's awareness. . . .[2]

— FRITZ PERLS

After spending some weeks videotaping various group discussions and Gestalt therapy work, including a discussion about video among members of our own media group, I spent a day editing the tapes into one master tape that our group was to exhibit. Editing and dubbing videotape is a tedious process that requires, along with lots of coffee and patience, the repeated viewing of all of the material being edited. There were two segments of tape in particular that I saw over and over again: members of the Gestalt group doing a projection exercise in which they conducted a dialogue with themselves as if they were the video camera, and a discussion among our own media group. As I was thinking about my own experience with Gestalt therapy, and now observing the work of others on tape, I began to see myself as I appeared on tape in our group discussion in an entirely new way.

What I began to see emerging on the tube was not my "topdog," nor my "underdog," nor my angry self, indifferent self, dancing self, "tiger" self — nor the introjection of my parents, nor any other parts of myself that I have become reacquainted with through Gestalt therapy. What I did see what someone new to me, someone I choose to call my "video subself." In this article I intend to describe the main characteristics of this odd new creature born of our electric environment, and to show how he relates to the theory and practice of Gestalt therapy.

In Gestalt therapy success can be judged by the extent to which a person moves from environmental support to self-support, takes responsibility for his own actions, and grows in awareness. In the Gestalt view, for a person to be self-supporting he must have a great deal of his own power and energy available for use. He must be able to expand his ego boundary (encircling that which he identifies as being of himself) to include more and more of that which he actually is, rather than that which he only thinks he is. He must discover in himself, and re-own, those elements of his personality that he has repressed in order to survive physically or psychologically. According to Fritz Perls:

> Everything the person owns can be recovered, and the means of this recovery is understanding, playing, becoming these disowned parts . . . and by letting [the patient] play and discover that he has all this (which he thinks only others can give him) we increase his potential. We more and more put him on his own feet, give him more and more ability to experience, until he is capable of really being himself and coping with the world . . . so what we are trying to do in therapy is step-by-step to re-own the disowned parts of the personality — until the person becomes strong enough to facilitate his own growth. [3]

Now, the video subself is not a disowned part of the personality, in Perls' sense. It is not properly a part of the personality at all, but rather a sizable part of a person's behavior over specific dimensions of time and space, abstracted through the video medium.

It is visible and audible — it can actually be seen and heard, and can be seen and heard fairly quickly in an ongoing situation (because of the technical ease and speed of feedback), which has the effect of expanding the present into the immediate past. The video subself is somewhat like oneself. It may not be fully recognized at once ("I'm not photogenic," "that doesn't sound like me," "the medium really distorts a person," "the picture is poor," "I'm not that heavy"), but is, in the main, accepted as being of oneself. Again, the video subself is one that behaves, both verbally and nonverbally. It exists in an environment, responds or does not respond to that environment, and can be seen and heard as it does this. The video subself should not, however, be seen as some hypothetical "objective" reality, being as it is a combination of the person and the situation he is in, perceived through the video medium (and subject to variations of color, lens focal length, distance, lighting, angle of view), in the present.

And perception itself is altered by the nature of the video medium. The video image, according to Marshall McLuhan, through its low picture resolution and two-dimensional electronic scanning system, involves the observer in depth in the image being watched. At a neurological level, the observer is required to participate, to fill in the blanks, to imagine in some way what is not there, to complete the gestalt.[4]

But to say that the video subself is not actually a part of the personality in the usual sense (and therefore has never been disowned) is not to say that it cannot be fully owned in the same way as are disowned parts of the personality in Gestalt therapy (as in Perls, above), thereby adding a new dimension to the personality.

To own means to include within the ego boundary, and this boundary can be flexible, allowing space to our new video subself. The ego boundary (between the organism and the environment), according to Perls, is more or less

> . . . experienced by us as what is outside the skin and what is inside the skin, but this is very loosely defined . . . is not a fixed thing . . . inside the ego boundary, there is generally cohesion, love, cooperation, outside the ego boundary there is suspicion, strangeness, unfamiliarity. . . .[5]

To fully admit the video subself within the ego boundary can give the personality the added dimension of a more or less objective (within the constraints previously pointed out) view of the behavior fostered by it — the outside experienced as inside — or to put it tritely, "seeing yourself as others (not individual others, but perhaps the average or mean of many others) see you." Allowing this view to become part of the personality can help to lessen the feelings of "suspicion, strangeness, unfamiliarity" toward persons and situations encountered outside of the ego boundary.

If we think that engaging and owning this video subself, as I have described it, is a worthwhile enterprise for Gestalt therapy, how can we do it? I think it can be accomplished by "understanding, playing, becoming" the video subject. Below are some exercises I have devised that I believe are appropriate to the task; they are suitable for Gestalt therapy groups, classroom situations, and for individuals working alone.

LIVE DIALOGUE /

For this exercise no tape is needed at all. Set up the video camera and recorder on live feedback. Face the monitor and carry on a dialogue with your video subself. Describe your video subself, and how you feel about him (or her). Then be your video subself and describe your real self and your feelings about yourself.

MIMICRY — EXAGGERATION /

In front of the camera, relate your here-and-now existence, while taping. View the replay and describe what you see and hear your video subself doing. Then play it back again and mimic the movements and voice quality of your video subself. Mimic just the voice quality (do not use words) and *exaggerate* everything. View this replay and be aware of how you are as you watch.

MIMICRY — OPPOSITES /

In front of the camera, describe your here-and-now existence, while taping. View the replay and describe what you see and hear your video subself doing. Then play it back again, and as you watch, mimic what you imagine the *opposite* movements and voice quality (again, use no words) of your video subself might be. Again, exaggerate everything.

DYADS (1) /

Tape a dialogue between you and another person for five minutes. Together, watch the replay of the tape. Continue your dialogue for another five minutes, with both you and your partner playing your own video subselves. Again, view this tape together and discuss any similarities or differences you see in the two tapes.

DYADS (2) /

Tape a dialogue between you and another person for five minutes. Together, observe the replay. Continue your dialogue for another five minutes while taping and become the video subself of your partner (he becomes yours). Together, look at this tape, and as you do, mirror and exaggerate your partner's movements and voice quality. To carry this to another level, tape this mirroring exercise, play it back, and mimic your partner's mirroring of your video subself.

LIVE DELAY /

Describe your here-and-now existence in front of the camera, while viewing the monitor live on ten-second delay (with the *sound off*). Tape this. View the playback (with the *sound on*) and repeat the entire exercise with the *sound on* throughout.

I believe that working with the video subself as I have suggested, or in similar ways others might discover, can enhance the Gestalt therapy goals of self-support, responsibility, and awareness.

Self-support is gained by re-owning parts of the personality that have been rejected. By owning the video subself, a person can learn, at a deep level, that it is he who is behaving as his video subself, and can include this behavior (in some sophisticated detail) within his ego boundary, thereby growing in self-support.

Responsibility is enhanced because the individual, to a great extent, becomes his own Gestalt therapist, lessening his dependence on outside authority to tell him what he is doing and how he is doing it. The person becomes the therapist; the video subself becomes the patient. The therapist's job of "feeding back the surface" of the person can, in good measure, be taken over by the person himself, working with his video subself. This can free the therapist to deal with frustration at the "impasse," when the person is suspended, without self-support and with environmental support not forthcoming, when he needs help.

Growth in awareness is facilitated through observing, role-playing, playing opposites, and exaggerating the behavior of the video subself. I think that intensive training with videotape can rapidly increase growth in awareness of both verbal and nonverbal behavior.

One final point. Getting in touch with our video image can be a rich, *self-validating* experience. For a couple of decades most of us have been receiving much of our experience of the surrounding world through the medium of television. For years we have been seeing the video subselves of others without seeing ourselves in the same way. By engaging and owning our video subselves, we correct this imbalance and validate ourselves as important sources of information. We might just find that we have a good deal more to offer than the greater or lesser "gurus" of our television viewing experiences. We will certainly come to know all of our selves better.

REFERENCE NOTES /
1. Marshall McLuhan, *Understanding Media: The Extensions of Man* (New York: McGraw-Hill, 1964), Introduction.
2. F. S. Perls, *Gestalt Therapy Verbatim* (Lafayette, Calif.: Real People Press, 1969), pp. 53–54.
3. Ibid., p. 37.
4. McLuhan, op. cit.
5. Perls, op. cit., p. 7.

7

GESTALT AND THE FIRST-YEAR TEACHER
— Melinda Rogers

Being in the now, experiencing, being aware, and being a first-year teacher — how do these relate, how do these affect one another, how do these merge into one total existence? As a first-year teacher I am suffering through all the doubts, dead ends, and frustrations that go hand in hand with working through a challenging situation. Yet I am also enjoying the warmth of sharing, the energy of discovery, and the excitement of never knowing exactly what will happen next with a roomful of eighth-graders. So far, this year has been one of learning and growth — not only in connection with my concept as a teacher but also as a total personality. A large portion of this growth is because Gestalt philosophy and work has brought me in touch with a larger realization of my strengths, with a larger awareness of choices and alternatives, and with a greater appreciation of, and trust in, my intuition. It is this growth — this use of Gestalt — and how it has added to and changed my actions and connections with education that I would like to share with you.

I began my first year as a teacher with a great number of shiny ideals and a philosophy of education that, if adopted by others, would change the world. I was no stranger to the classroom, having worked both as aide and student teacher, but it wasn't long until the pressures of teaching all day had me turned upside down. At the beginning of the day I was expounding belief in humanistic education, and by the end of the day I was telling students to sit down, open books, and shut up. I prepared extensive lessons, and if the kids liked them I was on top of the world. If they didn't respond with enthusiasm, I would be depressed and get revenge by making them do it anyway.

Weeks seemed like cross-country foot races where my endurance just barely lasted until Friday evening when I collapsed. The weekends were just long enough for me to catch my breath and wonder what the grand production would be for the following week. People kept telling me to slow down, don't try to cover so much, don't try to do and be everything for every child. But all I did was resent this interference. If I was going to be a teacher, I was going to be one of the best. I was going to conquer the challenge of teaching, and I thought that after a certain time of learning I would know all the tricks and skills and would only have to apply them. I didn't want or think I needed a philosophy for teaching. I simply wanted pat exercises, guaranteed to excite curiosity, spur growth, and set off a chain reaction of learning experiences for every child in my class. Also, I wanted a bonus thrown in — sure-fire ways of dealing with the "traditional" teachers in my school and with the administration. All I wanted was for someone to share all the secrets of being a great teacher — just tell me how to do it — and I would learn how to play the role.

I had been reading about Gestalt for almost a year, but it wasn't until I took the Gestalt Learning Theory course, where I personally experienced some Gestalt, that it all seemed to come together and actually become a dynamic source of power and a tool of insight for me. Slowly I came into touch with my strengths, and this sense of strength in turn allowed me to expand my ego boundary, to take risks. My intuition has always been strong, but I had never trusted it; now I feel it is like a sixth sense that not everyone has, and it is a great aid to me in working with people. Gestalt has also given me a means of getting in touch with what I'm actually doing, and thus I'm becoming aware that I have a choice, an alternative — to stop doing whatever I'm doing and do something else.

Of course, these personal changes also affect my approach to education and my concept of teaching. By being able to take more risks I allow myself more freedom in dealing with my students. I don't need to have guaranteed exercises. I can now try out things, and if they work, fine. If they don't work, I can examine and accept and learn from that failure. Perhaps the biggest change in this area is gaining the ability to say no — not to give "chicken soup." I don't always have this ability, this strength, even when I feel I should say no — yet it is becoming stronger. I am much better at frustrating a student when necessary instead of spoiling him with good intentions. I can now risk the animosity that saying no can bring about. I don't have to take all the responsibility for each child's learning. He must now begin to get in touch with his learning and assume responsibility for it himself.

Trust in my intuition is now one of my most valuable tools in working with individual students and at times with the entire class. I can generally sense when students are telling the truth, when they are upset, when they are angry, when they are bored, when they need a push, when they are to be left alone, and on and on, through the gamut of human moods. This sixth sense is immensely useful in contacting students and creating good rapport and trust. Of course, I am not one hundred per cent correct, nor am I always aware of my intuition. Yet now I feel a much greater awareness than earlier in the year, and I can enjoy the way my intuition helps me to see my classes as groups of individuals with individual needs, problems, and responses.

Taking time to be aware is perhaps the greatest thing Gestalt has helped me to do. I have always organized, structured, and planned broadly — flexible to an extent, but safe and orderly. I marched along trying to stay on the path I had planned and to reach the goal I had set. I seldom stopped to contact my feelings or my response as a total organism to any situation, for I always had "places to go, things to do, people to see." Now I stop and allow myself to contact myself. I still organize and structure and plan, but I have gained a greater flexibility, a greater range of actions. Often when I'm teaching I still get upset if things aren't going the way I anticipated, but now I stop and become aware of where my class and myself actually are, and then I have a valid choice of continuing in the planned direction or changing to something else. Also, if I am upset or angry or restless, I can touch this feeling and deal with it, not let it boil inside me and ruin my contact with all students for the day.

A person's philosophy of living is the basis for action, and there are practical everyday situations in teaching when this philosophy is tested, used, modified, and strengthened. How such things as lesson plans, curriculum designing, faculty relations and student-teacher relations are met and acted upon is a direct application of beliefs.

I feel more comfortable as a teacher in the classroom if I plan well. Yet, to be honest, when I plan well I experience some amount of stage fright because I have certain expectations which I fear won't be met. Though I still plan and organize and prepare because I feel it's basic to good teaching, I have broadened this concept to include planning for various reactions, for being flexible and in touch with the direction of the class, and for allowing students who can to assume responsibility for their learning. Gestalt has helped me gain this flexibility and openness (which I have not fully developed, by any means), and training has given me tools such as eye contact, voice intonations, body movement, and intuition, to help me "read" my class. I no longer feel so tied to the idea of getting through a certain amount of material. Curriculum is not the essense of education — the individual is. Of course, being the practical person I am, I do want concrete tools to work with in changing and improving the body of material that children learn. Curriculum must provide learning of all types, must teach students the process of learning, must include affective experiences, discipline, interaction, and cognitive exercises. The specific designation of what is to be learned should slowly and carefully be handed over to the student as he matures. Deciding what should be studied is not all *my* responsibility. Students and I can share this responsibility and can share in the creative process of curriculum design.

As a student teacher I was particularly frustrated by my master teacher and the conflict between his approach to teaching and mine. I went to him, seeking the rules of teaching and received only reassurance that I could learn the rules on my own. I can't say that Gestalt work has provided me with all the answers in this area, but for some reason I don't have to play disciple anymore. For the most part I like what I'm doing and I don't have to sell it to anyone else — I don't have to convert anyone else. I can share and be open to others, and that's enough. I can work with most others on our faculty, can appreciate them, and simply try to be an example of what I believe in. I must admit, though, that I still have periods of frustrations and I still resent unwanted intervention from the administration. So, as you can see, this is not a closed or solved problem area, but rather one in which, hopefully, I will continue to grow and learn.

Teacher-student relations, I feel, are the keys to education and can determine whether the education is good or bad. They are not the only keys to the learning process, but they are important ones. One of my stronger areas has always been good rapport with students. Being close to their age, it is easy for me to empathize with many of their hassles and problems. Working with Gestalt is adding another degree of enjoyment and skill in this area. When a student comes in to talk I am not so concerned with why he did this or that, but rather with getting him to become aware of where he is now, to become aware of his choices, and to realize he has responsibility for whatever decision he makes and whatever action he has already taken. I am not a perfected Gestalt therapist, but I do believe in it as a valid approach in working with students; and from student feedback, I think they feel it is straightforward and honest, and hard on them. Personally, I am now more in touch with my own strength, so I can risk being honest and straightforward with students. I can risk being me, say no when necessary, not try to be "the perfect helper" at all times for all students.

My concept of myself as a teacher has changed during this first year. I've been frustrated, joyous, exhausted, excited, depressed, and content. Gestalt has helped me to grow and to broaden as a person, has given me the tools to work more effectively with my students, and has expanded my ability to perceive. I am no longer a "teacher" — I am teaching. I have gained flexibility, trust in my intuition, and freedom to take certain risks. I have matured as a person, and this enables me to make better contact with the world I live in — to enjoy its richness. I am becoming aware and open, confident and relaxed. I am a good teacher, but I have much to learn. Gestalt is one of the many means by which I can accomplish growth.

8

GESTALT AND THE SUBSTITUTE TEACHER

— Victoria Grizzard

The role of the substitute teacher is a difficult and complicated one, and guidelines are virtually nonexistent. A substitute must deal with the attitudes and expectations of the principal, the regular teacher, and the class. The principal wants the class controlled, the regular teacher wants certain material covered, and the class wants freedom and fun — a break from their normal routine.

I believe that Gestalt principles offer direction and guidance that are especially valuable for the substitute teacher, and in this article I would like to relate how I have applied some of these principles to my own lively and often tumultuous experiences as a substitute teacher in the elementary school.

To function in the role of the substitute, I must be in touch with my own identity as a teacher, instead of adopting the role of the absentee teacher. I must make it clear to myself and others that I am not stepping into someone else's shoes, that I have my own two feet to stand on, and that I do not intend to follow in someone else's footsteps, even though I am willing to move in the same direction.

Younger children (kindergarten to grade three) are usually warm, open, receptive, and friendly toward substitutes. Those in grades four and five are less predictable, and those in grades five and six are the most challenging and testing. When I meet classes for the first time, I like to begin by introducing myself, letting them know that I am a regular, "real" teacher, that I have a child, and that I would appreciate their taking care of me and teaching me their routine procedures, schedule, and class layout. I let them know what kind of mood I'm in, that I enjoy jokes and humor, but not always at my expense. I tell them what their regular teacher has left as their assignments. I also let them know that as a substitute I can choose which classes or schools I want to work in or return to, and that I like to work with students who learn something from me. At the end of the day I take five or ten minutes to find out what they learned that day. I also try to include one special lesson of my own (an affective or confluent experience), even if it means omitting part of the regular plan.

Then I ask them to tell me their names and something about themselves, something they like to do, something they want to do today, how they feel about having a substitute, what they expect from me, what they would like me to know about them. Taking time for this round of introductions has proved very effective/ affective — almost as if the personal contact establishes a personal commitment to work together and be open and honest.

I make it clear that I do not want to act as a babysitter or a policewoman. I do not plan to teach them how to behave — they already know that. I want to share my knowledge and ideas, which may be new or a different version of what they have been learning, and they can show me their way, but for the most part I expect them to work independently.

I let the class know that usually I leave a note for the regular teacher about the work we complete or do not complete. I do not report on behavior problems or personal conflicts — I feel that those are between myself and the students and should be finished before we leave. I do leave positive comments about various students who are kind and helpful.

"Affection is the tendency to make friendly contact. . . ." [1] As a substitute I need enough ego strength and courage to reach out to young strangers for friendly contact. My willingness to encourage and my ability to understand at what point a student can help himself can facilitate growth and contact.

While supervising a math test (grade six) I let the students know that I was available if they were stuck. By rephrasing their questions and returning them to the students, I was able to promote more thought and they were able to make new connections. I understand the futility of answering questions directly. As I circulated, I encouraged students who worked independently as well as those who sought help. The atmosphere changed from cold and sterile to warm and productive.

I am aware that I represent an entirely different reality to each student, depending on his interests, needs, and tools of perception. One student may see me as a target for repressed aggression, another as an exciting change, as a listener, as a friend, as a critic, or as a confidant.

In order to attain an organismic balance between the group and myself, we must both be in touch with our needs and wishes and share them openly and clearly. A simple item such as seating arrangement can affect me; changing the seating arrangement certainly affects the students. I find it necessary *to ask* if they will accommodate my need, and at times it is necessary for me to accommodate theirs.

If I maintain awareness of the figure-ground phenomena and am really in touch with myself, then I have the confidence to deal with difficult situations in the classroom and to recognize my environment as one I share with the individuals as well as with the class as a whole. I am not totally responsible, though. I cannot and do not wish to control or direct all the situations and environment. As I remain aware, I am better able (in a considerate manner) to help the student seeking attention to become aware of his exhibitionism, and to draw upon other class members (by way of feedback) to help change this exhibitionism into concentration on objects, others, or his work.

If I try to control with a heavy hand, I meet resistance and resentment, not only from the attention-seeking, disruptive individual, but from other class members (often his friends) who are offering support against an outside adversary.

Taking the time to let them state their demands in various ways (i.e., write down or verbalize what they expect or want today, now, from me, the substitute teacher), whether I agree to them or not, often satisfies and eases the tension of uncertainty and lets the students know I am interested in them and their demands and will respond positively to any reasonable request. This often allows the shy student to express his needs and desires.

In one class (upper elementary, grades five and six) with which I was going to spend a week, I sensed a great deal of discontent, agitation, and resentment as soon as I entered the classroom. I overheard a few disparaging comments about me exchanged among the students. (Substitutes are not supposed to have ears, much less feelings.) I started out by stating what I sensed, what I had heard, what I was feeling, and asked what they were upset about. (They had known that their regular teacher would be absent, and had had a substitute the previous week who did not want to continue working with this "difficult" group.) At first they exchanged looks and glances with each other, made a few wise comments and challenges — "what's the use of telling you, you won't do anything about it." Then a few students expressed complaints and resentments toward the previous substitute, about events that had taken place that week.

I told them that I could do nothing about the past or the other teacher, but if they could change their complaints into requests or demands for today, or this week, I would be glad to deal with them. There was a mini-explosion. Everyone wanted something or didn't want something; they were talking and shouting all at once. I called for order. I realized that there was no way I could get to everyone, and we had a schedule to adhere to that involved other classes. After listening to a few students (some making impossible requests, such as "no school," others making reasonable demands, like "less homework," still others saying simply, "don't shout at us"), I asked them to take out a sheet of paper and make three columns. The first column was what they wanted or expected from me, the second what they wanted for themselves, and the third was what they wanted or expected from the whole group. They spent fifteen minutes on this before their next class.

I had no idea what I would do with all this information, but the class seemed more relaxed; the rest of the day was productive, with only a couple of minor conflicts. Throughout the day various students asked me what I was going to do with their papers, and they told friends in other classes (who also had various classes with me) about the papers.

After school I read all the papers, learning a great deal about the individual students and the group. One student wanted me to stop his brother from hitting him; several boys didn't want me to pick Jane as my assistant (even though they knew she had been selected as assistant by their homeroom teacher); one girl wanted me to send rowdy boys to the principal. I tabulated the results, made three charts stating all the demands and expectations, and put them up in the room. The next morning they excitedly read the charts — some identified their contributions — and we started this day much more congenially. I had spoken to Jane privately and explained that I appreciated her capabilities, but that I would call on others to assist me, and that if any serious questions came up I would check with her. She said she felt good about that; she hadn't asked to be picked as assistant in the first place.

No one asked me anything all week about my decisions in regard to their demands (I did cut back on the amount of homework assignments) and the week was pleasant and rewarding. On Friday, I asked how they felt about the week and which of the demands and expectations they felt had been met and which ones they felt had not been met. Their responses were enthusiastic and positive.

I have also used the resentment/appreciation exercise at the end of a day. I sometimes change the terms to: I didn't like, I felt bad about, I enjoyed, I liked, depending on the class and grade level.

Substitutes especially need to be aware of the balance between the means-whereby and the end gain. As a substitute I need self-awareness and awareness of the group. I need to know what my goals are (i.e., carrying out the plans of the regular teacher, making human contact with the students, etc.) and to have a repertoire of techniques and plans (games, activities, lessons) to achieve various goals. I have spoken to many kind, intelligent substitutes who have either the means-whereby or the end gain but not the complete Gestalt. Some older, experienced substitutes have a collection of sure-fire, prepackaged activities and lessons that they use (with little or no variation for class or level) to keep children busy and produce a take-home product; some younger, inexperienced substitutes want to make real contact with the children, but they have only the plans left by the regular teacher with which to work.

Having a packet of ideas, possibilities, techniques, and lessons is great, but being flexible, planning and consulting with the actual students, is also essential. Being willing to accept a no from the class when they don't want to do the great preplanned lesson, and being willing to go with their requests (when reasonable) is evidence of flexibility, consideration, awareness, and life — qualities that students really respond to.

I have found that being honest and giving students a fair choice results in real two-way contact and communication. In one class (upper elementary, grades five and six) I told the students what I had to offer — an imaginary trip and drawing — and asked if they would be willing to try it. Five boys said they wanted to play a game instead. I said no, that the game would intrude on what most of us wanted to do, that they would have to think of a more quiet activity. They opted for free drawing.

During the "Train Fantasy" the five boys would stop and listen; when we got to the drawing part, they were curious to see what the others were drawing, and one of them began drawing a picture in terms of the fantasy trip. They listened, and the one boy participated when we shared the drawings in terms of projection (I am an old train, I'm going, I am the tracks).

Children are very much in touch with their biological needs. They have a good feeling of themselves and are well aware of their capabilities and limitations. A substitute can give fresh encouragement to develop their abilities and transcend their limitations. Teachers who uphold impossible standards of behavior — sit still, don't talk, write for long periods of time — turn the life of the class into hell.[2]

In dealing with behavior problems — disruptive children — I try to avoid the mistake of striving for perfection instead of development. Robbie can't work as quietly as I'd like him to, but he can work more quietly than he is now doing. I ask for the possible, not the ideal. Instead of punishing a disruptive student by canceling his recess, a common practice — very often he needs physical activity in order to settle down and cooperate — or publicly reprimanding a student, I use personal contact and find it much more effective. If he avoids eye contact, I ask him to look at me and tell me what he is doing. Usually this contact and awareness is sufficient. I might ask if he feels a need to say something or move about. Often it is attention the student seeks and now that he has it, he is satisfied. If not, I may tell a student that the rest of us are busy, that he is interrupting our reading, that he should go outside, jump up and down or whatever, and come back in when he is ready.

In one reading class (lower elementary, grades one and two) I asked a boy who was tickling his neighbor what he was doing, and he said, "Nothing." I asked him to ask his neighbor what he was doing.

NEIGHBOR: You are making me laugh.

ME: Jack, do you enjoy making people laugh?

JACK: I don't know.

ME: Would you try something?

JACK: Sure.

ME: Come up front and make all of us laugh without touching us.

Jack came forward and started taking funny poses, flexing his muscles, etc. Then he added comments about himself: "I can climb trees like a monkey and get bananas. . . . Bobby, wanna banana?" Sure enough, he had us all laughing. I asked the group if they enjoyed Jack. They said yes. I asked if anyone wanted him to continue to do so by tickling. They said no, they wanted to get back to reading. I asked Jack if he would sit down and read with us. He did.

Being aware of projections not only protects my ego, but enables me to guide students toward assimilating their projections and seeing themselves more clearly.

In a literature class (middle elementary, grades three and four) we had finished sharing an enjoyable story and our feelings about it. The students returned to their seats to do independent work. I circulated and gave help and encouragement. I noticed Anne teasing her neighbor. I said nothing. I watched her. She saw me watching and stopped. Five minutes later her neighbor came up to me and asked me to tell Anne to stop pulling her paper, because she couldn't work. The three of us went out into the hall and I asked Jill to tell Anne what she wanted.

JILL (*to me, angrily*): I want Anne to stop bothering me!

ME: Tell her.

JILL (*softer voice, not so angry*): I want you to stop pulling my paper.

ANNE: I was only kidding.

JILL: But I told you before to stop it.

ANNE: O.K.

Toward the end of the class I went over to Anne to see how she was doing and to ask if she needed help. She curtly said no. I asked what she was angry about. She said I was a skinny, mean teacher and she didn't like me. She wanted her regular teacher back. He was rounder, smiled more, and wasn't mean. (Anne was very round, chubby. Jill was very thin.) I asked her if Jill had been mean to her. She said yes. I asked how, and she said by telling on her and getting her in trouble. I informed her that she was not in trouble and that I felt bad that she didn't like me.

When working with younger children (kindergarten to grade three), I am very aware of their use of "proper ego language." The avoidance of responsibility and the avoidance of the first person singular is very evident in regular classrooms as well as in special problem cases.

"Correct ego language, e.g., correct identification, is the basis of self-expression and confidence." [3] As a substitute teacher I must be open and honest, and use "I" to express my feelings, wants, demands, appreciations, and resentments, rather than divorce myself from the situation and give out instructions like an automaton: "Read pages 273 to 296, and answer the questions." What does that statement have to do with me? How does it relate to the students? They respond much more positively to: "I would like you to read quietly pages 273 to 296, so that I will have time to prepare, and then we will decide how to handle the questions — have open discussion, answer the questions orally, or work with a partner."

The teacher can help a great deal with the "I," especially in building self-image and helping children assimilate disowned parts of their personalities. The correct use of "you" is more complicated, because it involves interpersonal relationship as well as projections. [4]

In a kindergarten group (a half-hour reading class) some of the children remembered that I had been in their class two months before and that I had read them a story. I asked them to "write" (say) a short story about me and I would write it on the board. They could say what they remembered, what they liked or didn't like about me, or look at me and describe me. When they gave phrases like "pretty hair" I asked, "Who has pretty hair?" "You have pretty hair." "Who says so?" "I say so." "My hair looks pretty to you?" "Yes." "O.K., then let's write 'her hair looks pretty to me.'" The next student gave "your eyes." "What about my eyes?" "I like your eyes." The rest of the story: I'm mad at her, she is mad at me, she likes me.

I decided to deal with their concerns and projections about my liking or disliking them. I asked them to say their names and to say what they liked about themselves, expanding their sentences to include or begin with "I." One shy girl couldn't say anything. I called her to me and asked her to whisper in my ear what she liked about herself. She whispered, "I don't know. Nothing." I asked if it was O.K. with her if I asked the group for some help. She nodded. I asked the group what they liked about Mary, and had them begin with: I like her smile — her smooth hair — her, because she shares with me. Mary was beaming. After that, whenever I met Mary at recess time or lunch time I asked her what she liked about herself. The first couple of times she repeated what her classmates had said. Later she would smile and come up with something new. "I like the way I skip."

In another kindergarten class I encountered a vivacious, energetic little girl who was always telling others what to do during free-choice time. When things were not going the way she wanted (she was in the group using large building blocks), she came over and insisted that I tell the others how they should be building.

ME: How should they be building?

POLLY: I want the big blocks on top, and they won't listen.

ME: How can you get them to listen?

POLLY: I told them what to do.

ME: How can you get them to listen?

POLLY: They won't.

ME: Then what can you do?

POLLY: I could put the blocks up myself.

ME: Who gave you all the answers to your questions?

POLLY (surprised, questioningly): Me?

ME: I'm going to give you a magic finger, and every time you point it at someone else, look at it and see if it has something to say to you.

Polly walked away holding up her index finger. Later she came to ask me what to do next. Before I could answer she said, "Oh, I know — I should ask my magic finger." She left and found her own activity.

In the same kindergarten, during free choice, John had taken Peter's special STP car. Peter was crying and sobbing, but John wouldn't give it back. I went over and asked what the problem was. John quickly handed Peter his car. Peter was still sobbing. I asked John if he could tell how Peter was feeling.

JOHN: I don't know.

ME: What is he doing?

JOHN: Crying.

ME: Who is crying?

JOHN: Peter is crying.

ME: Do you know how he feels when you take his car?

JOHN: I don't know.

ME: O.K., let me have your shirt. (*As I reached out, John stopped me by protecting his shirt. A few tears came to his eyes.*) How do you feel if I want to take your shirt?

JOHN: Bad.

ME: Who feels bad?

JOHN: I feel bad.

ME: Do you know how Peter feels now?

JOHN: Yes.

Students of all ages are taught to ignore their body and body functions and concentrate on their thinking. Children of elementary school age, especially, identify with their bodies. Having to sit quietly for long periods of time is unnatural for them. "We all require, at least occasionally, a respite from the stress which profession and society lay on us, a regression to our natural self." [5] Recesses are for getting rid of excess energy so that children can work more efficiently, mentally, back in the classroom.

Physical education often has as its goal the development of physical skills and abilities, but quite often it does not deal with the students' feelings about their assets or deficits. Feelings become more confused and abused when the class goes out for a half hour of baseball or volleyball, and students who don't do well are berated by their classmates.

Perls' body-concentration exercises can be very helpful for the substitute teacher as long as they are adapted to the actual situation and the real needs of the children at the appropriate time.

"If properly understood, relaxation can be a help in acute emergency . . . addressed to someone over-tensed and over-excited. Relaxing in this case means letting go of the hanging-on attitude, getting one's bearings, switching from the blind emotional to the rational aspect, recovering one's senses. In such cases relaxation even as a short interruption of the tension can work wonders." [6]

When a situation or a group becomes filled with tension, or the children are very "nudgy" and annoy one another, punitive measures usually make matters worse and create more tension, with resentment toward the teacher thrown in. And if the teacher is a substitute, a mini-explosion may occur.

When groups (kindergarten to grade three) have become overexcited or superactive, which happens when we are working creatively and freely, I have asked the children to lie down on the floor without touching their neighbor, to feel how they are breathing, to trust me that nothing is going to happen or be done to them, to place their palms up, close their eyes and relax, feel the floor supporting them, think of a special place where they like to be alone, and use their imagination to go to that special place. I wait a few minutes, then tell them to open their eyes very slowly, without saying a word, and slowly sit up. If time permits, I ask who is willing to tell us where their special place was, and what they were doing there. (When I have returned to classes for a second time as a substitute, students have excitedly requested by "relaxing" or "special place" exercise.)

By dealing in the present, the substitute can create an atmosphere of interest and excitement by relating to the students as they are now, not as they were in past performance. Students usually speak expressively and emotionally in the present tense except when they say something like "he always does that." Then they have found a scapegoat and begin dwelling on past misdeeds.

One of the standard "jokes" played on substitutes is for the students to change their names. Is this their way of experimenting with a new, present identity — completely divorced from previous behavior? In asking how they feel about my being there, instead of their regular teacher, I can quickly assess whether they are aware of me as a person, or are reacting to me in terms of past experiences with substitutes. I deal with sentences that begin "Whenever we have a substitute" or "The last time we had a substitute" by countering with the question, "What about right now?"

REFERENCE NOTES /

1. Frederick S. Perls, *Ego, Hunger and Aggression* (New York: Random House, 1969), p. 23.
2. Ibid., p. 271.
3. Ibid., p. 219.
4. Ibid.
5. Ibid., p. 229.
6. Ibid., p. 230.

9

GESTALT THEORY AND PRACTICE AND THE TEACHING OF LITERATURE

— *Thomas Yeomans*

As its title indicates this article deals with two educational practices and the possibilities of their relationship. Writers, literary critics, and educators have given the second part of the title, the teaching of literature, much attention over the years, and have hotly debated its promises and problems since the beginnings of literary culture. The first part, Gestalt theory and practice, is a newcomer, and psychological theorists and clinicians have only begun to examine, amplify, and appraise it. At the moment both occupy largely disparate environments, each with its own issues, controversies, and hypotheses — teachers of literature know little of Gestalt, Gestalt therapists know little of the teaching of literature — and in this I see a loss, for there are many ways in which the two can be related and be of service to each other.

This is particularly so in the expanded possibilities Gestalt theory and practice offer to the teaching of literature, and I will be concerned here mostly with this aspect of the relationship. In dealing with this topic, I plan, after some preliminary discussion of theories of teaching literature, to set forth the theory I find most valuable of those available and then to indicate how Gestalt can be used to put this theory into better practice than it now experiences. I intend to demonstrate that Gestalt contains powerful techniques and approaches to learning, readily adaptable to the problems of teaching literature, and to argue for a close connection and interfusing of these two realms of educational activity and concern. Hopefully, a time will come when the two are no longer strangers.

Theories of teaching literature fall into two main, and mutually hostile, camps. The first theory, and at the moment the predominant one, holds that a work of literature is an artifact to be examined with discrimination and analytical skill in order to arrive at some knowledge of how, and how well, it is put together and, secondarily, to arrive at some knowledge of what went into its making. This approach borrows the so-called "objective" scientific method from the physical sciences and applies it to literature, the basic assumption being that the more you know about a work, the better you will understand it. It thus makes great use of the fields of literary history and criticism, as well as, of course, the technical aspects of poetics, aesthetics, and formal analysis. The work of art is viewed as a complicated, delicate, and beautiful machine, whose workings can be fathomed and understood through the processes of careful intellectual analysis.

This theory has led, in practice, to an enormous collection of scholarship on literature. Not only are the classics exhaustively and repeatedly reviewed, but commentaries appear on books whose print has scarcely dried and whose authors are still in mid-career. It is easy to obtain more information than you might want to know about any writer, be he famous or obscure — his life, his times, his works, his place in the Great Tradition. Generations of literary scholars have compiled such a vast range of material that a life time spent in reading cannot command it, all of which is valid and valuable, except that the essence of the original work is often lost in the midst of this morass, along with the experience of itself that the work offers the world.

Basically, this theory emphasizes the importance of tradition over any particular work and uses the literary tradition to judge new works. It takes the long and objective view, and is more concerned with the received canons of taste than with immediate and unique experience. It is a theory of literature espoused, for the most part, by scholars, university professors, and "academic" writers whose roots lie in European culture and scholarship and, more recently, in the New Criticism and other schools of formal literary analysis. It is a conservative theory, valuing the Great Works and seeing itself as responsible for handing down a given and inherited cultural milieu to the young. In its proceedings the theory is very remote from the initial creative impulse and act that spawned the work, and few artists follow it; most artists are rather hostile to its formality and at times its pomposity.

At the opposite pole from the traditional theory of literature lies the second approach — the gut-level theory of literature. According to this theory, literature is to be experienced as an immediate, gut-level happening to which each person's response is of equal value, and the work is validated by its mere existence. Here, there is no need of analysis, criticism, literary history, or aesthetics, for each person gets what he gets, with emphasis placed mostly on how he feels about the poem or story, on how it affects him. Artist or critic, the conventionality of language and form are completely ignored, for the reader's personal reaction is held paramount, and learning is assumed to result from this experience in and of itself. If a poem makes you cry, it's got to be good; a novel makes you laugh, so you love it. Emphasis is placed on the here-and-now response to, and interpretation of, a work of art, and little attention is paid to its place in a tradition, its genre, its relationship to other works of art, literary or otherwise. All secondary sources of knowledge are considered unimportant compared to that gleaned existentially from the event itself, knowledge which often is expressed by such appreciations as "that was far out" or "what a bummer."

In writing of these theories I find it hard to resist satire or irony since both techniques obviously are exaggerated; but each is important as an antipode to the other and, in a sense, each exists because of the other. Each polarizes the other — one driven toward mind and knowledge, the other toward mindless experience. Neither speaks fully to the literary experience itself, though each contains a partial truth. And both are powerful influences today on how literature is taught in and out of schools.

A third theory, which falls between and synthesizes these two extremes, is the process or growth theory of literature. This theory emphasizes the processes of literary development and of learning to express oneself through the medium of language. Instead of beginning with the work, it starts with the person. More specifically, the theory focuses on the person's relationship to his language as a vehicle for self-discovery, growth, and increasing existential understanding of self and world — holding that a person's first responsibility is to himself, not to any given tradition and/or body of knowledge — and then works from these foundations toward and into the literary culture.

Unlike the gut-level theory, the growth theory respects and uses tradition as a resource for expanding and deepening the literary response. It does not treat a work either as totally isolated and immediate (as does the tradition theory) or as totally fixed in product form, but views it, rather, as a stage in a literary growth process through which both artist and student are passing. Both are human beings; both have language in common. One undoubtedly is more skilled in the use of language than the other; one is perhaps more sensitive and open to his experience, but both are connected by a process of seeking and growing, and this allows mutual respect and learning. Emphasis here is placed on the creative process as a connection between artist and reader; contact through works of literature is seen as an opportunity for expansion of consciousness, growth in language skill, and deepening of understanding of the possibilities for using language. Given this, each progresses as he can, perhaps to be a gifted writer, perhaps not, but in any case to obtain through writing and reading a wider and richer experience in and of the world.

Specifically, this theory first gained visibility at the "Anglo-American Seminar on the Teaching of English" held at Dartmouth College in the summer of 1966, and several publications that resulted from that event. All stress various aspects of growth, response, and creativity in the learner.[1] Clearly, this theory of literature combines the best of our first two theories without going to either extreme, and thus represents a synthesis of the two. Literature is considered as an immediate and an informed encoding of human experience, arrived at best by working with a student's immediate concerns and encoding system (his language), and expanding from there into wider ranges of literary expression. The literary tradition is maintained and valued, but it is reversed in that the individual's sensibility now grows out from his center to include more and more of tradition. In this way a student will eventually get to the Great Works, if it profits him. He is free to choose and create his experience with literature from the vast resources which a good teacher will make available to him. And always he is in touch with his creative center which, in conjunction with his environment, chooses, directs, and evaluates his learning experiences and the course of his development. Analysis and synthesis are both necessary to this process as the student grows as a reader, writer and, most important, as a person developing toward emotional, intellectual, and moral maturity.

We have, then, three theories of teaching literature: the traditional, the gut-level, and the growth. The third is the theory I have found most useful in my teaching, and it is its practice that I want to improve through the use of Gestalt learning theory. To move in this direction I will first draw some general parallels between Gestalt and the growth theory, where theoretical connections can be made and practice generated, and then I will propose a few specific exercises as concrete examples of what might be done in the classroom.

On the theoretical level, the most obvious parallel between Gestalt and the growth theory is the central position occupied by the person and his growth process. Gestalt theory is a growth theory which views the individual as incomplete and/or divided against himself and works to assist him in removing blocks to his growth and in re-owning disowned parts of his personality. Thus it is person-centered, and the very arrangement of the classical Gestalt session stresses this. The therapist sits beside the patient, watching what is happening and making explicit what he sees while the patient works on his difficulties-problems-blocks, with the empty space in front of the patient filled with his own obstacles. His work is with himself as he opposes himself; the therapist only assists. Here "learning is discovery," [2] not instruction, and the therapist and other members of the group serve as resources for use in discovery and expanded awareness, which the patient (or in the case of a class, the student) gains by himself for himself. Obviously, the growth theory of literature would endorse these same tenets and arrangements.

A second parallel is the concept of responsibility. Both theories stress the learner's responsibility for what he does or does not learn, and insist on his evaluation of what he has or has not accomplished. He, not the teacher or therapist, is responsible for assessing his own strengths and limitations, and for dealing with his frustration caused by the gap between who and where he is and where he wants to go. Too often other theories or therapies allow a student (patient) to make the teacher (therapist) responsible for his development by getting the professional to help him, to do for him what he can really do for himself. In Gestalt learning the therapist lets the frustration work in mobilizing the patient's resources so that he can get through the impasse or block by himself.

This experience leads to the development of a second responsibility (a favorite definition of Perls' was "responsibility spelled with an 'a' ") — the ability to respond. The patient breaks through his own rigid responses (Perls terms this "character"), and in the process becomes more open and able to respond freshly to an environment which is constantly changing and never the same again. Clearly, this is just another way of talking about traditional versus individual and informed sensibility responses to literature. In the growth theory of literature the teacher works to assist a student in responding freshly and immediately to a literary work, unhampered by traditional clichés and attitudes, and encourages him to take responsibility for his response and for what he knows and still needs to know.

A third parallel is the emphasis on present, here-and-now experience. The Here and Now is the medium in which Gestalt therapy works. Again and again the patient is asked: "What's happening now? What do you experience here and now?" Speaking or writing about awareness continually encourages this orientation also, and a patient is constantly urged to be aware of how he is feeling and of how he is dealing with a problem or conflict "right now" rather than thinking and speculating about why he is where he is. In dreamwork the therapist insists that a patient retell his dream in the present tense, and experience and work with it in that tense. In relation to the group he is asked to make "I" rather than "it" (or indirect) statements and, all in all, he is held as much as possible to an awareness of his immediate experience. In this way he comes to be more comfortable and more in touch with himself and his responses to his internal and external environment — much as in the growth theory of literature when, through immersion in the present state of his reading or writing, a student experiences fully and freshly his response and is able to grow from this. Note, however, that here the growth theory goes beyond Gestalt, for, as I have pointed out, it works also with the "whys" of literary study, and is not just gut-level. However, the point is that this is where it starts, in the here and now, and Gestalt can do a lot to intensify this basic experience out of which a literary sensibility is built.

A fourth parallel between Gestalt learning theory and the growth theory of literature is in the concept of polarities. Gestalt finds an opposite for every situation or feeling and works to achieve a balance at a point of "creative indifference" where the two extremes become integrated.[3] Rather than an either/or therapy, it is a both/and therapy, leading to richer experience rather than one-sided, impoverished existence. Growth literary theory works to achieve a comparable balance between the emotional and intellectual components in literature and between the literary tradition and the individual sensibility. It denies neither pole as the other theories do, but works with both, exploring the tension between them and seeking integration in the experience of reading, writing, and discussing literature, be it written by other students or by Shakespeare or Homer.

The fifth parallel is the concept of the organism-in-its-environment. Gestalt holds that all responses are a response to something, that every organism of necessity must relate to an internal/external environment. Nothing exists outside of a particular context — one which is constantly shifting and changing. In literary theory we come closer to the traditionalists, which is fine, for this is the way to use what we know of the life and times of an artist — to illumine his growth process. The difference is that in growth theory the environment never becomes more important than the organism itself. The artist remains in the center of his world, responding to it as it shifts, and we see this; but we also know that it is to him that we are most immediately and meaningfully connected, not to his world in and of itself.

A final parallel lies in the Gestalt concept of ego boundaries. Much of Gestalt therapeutic work concerns itself with making clear what is inside and what is outside a person's ego boundaries. Do they include only what is existentially him, at any given moment, or have they expanded to include introjections and retroflections, or have they shrunk because of projections and disowning? [4] As a person sorts this out he regains his power and is increasingly sure of who he is and is not. In literary growth theory this concept is very useful in helping a student both to immerse himself in a new literary experience (ego boundary expansion) and to sort out what is useful or not useful to him in the experience (assimilation and ego boundary clarification). Ego boundaries shift constantly. At times expansion is appropriate, at times contraction. The trick is to know when, and what's there. With a literary experience the trick is to be open, yet not lose oneself permanently under the weight of introjected knowledge and projected creative power (in the case of the tradition theory), or introjected total creative power and rejection of all knowledge (in the case of the gut-level theory). A good literary experience expands ego boundaries and consciousness — something new is taken in — but in order to maintain growth of the individual sensibility some sorting and evaluation (assimilation) is necessary.

These, then, are the main and most useful parallels I see between the two theories. I draw them in the hope that they will generate approaches in the teaching of literature that make use of Gestalt theory and practice. To further this end, we turn now to a few ways in which Gestalt learning theory might be applied to the actual teaching situation. Clearly, the following suggested exercises and approaches are representative at best. Further, the best applications will most often emerge from the response of the trained teacher to a specific situation, and they are offered in this spirit. Not all arise from the immediate discussion, but are based on Gestalt theory and practice, and so provide a starting point for further thought.

EXERCISES /

1. Conceive of an essay as a figure/background phenomenon. A series of figures emerge and re-merge, making a series of gestalts which the reader experiences and the writer can shape. Conceive of sentences within a paragraph in the same way (topic sentence as major gestalt). Conceive of words within a sentence in this way.

2. Use projection techniques:
   a. With parts of speech, punctuation, misspelled words. How do you feel as a verb, a noun?

    b. With words in a sentence to explore relationships (grammar). Students could "play" the different words.

    c. For work with diction and word choice. Become the paper, poem, essay, or sentence. What do you need? Dialogue between two word choices.

3. Explore polarities in word meanings and vocabulary work.

    a. "Play" words and their opposites.

    b. Find points of creative indifference between them.

4. Dream-work a word. Explore its associations and become parts of the resultant fantasy. Get at images embedded in the word.

5. Use chair dialogue (a student working with an empty chair in front of him in which he places whatever is troubling him) for working through writing blocks. The student puts himself in the chair and tells himself what he needs. Explore topdog/underdog. This approach also fosters responsibility for writing problems and self-evaluation.

6. Use Gestalt therapy format for getting student in touch with himself. Use Gestalt games for expanding awareness. Use material evoked as a source for writing.

7. Have students write daily awareness continuum.

8. In writing dialogue use the chair technique to explore disagreements on an issue or tension between two or more characters.

9. Use projection exercises to improve identification with objects, animals, plants, people, etc. Training of the imagination.

10. Use contact/withdrawal and feelings/behavior to explore different simultaneous levels of experience.

11. Use fantasy exercises and dreamwork as a way of supplying material for work in writing.

12. Use avoidance principle to get student in touch with the kinds of writing or situations with which he has trouble and is avoiding.

13. Treat a poem as an environment with different gestalts. Become parts of the poem. Create and explore its environment.

14. Use projection techniques with characters in a novel. Play them and/or the real self within context of the novel and/or the classroom. Work with characters in the chair. Explore identification. Explore polarities in characters using techniques of reversal and exaggeration.

15. Present a novel or story as a dream. Do dreamwork with particular episodes or situations.
16. In drama, deal with characters as splits in the playwright experience. Explore their relationships, using the chair technique.
17. Explore illusion/reality relationship in dealing with characters in a play.

In general students can be encouraged to stay in touch with themselves in both reading and writing (and in all their work) by using the techniques of Now statements and shuttling. This will insure that they are open to what they are learning or doing while they are involved in it, and that they will take responsibility for choosing to withdraw from that activity.

We have come a fair distance, and now I want only to state again my initial hope that practitioners of Gestalt theory and growth theory will make increased use of each other's work. I have tried to demonstrate here that Gestalt offers tremendous possibilities for improving the teaching of literature, and that it is a natural resource for enriching people's experience with, and understanding of, language and literature. Obviously, much still needs to be done in relating precisely and in detail, these two activities. But in myself I now feel a beginning.

REFERENCE NOTES /

1. Publications resulting from the "Anglo-American Seminar on the Teaching of English," Dartmouth College, summer 1966: Douglas Barnes (ed.), *Drama in the English Classroom*; Arthur Eastman (ed.), *Sequence in Continuity*; Albert Markwardt (ed.), *Language and Language Learning*; Paul Olson (ed.), *The Uses of Myth*; James R. Squire (ed.), *Response to Literature*; Geoffrey Summerfield (ed.), *Creativity in English*. [All published by the National Council of the Teachers of English, Champaign, Ill., 1968.]

Also from this conference:

Herbert J. Muller, *The Use of English* (New York: Holt, Rinehart & Winston, 1967).

John Dixon, *Growth Through English* (London: Oxford University Press, 1967).

2. F. S. Perls, *Gestalt Therapy Verbatim* (Lafayette, Calif.: Real People Press, 1969), p. 25.
3. F. S. Perls, *Ego, Hunger and Aggression* (New York: Random House, 1969), p. 19.
4. Ibid., pp. 107–184.

10

"BEYOND" GESTALT THERAPY

— George Isaac Brown

The title of this article is partially in quotes because I want to differentiate between what many narrowly perceive to be the end-all of Gestalt therapy and what I believe to be a more realistic, holistic, and practical conception. The latter point of view, incidentally, was posited by Perls himself, though perhaps not conspicuously during his lifetime. Thus, what I have to say goes beyond Gestalt therapy as practiced by many, but not actually beyond Gestalt in its essential nature and composition. The narrow view seems to be prevalent enough in practice today to warrant a differentiation, for its limitations have serious therapeutic and educational implications.

Frederick Perls, the founder of Gestalt therapy, or, as he preferred to call himself, the re-finder of Gestalt therapy, consistently and vigorously attacked the neurotic attempts of his patients or clients to manipulate him. They tried to con him, and all other people around at the time, into giving them support in whatever neurotic role they chose for themselves at the moment. Perls, however, skillfully frustrated these attempts.

Sometimes the client had a variety of roles or games from which to draw. Some examples of these were playing helpless or stupid, playing the seducer or the bulldozer. An example of the helpless game is when statements like these are made: "I really try, but things never work out for me when I do it alone." Or, "You have to do this for me. You're so much stronger (capable, competent, resourceful, etc.) than I am." This game can continue ad infinitum and works es-

This article first appeared in the *Journal of Contemporary Psychotherapy*, vol. 5, no. 2 (Summer 1973). Reprinted by permission of the editor.

pecially well for sucking in people who want to help others. The stupid game is characterized by statements like: "I just don't understand. You'll have to explain it again." And again and again. Or, "You know so much more about people than I do. You tell me what to do." Whatever suggestions given are each swiftly and effectively sabotaged by the client. The role of seducer is an obvious one and also highly effective. Nearly everyone likes to be seduced. The bulldozer is a combination bully and loudmouth who will not listen and who has tunnel vision. These are only four examples among many of the roles or games that environmental manipulators can play. It should be noted that the client, while manipulating, sincerely believes that he is incapable of doing for himself what he imagines others could or should do for him. Sometimes he even believes there are things others should do to him.

By frustrating these manipulations, Perls hoped first to help the client become aware of what he was doing, as he attempted to manipulate. Through other methods of Gestalt, Perls then hoped to help the client experience *how* he was doing what he was doing. Perls described this process as moving the client from a position of requiring environmental support to a stance of self-support. Among the more or less poetic metaphors he used to describe the condition of self-support, perhaps the most acceptable description for conventional discussion is "learning to stand on your own two feet."

Because most of us have learned all too well a variety of manipulations to use in order to obtain environmental support, especially the support of other persons in our environment, and because our learning has its roots in our childhood, and because in our families or educational institutions we have seldom been given the opportunity to experience or learn alternatives, we continue to use what we know — these manipulation roles and games. Consequently, instead of responding to each situation in which we find ourselves, in ways appropriate to that situation, we may distort or deny our perceptions of the situation. Through our manipulating roles and games we may attempt to modify the situation so that it will better fit how we imagine we are and thus maintain our status quo. Our status quo stems from how we experience ourselves and, especially, includes the limitations we imagine ourselves to have. These limitations are in fact a consequence of the narrowness in our choices of ways to be, or respond to the world around us. In other words, through the well-learned manipulation roles and games that we skillfully use, we enslave ourselves in a no-growth prison fraught with impasses. I should point out that this process is not usually a conscious one; most of us believe that we are indeed responding realistically to whatever is occurring within ourselves or in the universe around us. The actual condition of our narrow existence, however, is simply a consequence of limited choices.

What Perls was trying to do when he frustrated the attempts at manipulation by a client was to demonstrate dramatically that at least for this one time such ways of responding or reacting did not work. Thus the client would have to find other ways to act.

Using Gestalt-styled feedback, Perls provided structures with which the client could work. These took many forms, such as the use of exaggeration, experiencing one's polarities, the use of dream-work wherein projected aspects of personality are re-owned through re-experiencing the symbols occurring in dreams, other methods of re-owning projections, topdog-underdog dialogues, going into one's impasse, and a number of other techniques. Perls thus helped the client to discover, by himself and for himself, other ways to be and other parts of himself that were available for use by him. The energy previously dissipated in manipulations became more and more channeled into growth and creativity. The client discovered new strengths and resources, sometimes inside himself and sometimes in the environment, which then became available for him to use in healthy ways in contrast to the former neurotic games. As the client began to discover and experience the strengths, resources, and abilities he had had available all along, within and outside himself, the client moved from environmental support to self-support. Thus he gradually learned to stand on his own two feet.

This process can be a long and arduous one. As Perls trained others to use Gestalt, he emphasized the aggressive role of the Gestalt therapist, because many therapists who trained with him came out of other schools of therapy, and many of these schools commonly stressed a supportive role for the therapist. Thus it was easy for clients to con these therapists or to suck them into the games they, as clients, played. To counteract heuristic sets which these trainees brought with them, Perls stressed the role of therapist as frustrater instead of supporter. As a consequence, many of the individuals who trained with Perls came to the conclusion that the *ultimate* goal of Gestalt therapy was to "help" the client stand on his own two feet by frustrating him — that was all there was to it! And these therapists passed on their mistaken idea to those they trained.

Although such a goal is an important one as far as I am concerned, it is a means toward an end — *not* an end unto itself. To best illustrate my point I want to describe an incident that occurred in a workshop with Fritz Perls, which was attended by my wife. Perls was talking about relationships between men and women and how people who are married, or who are together in other primal relationships, manipulate one another. He implied that men and women formed relationships with members of the opposite sex to use each other to achieve their own ends. Thus what is formed is a relationship of mutual manipulations, however these may be disguised. My wife spoke out in disagreement and said something to the effect that sometimes she did things for me just because she wanted to, or because she knew I needed something and she got joy out of giving it to me. Fritz turned to her and said, "Oh, that! That's an act of love!" End of statement.

In Perls' first book, *Ego, Hunger and Aggression*, he carefully describes a process he calls the extension of ego boundaries. In treating the phenomenon of love, Perls states that it is quite possible for one person to extend his ego boundaries to include at least one other person, and to take this other person as seriously as he takes himself. This is similar to the concept of Martin Buber's "I-thou" relationship.

In the introduction to Perls' *Gestalt Therapy Verbatim* can be found the Gestalt "prayer":

I do my thing, and you do your thing.
I am not in this world to live up to your expectations
    and you are not in this world to live up to mine.
You are you, and I am I.

And if by chance we find each other, it's beautiful.
If not, it can't be helped.

A commercialized version of the "prayer" is being sold widely in poster stores, illustrated by a picture of a boy and girl "finding each other." The last line of the text has been omitted — which may help sales, but destroys the essence of the message. However, the fifth line is there: "And if by chance we find each other, it's beautiful." This line is equally as important as the omitted last line. Unfortunately, there are many who consider themselves Gestalt therapists who have omitted this fifth line from their own values, which underlie and govern their therapeutic behavior. They forget that some people do find each other. And when two people come together without demanding too much of each other, the experience can be beautiful.

Please remember that these conditions exist in an existential context — that is, all elements, qualities, and characteristics of the relationship between two people are subject to change from moment to moment. The change may be manifested by the extremes of an explosion of mutual disgust on the one hand, to an ever-evolving series of delightfully fresh discoveries on the other, as the two continue to experience each other. Most loving relationships have highs and lows, but they are usually shifting back and forth in the continuum between these two extremes. Those who are truly fortunate, I believe, are those who, out of commitment to each other, work hard on their awareness of themselves and their partners and who strive to communicate this awareness to each other when appropriate. I say "when appropriate" because the fortunate ones have learned to differentiate between when it is crucial to communicate and when it is best to be quiet.

The question to be asked by anyone practicing Gestalt therapy or anyone engaged in the Gestalt learning process is this: After the individual can stand on his own two feet, what then does he do? Just stand there? It seems obvious that one would next want to move. It further seems obvious that one would probably want to move *toward*, as well as *away from*, and that the direction *toward* could have at least another human being as its goal. This could further develop into a movement toward many human beings, or perhaps toward all human beings, or perhaps even ultimately toward all manifestations of life and energy.

What I propose in no way negates the need for individuals to learn to be self-supporting. I simply want to point out again that this is not an end unto itself — it is only one part of a process. For each of us there is in this process an ultimate goal: The expanding capacity for healthy love, experienced in a real universe.

TWO

The Theory of Confluent Education

The articles in this part focus on the theory of confluent education. For its development the writers have drawn on various sources. Chief of these, as mentioned previously, is Gestalt therapy. A second major source is Psychosynthesis. This is an approach to human growth and development that Roberto Assagioli, an Italian psychiatrist, has developed over the past sixty years and that recently has attracted increasing interest among psychotherapists and educators in the United States and Canada. Assagioli, trained as a psychoanalyst, felt that analysis in itself was insufficient to explain and heal psychological and spiritual suffering. As early as 1910 he began to develop an approach that worked toward synthesis as well as analysis, toward the integration of all aspects of human experience — somatic, emotional, mental, and spiritual. The sources from which he drew his techniques to facilitate this synthesis were many and varied, but the criterion for the use of each was: will his approach help this particular person experience a greater degree of integration and harmony with his personality and in relation to others and to his environment? Assagioli has drawn both on Western (Jung, particularly) and Eastern psychologies, and thus provides a very broad and comprehensive view of man and the course of his development throughout his life. The implication and applications of Psychosynthesis in education have only begun to be worked out, but its theory and practice hold great promise for the field.

Beyond drawing upon these two major sources, the theory of confluent education, is eclectic and creative, as these articles will indicate. Confluent education has moved more quickly on practical levels than it has on theoretical levels. Nevertheless, these articles represent a very solid beginning for the delineation of the theory behind the act.

The first article, "Human Is as Confluent Does," by George Isaac Brown, provides an overall introduction to confluent education, an historical analogy, and a description of projects at different educational levels.

Stewart Shapiro, author of the second article, provides a process for deciding what confluent education is, what it is not, and what is related to confluent education.

John Shiflett's article, entitled "Beyond Vibration Teaching," is one of the first attempts to combine confluent approaches with the work of Gerald Weinstein and Mario Fantini, who have directed their efforts primarily toward developing a curriculum of affect which deals with student concerns and blockages.

Thomas Yeomans' article, "Search for a Working Model," integrates Gestalt with Psychosynthesis to describe the educational process of confluence which occurs in learners as the result of confluent education, and outlines a model of personality based on these two theories.

The last article by Steven Bogad places a deserved emphasis on process, as against product, for the teacher and student alike, particularly in work with the affective components of confluent education.

11

HUMAN IS AS CONFLUENT DOES

— George Isaac Brown

To become more human, whether through the humanities, the sciences, the arts — whatever the discipline, process, or vehicle — I suspect has been a goal of some men for as long as men have been in existence. As men sought to bring meaning to their existence, as they struggled to make sense both of their universe and themselves in that universe, and with that sense somehow to improve their lot, they unavoidably were confronted with the use of their own powers to accomplish this. These powers were inevitably connected in some way to their human qualities: their intelligence, their knowledge, their sensibility, their creativity, and their capacity to relate in wondrously complex ways to one another.

We continue the search for ways to bring our humanness to fuller realization. Emerging in our time are approaches to human growth and learning, such as confluent education, that can help resolve some of the conflicts and what might appear to be, at first glance, the contradictions between what some have held to be most important and what others have held dear.

For example, the Age of Enlightenment initiated the expanded use of analysis in acquiring knowledge. Ellenberger comments, "The Enlightenment's most fundamental characteristic was the cult of reason. . . . Reason was opposed to ignorance, error, prejudice, superstition, imposed beliefs, the tyranny of passions, and the aberrations of fantasy." [1] The "error" of the Age of Enlightenment lay not in its goal of reason but rather in the means toward the goal. As it moved

First appeared in *Theory into Practice*, vol. 10, no. 3 (June 1971). Reprinted with permission.

beyond the Baroque period, where there was emphasis on models of the ideal man, in its enthusiasm for analysis, an exaggerated reaction to the Baroque period occurred. There developed an over-confidence in analysis as the way toward reason and an over-confidence in reason itself. In the least the advocates of reason seemed to show a lack of awareness that the very qualities in society which they were attempting to defeat — ignorance, fear, prejudice, the tyranny of passion, and the aberrations of fantasy — were in effect influencing their own process of analysis. The advocates of reason had little cognizance of how the quality of synoetics, as described by Phillip Phenix,[2] and elaborated by Michael Polanyi [3] as personal knowledge, affected that very reason which the men of the Age of Enlightenment were using to try to eliminate the distortions of pathological emotion. In short, they were contaminated by elements, and then used the contaminated process to try to eliminate these elements. Understanding this, one begins to apprehend how limited the process of reason was, both in terms of those who would use it and the success of those who did use it.

As a reaction to the ostensible limitations of the Age of Enlightenment the period of Romanticism emerged, counteracting the values of reason and the strictures of society. Romanticism was antithetical to reason in the sense that it stressed feelings, the irrational, and the individual. But, again, an exaggerated response characterized this reaction through attempts by the Romanticists to deny or repress the intellect and its use. Furthermore, their stress on affect was also in a sense contaminated by the intellectual mode in "knowing" what they were doing and feeling, and by the use of this mode through language (abstract symbols) and unavoidable theoretical systems, no matter how formal or informal these systems might be. The lack of awareness on the part of the advocates of Romanticism of the paradox resulting from making use of rationality in their drive toward irrationality, no doubt had significant effects on the manifestations of their goals.

Now, if it were possible in some way to combine the values of the Age of Enlightenment and the Age of Romanticism and to try to find some central point between the polarities of reason and the irrational, as represented by the two periods — or in more classical terms, the Apollonian and Dionysian polarity — we might have an holistic and valuable synthesis.

Confluent education is an attempt to integrate the Apollonian and the Dionysian, the Age of Enlightenment and the Romantic period, head and heart, mind and body, howsoever the basic polarity common to all may be hallmarked, so that like two brooks flowing together into one stream, each merges into the other, losing its boundaries to a greater whole. Confluent education is essentially the synthesis of the affective domain (feelings, emotions, attitudes, and values) and the cognitive domain (the intellect and the activity of the mind in knowing).

Confluent education, however, also includes learning experiences wherein may exist an interplay between affectivity and cognition, where frustration and tension in appropriate degrees resulting from this interplay are seen as valued conditions, directly related to healthy growth and development. The unending interaction of self with universe inevitably produces an interplay sequence of (1) conflict, (2) confrontation, (3) persistence, and (4) some degree of resolution or finishing up. It is through this interaction that we grow, whether the self-universe interaction be immediate or an outgrowth of subsequent recollection and reflection. Interplay as a process may be subsumed under the taxonomical umbrella of integration. The description of confluent education is so worded here to offset assumptions that confluent education always connotes a smooth and pleasurable series of lovely learning experiences where affective experience is interjected to add positive excitement to cognitive learning.

The putting together of the affective and the cognitive through conscious teaching acts is an attempt to make both the educational process and its product, the student, more human. Along with other characteristics, being more human means exhibiting more intelligent behavior; that is, the use of the marvelously unique human mind in a context of reality where feelings influence the mind and the mind, feelings, but where these feelings, too, arise from the same reality context. Feelings are undesirable which distort or deny reality and thus trigger mind into similar denials or distortions which, in turn, affect behavior. The consequent behavior may be defined as unintelligent to the degree that it does not fit reality.

Reality, at least operational reality, should not be conceived of as a constant. Rather, reality should be existentially considered as being in continual flux. This seems useful when explaining the function of reality in an educational process. As a consequence, the individual must learn to experience himself and the part of the universe in which he finds himself, directly or indirectly, from moment to moment. In order to do this he must be able to differentiate between the ways he would like things to be, or imagines they ought to be, and the way things are. To do this is to make a more optimal use of mind in contrast to using mind to create fantasies or illusions founded on, and interlaced by, distorting or reality-denying feelings. Fantasies and illusions help an individual evade the unpleasantness, frustration, and challenge of reality. What is sought here is a more intelligent use of mind so that individuals will not avoid taking responsibility for that large portion of their existence wherein potentially they could take responsibility. The healthy integration of the cognitive domain and the affective domain through the approaches of confluent education includes ways to learn this kind of personal existential responsibility.

An illustration of such confluent approaches can be found in one of our DRICE projects — I will explain DRICE later — wherein secondary school teachers focus on teaching responsibility as a means of increasing achievement. This takes the form of personal responsibility for what one does or does not do. I hasten to add that this process of responsibility training is not strictured by a Puritan morality whereby students *should do or be* such and such. Rather, learning experiences are structured first to help the student get in touch in a personally meaningful way with his first person singular, with the "I" of his existence and behavior. He then has opportunities to become aware that this "I" is or is not acting in certain ways, and to become aware of how much he may be blaming others for his behavior. Eventually, through further structuring, he may discover how in the existential now he, himself, is ultimately making his own decisions and choices, even when he opts to do nothing. Part of this last step may also in-

volve a growing recognition of his own strength and abilities — a cognizance of what he has available both within himself and in his universe "to do" with, or perhaps even "to be" with. As the student becomes more in touch with his interior and exterior reality, he can
also take more and more responsibility for his own learning. The
teacher's function in this project, then, is to help increase the
learner's awareness of his strength and capabilities rather than to
judge his performance, as in the more conventional teaching role.

Related to the problem of learning how to take responsibility is
learning how to make choices and to act on those choices. There may
be semantic difficulties with this concept because the word "choice"
could represent to many a kind of bind. We may believe that once
we have made a choice, somehow or other we have placed ourselves
in a box and are stuck there, imprisoned by the choice. Instead, in a
sense, each choice can open up many kinds of alternatives. For example, take the teacher who places a high value on confluent education and finds himself in a traditional school system. If this teacher
is strongly committed to more use of confluent approaches to education and makes this choice, he is now able to look at the system with
this end in mind. He begins to find all kinds of little nooks, crannies,
and crevices he had not seen before because earlier he had no need
for them. All of a sudden, using these discoveries, he can begin to
maneuver with an increased degree of freedom. If he had not made
the choice, he would continue to be owned by, and locked into, the
system.

The process of making choices is seldom a clear and clean one.
This contrasts with most formal educational practice, in which explicit demands are made of students to find right or correct answers
to problems along with implicit connotation that if the student
cannot find correct answers there is something wrong with him.
Most of life consists of a series of ambiguities, and often of paradox-
ical situations. The choices we make are not easy because the various
alternatives that exist for us may possess equally attractive features.
When we decide to marry, when we decide who our friends are going to be, what jobs we are going to take, and what to have for
dinner, all of these decisions may be fraught with ambiguity. In the

widely distributed comic strip, Mary Worth states the case most simply when she says, "There are no final examinations in life."

In a chapter in *Behavioral Science Frontiers in Education*,[4] Barbara Biber, formerly of the Bank Street School, complains of the limitations of Senesh's attempts to introduce principles of economics into the elementary school. One of Senesh's approaches was to divide first-grade students into two groups: one half of the children each made a complete gingerbread man on his own; the other half formed an assembly line with one child rolling out the dough, another stamping out the gingerbread man, someone else putting in the eyes, etc., down to the final step when a child took the gingerbread men out of the oven. Senesh's objective was to show how many more gingerbread men could be made using an assembly line. Biber commented that Senesh overlooked completely the fact that the gingerbread man made by the individual child became a beloved gingerbread man. Biber's point is a telling one.

Extending this lesson, however, using confluent approaches, one might have the children remain on the dreary assembly line, perhaps all day, or at least to the point of beginning to feel what it was like to be doomed to an existence of placing right eyes on a gingerbread man, day after day. A large number of people in our technocratic society are faced with this kind of frustration and despair. We are told that society needs assembly lines because of the demands for increased production. At the same time we know of the dramatic need of individual members of society for some sense of fulfillment, for actualizing or realizing themselves in some way. So we now have a polarity, a direct confrontation between the needs of individuals and the needs of society: that individuals need to feel that they are doing something personally meaningful in a major area of their lives, that they are exercising their potential creativity no matter how humble the work, that they are doing something which makes them feel less like a part of a machine and more like a human being; but the society in which these individuals live demands increased production, and the individuals themselves may be partially responsible for these demands. Thus we have a classical ambiguity — in effect, almost a paradox. What is the answer? There is no single answer. There are many possible answers.

Children can appreciate this ambiguity by experiencing it, even though they may not like it any more than grown-ups do. Think for a moment of any time in your own formal schooling when you might have been taught about polarities or ambiguities. Perhaps a poetry class — but how many English instructors make clear the connection between ambiguity in poetry and ambiguity in students' lives?

The point is that teaching about the existence of ambiguities and learning how to make choices, and to act on those choices, is available in many disciplines. We have only to become conscious of these opportunities and of how such learning can contribute to the humanizing of ourselves and of our students.

In translating theory into practice it is essential that what teachers preach in confluent education is also what they practice. This means that educators must be provided with training programs so that they may personally experience the techniques and effective learning approaches they will use in the role of instructor, and at the same time have opportunities for personal growth. I want to stress that the focus on personal growth is to be on feelings in the teaching role as opposed to personal, private areas outside the professional role. Obviously, at times these may overlap. However, the intent, function, and focus of personal growth in this situation can, in my experience, be legitimately justified only through a focus on professional behavioral outcomes. There are also practical reasons for this focus — individuals will be much more willing to accept the risks they anticipate than if they view this "therapy" with its accompanying negative connotations. One example of this is the "What's wrong with me?" response when personal growth is suggested with approaches which might possibly encompass all sectors of the individual's existence.

Until the educator can himself grow, he will tend to be stuck with cookbook approaches to confluent education. He will be deprived of the opportunity to improvise and to invent learning structures that might be uniquely appropriate to his own classroom situations. Thus he remains a technician instead of becoming an artist, limited in his opportunities to be creative and to fulfill himself in his work. And, at the same time, his students also are deprived, for the spark of creative enthusiasm can be infectious. The quality of teaching affects the quality of learning.

Where can the teacher, who has been intuitively approaching the problem of integrating affective components into classroom practices, begin structuring his teaching and the curriculum? There are two questions which can be helpful for use when beginning consciously to structure a more confluent approach to education. The teacher can continually ask:

1. How does the student feel *now* about the content of what I am teaching?
2. Is there any way to establish a relationship between this content and the student's life?

These questions can help the teacher focus on affective dimensions of his curriculum and teaching methodology and, in some cases, may assist him to present the content in ways which can be more relevant, exciting, and challenging to his students.

I intentionally avoid the question of how or when to change the curriculum on the basis of these two questions. At this point, the selection and design of curriculum within a confluent context is premature on any grand scale. Of course, individual teachers or departments or school faculties may begin to innovate curriculum on their own initiative as desirable changes become obvious. But for many teachers it is enough to begin to attend to the significance of affective components in learning, not only affectivity in what motivates students to learn, but affectivity which sustains the learning as well.

An extensive description of initial work in this area may be found in *Human Teaching for Human Learning*.[5] Through a Ford–Esalen project, a pilot program was established to explore ways to incorporate affective learning activities into the curriculum. Working with a small staff of elementary and secondary-school teachers we found it was possible to grow professionally through experiencing these activities ourselves, and then translating some of the activities for use in the classroom.

Building on this initial exploratory project, we have been involved for the last three years in DRICE (Development and Research in Confluent Education), a center funded by the Ford Foundation, which involves a number of projects at various levels of formal education. At the present time DRICE includes four projects:

1. Curriculum development in English and social studies at the secondary school level (mentioned earlier in this chapter). The focus here is on responsibility and its relationship to achievement.
2. Closely related to the above project is one involving English instructors in junior or community colleges.
3. A project exploring ways to utilize a variety of affective approaches in the teaching of reading. This project is being conducted in the San Francisco area in collaboration with the Esalen Institute.
4. An elementary school project focusing on the development of confluent curricula in social studies.

A fifth DRICE project, which had to be phased out because of changes in the State of California teaching credential requirements, involved a combined teacher-training and empirical study. Here a group of graduate students in a fifth-year elementary training program were provided with special courses focusing on personal and professional growth, based mostly on principles of Gestalt therapy. Personality and teacher-behavioral measurements were made using pre- and post-test measures. Comparisons were then made with control groups.

One principle of all the projects is to have participants involved as much as possible in decisions relating to their training and other project processes. A second important principle is that no one has to do anything he does not want to do. On the one hand, this means that no activities in the project are dictated by administrative edict or consultant injunction or expert dictum. On the other hand, though resource persons may be recruited, responsibility for what goes on or does not go on now becomes that of each individual in his role in the project.

One of the unique contributions to education which confluent education can make by introducing affective components is that what is now conventionally accepted as curricula at all educational levels can be brought back to life. After all, curricula once had its source in some living reality. It lost its vitality as it became an end instead of the means it was originally, a means toward helping the student develop and utilize those characteristics which make him a human being.

Thinking about education in confluent ways can help restore revitalizing juices to education. Man has a mind. Man has feeling. To separate the two is to deny all that man is. To integrate the two is to help man realize what he might be.

REFERENCE NOTES /

1. H. F. Ellenberger, *The Discovery of the Unconscious* (New York: Basic Books, 1970), p. 195.
2. P. Phenix, *Realms of Meaning* (New York: McGraw-Hill, 1964).
3. M. Polanyi, *Personal Knowledge* (Chicago: University of Chicago Press, 1958).
4. B. Biber, "A Paradigm for Integrating Intellectual and Emotional Processes." In E. Bower & W. Hollister (eds.), *Behavioral Science Frontiers in Education* (New York: John Wiley, 1967).
5. G. I. Brown, *Human Teaching for Human Learning: An Introduction to Confluent Education* (New York: Viking, 1971).

12

DEVELOPING MODELS BY "UNPACKING" CONFLUENT EDUCATION

— Stewart B. Shapiro

Confluent, or humanistic, education is a relatively new and rapidly developing field of inquiry and practice. As with many other promising and innovative approaches to education, its practice has far outstripped its theoretical development. While some preliminary conceptual models have been developed by George I. Brown,[1] Richard Jamgochian,[2] and John Shiflett,[3] and a more complete model by Weinstein and Fantini,[4] there remains much to be done. After several years of exposure to these approaches, teachers still persist in asking the question, "But really, what is confluent education?"

The purpose of this article is to present the "unpacking exercise," a new approach to the development of models for confluent education. The aim of this approach is to define and explicate further this complex array of techniques, concepts, values, settings, and people, as a preparation for building meaningful models.

THE "UNPACKING METHOD" /

Most interesting concepts like confluent education are emotionally, philosophically, and semantically "loaded" or "packed" with many connotative meanings for various individuals. Perhaps that is one reason why they are interesting and vital ideas.

In order to become more aware of the richness of meanings and the uses of this complex approach, and to increase the ability to communicate these ideas to others, a six-person team in the Ford Foundation's Development and Research in Confluent Education

(DRICE) project, engaged in a systematic attempt to "unpack" or explicate the concept of confluent education. The team participated in a technique adapted from "Thinking with Concepts" developed by John Wilson,[5] an English professor of philosophy. This approach is designed to explore and define the domain of meanings of any concept by following eight systematic steps in analysis. The outcome of this DRICE project was to be a cognitive map or model of confluent education.

PROCEDURES /

The six-person team moved through a series of steps which involved making various statements about confluent education. These statements were written independently and then were reviewed for consensus or prominent themes. These themes, or "findings," were used to form general conclusions or a conceptual "mapping of the territory" of confluent education. The objective was to achieve only a rough mapping, in view of the fact that the frontiers and borders of this complex concept are difficult to formulate precisely.

The steps in analysis consisted of:

1. Model cases
2. Contrary cases
3. Related cases
4. Borderline cases
5. Invented cases
6. Social context
7. Practical results
8. Language results

The various findings were then synthesized in a summary statement.

1. Model cases

Model cases are those instances of confluent education which are considered to be "pure examples." They are events about which could be said, "If *that* isn't an example of confluent education, then *nothing* is." From these cases the essential features are extracted and then the procedure is repeated with a second round of model cases. If the so-called essential features do not appear on the second round, they are discarded.

2. Contrary cases

Here the sharpening of discrimination of essential features is continued by examining cases that are classic examples of the opposite of confluent education. It can be said about these cases, "Whatever confluent education *is, that* certainly is *not* an instance of it."

3. Related cases

In this step, concepts similar to confluent education in their usual meaning are examined. The team wanted to examine how the concept of confluent education fits into a class or network of related concepts. Circumstances in which terms like confluent education could be used were examined in order to clarify the essential criteria for the class of concepts of which confluent education is a member.

4. Borderline cases

This involved cases in which there was some doubt of the usage. It included examples which have *some* but not all features in common with confluent education. The team looked for important features which were missing or different in the borderline cases and which kept them from being model cases. This, again, served to emphasize the key feature which served to delineate confluent education from other concepts.

5. Invented cases

Here the task was to invent an imaginary (e.g., science-fiction) example of confluent education in order to broaden an ordinary experience with it. This might help, at the same time, to clarify its "central meanings" and to map out its uncertain frontiers. Another purpose of this step was to be a reminder that the "unpacking" approach is *essentially imaginative,* at least as much an art as a science, and certainly an enterprise in which there are *no right answers.*

6. Social context

Questions about the meaning and use of confluent education were asked in the context of particular circumstances in everyday life (e.g., the classroom, the workshop, the home). In this procedure the team tried to determine *who* would be asking the questions or making the statements, *why* they would want to do this and *when* they would be most likely to do it. Examples of real-life situations were examined for the feeling tones, anxieties, and politics of both the speakers and the audience.

7. Practical results

In this step the team considered whether questions or statements about confluent education make any substantial difference in the everyday life of the people involved. This was done to discover how statements about the concept can affect actual behavior.

8. Language results

Even if it was concluded that confluent education does *not* have a central meaning, it might still be possible to say that it is more sensible or useful to adopt *some* meanings rather than others. In this step an attempt was made to tie down some particular meanings of confluent education as contrasted with other concepts.

9. Summary statement

Following the above steps, the team reviewed each of the statements and cases to see if they held up. After certain revisions were made, the domain of meaning of the concept of confluent education was roughed out. A summary statement which is a tentative "unpacked" definition of confluent education was then made.

FINDINGS /

1. Model cases

The *essential features* of confluent education which emerged are:

a) A context or climate of *two-way openness to learning*. Confluent education has a structure which includes *intentionality* to learn and support for the learning of both teachers and students. Setting this climate is considered "shaping behavior," and intentionality includes awareness of the teacher's own values, patterns, and selective reinforcements of the student's responses.

b) Awareness of *self* as a legitimate object of learning (for teacher and student) and *deliberate attention* directed to this learning.

c) Subject matter which is closely related to the significant *personal needs* and feelings of the students. The major criterion for inclusion of any subject is the extent to which children (students) can come to feel significantly related to it.

d) *Experienced-based learning*. This means learning that is closely tied to the direct contemporary experiences of students, and learning in which inferences and abstractions are drawn after the concrete learning experience itself.

e) Awareness and intention to develop convergent and *cognitive processes integrated with,* or parallel to, other learnings. Other learnings involve action and will, as well as affect.

f) Encouragement of the expression of *feelings* by both student and teacher.

g) Use of *feedback* to refine and develop learnings.

h) Encouragement of divergent *imaginative thinking*.

i) *"Re-subjectivising"* of meanings. This involves the re-creation and internalizing of external, social, and transpersonal meanings, and perception and knowledge. In some ways it is the opposite of what Phenix [6] describes as the process of aesthetic creation (i.e., objectifying the subjective).

2. Contrary cases

Cases contrary to confluent education involve:

a) Denial, absence, or *inhibition of "personalness."* Personalness includes significant feelings, needs, states of being, motivations, etc. Denial or inhibition could include stimulation of needs followed by nonresponse or suppression (cf. Torrance's [7] concept of a responsive environment).

b) *Absolute or near-absolute teacher control* over classroom events, either directly or indirectly expressed; none, or very little, learner participation in shaping the experience.

c) The presence of significant *affective arousal* in student and/or teachers *with no awareness;* acceptance or use of this affect by the central person in order to facilitate learning.

d) *One-way flow of information* or feeling from teacher to student group.

e) *No learner responsibility* for choice or variation in modes of learning.

f) *Denial by the teacher of authentic (existential) expressions* in students and *denial of authentic interaction* among students or between teachers and students.

g) Primary emphasis on the manipulation of *"extrinsic knowledge"* (i.e., knowledge completely removed from "here and now").

3. Related cases

Cases related to confluent education:

a) Confluent education and related processes focus on both *feelings and cognition.*

b) They include *content, process, and evaluation.*

c) They take account of both *shared and individual interests.*

d) They can use affect as *instrumental* in learning cognition and vice versa.

e) They involve *intentionality* with respect to both affective and cognitive learnings.

4. Borderline cases

Confluent education and borderline cases:

a) Confluent education involves a *smoothness* or flow *in the transition from affect to cognition*. Affect and cognition are coexisting modalities and their interpenetration is facilitated. The transitions are neither extreme nor abrupt.

b) Confluent education includes a third dimension, distinguishable from cognition and affect. It could be called the "*observer dimension*" and involves feedback and processing of cognitively- or affectively-oriented experiences, roles, or learnings. This *processing dimension* includes observations and comments on the degree of integration and transitions between affect and cognition.

c) Confluent education includes the *learner option* to move from personal feelings to cognitive learning and vice versa. This means learner/teacher negotiation of the pace pattern of moving back and forth between affect and cognition.

5. Invented cases

Confluent education and invented cases:

a) Curricula and learning experiences could be primarily *centered around human needs* (cf. Weinstein and Fantini's Curriculum of Affect [8]).

b) *Technology could be harnessed* for immediate teaching and feedback on progress toward human goals. The independent variable could be the child.

c) The variety and *options of experience* could be greatly increased and could include pleasure as well as self-control.

d) Teachers could be resources primarily, and learning experience could be student-centered. This would mean *learning about self first*, particularly personal styles of assimilation and accommodation (cf. Piaget [9]).

e) *The unlearning by teachers* of some of their previous positions and assumptions might have to precede expanded learning by students. The student might become the teacher and the teacher the client or primary learner. Adult leaders might also be the major clients of expanded confluent education, particularly when it provides a model of unlearning "hardened sets." Society could capitalize on divergences with *children as the primary learning models* rather than adults (cf. Shapiro [10] and Jackins [11]). This might also result in a crucial learning for many people: resistance to manipulation.

6. *Social context*

Confluent education and social context:

a) Translation and *transmission of the concept* of confluent education is often difficult because it is controversial, complex, not immediately obvious, and presumes a preparatory mental set (heightened self-awareness) which runs counter to the traditional Western separation of thinking and feeling.

b) Consideration of *resistances* to confluent education might indicate "warm-up" or readiness techniques such as fantasy or relaxation exercises (affect-cognition-action bridges), or a presentation of examples of confluent education to indicate how closely related the concept is to the concrete personal experiences of the audience.

c) Ordinarily, the pressures of the social context in which the concept would be communicated requires *a sharing of common frames of reference* and building an atmosphere of safety and trust.

d) The medium in which the messages of confluent education are communicated usually require both *evocation of feelings and the stimulation of inner dialogue* in the audience. To overcome the difficulties in translation and language, and to facilitate internalization of the concepts, the receivers of the message would be stimulated to "talk (think) to themselves" and to "talk (think) out loud about what confluent education means to them."

e) The *goals* of confluent education are to increase *intelligent behavior*, defined as appropriate responses to "reality."

f) There was a commonly held *personal apprehension* among the DRICE team concerning the making of statements about confluent education to parents, teachers, administrators, colleagues, the community, etc. Acknowledgment of the "threat-potential" of these concepts to the predominant existing values, norms, and roles of educators and the community was unanimous. This, along with the awareness of the *risk of change*, and anticipated opposition to the whole idea of confluence, elicited considerable personal anxiety from the DRICE team in the role of communicator to the public.

7. *Practical results*

The practical results of confluent education:

a) Statements and questions about confluent education tended to make the DRICE team more aware of the *potential for confluence* in themselves and others.

b) Confluent education structures and reinforces the assumption of *responsibility* and accountability by the leaders and participants for the integration and growth of the whole person.

c) Confluent education involves nonaccidental, *deliberate*, purposive, but flexible efforts, to facilitate co-participants in attaining increased wholeness and spontaneity.

d) Statements and questions about confluent education, plus the "unpacking" exercise itself, led to *behavioral changes in the members of the DRICE team*. These changes included renewed intellectual curiosity, the reading of "new" books which were rejected previously due to an "affective bias," and the attracting of certain more cognitively-oriented individuals to the graduate program in confluent education at the University of California at Santa Barbara. The exercise generated some excitement and renewal in the DRICE program via a temporary task-oriented subgroup which, it was felt, contributed to the supportive, nurturing quality of the social matrix of confluent education.

8. *Language results*

Confluent education and language:

a) Attempts to unpack the concept confluent education led to *tentative definitions* along the route of the exercise. One such definition is: "Confluent education is the deliberate evocation by the design of responsible agents (leaders and/or participants) of knowledge, skills, attitudes, and feelings which tend to produce increased integration in the individual and society (differentiated unity)."

b) Confluent education is *identifiably distinct* from:

1. experienced-based education
2. psychological education
3. affective education
4. emotional education
5. personal-growth methods

in that confluent education also includes:

1. external structure which integrates subject matter and personal awareness
2. an intellectual component
3. abstract knowledge or information

c) Confluent education is *related to humanistic education* in that the former is subsumed under a general humanistic philosophy of education, but it is more precise. Confluent education indicates or implies procedures and plans of action to implement the goals of personal and social integration.

d) The *general "explicit contract"* of confluent education is, in the last analysis, between co-participants in the mutual facilitation and actualizing of confluence in themselves and society. This contract explicitly states:

1. structure, subject matter, intentionality, and responsibilities
2. mutuality of learning
3. commitment to growth
4. recognition of needs, strengths, and special resources

SUMMARY STATEMENT /

As one consequence of the foregoing analyses, the DRICE team formulated the following working definition of confluent education:

"Confluent education is a deliberate, purposeful evocation by responsible, identifiable agents of knowledge, skills, attitudes, and feelings which flow together to produce wholeness in the person and society."

The following are the necessary elements:

1. *Participation* (P). There is consent, power-sharing, negotiation, and joint responsibility by co-participants. It is essentially nonauthoritarian and nonunilateral.
2. *Interpenetration* (I). There is interaction, interpenetration, and integration of thinking, feelings, and action.
3. *Relevance* (R). The subject matter is closely related to the basic needs, life, and meanings of the participants.
4. *Self* (S). The self is a legitimate object of learning.
5. *Goals* (G). The social goal, or purpose, is to develop the whole person within a humane society.

Confluent education is distinguishable from affective education, psychotherapy, or personal growth methods per se. It is subsumed under the general humanistic philosophy of the nature of man which also encompasses affective education, personal growth, and the humanistic philosophy of the nature of man which also encompasses affective education, personal growth, and the human-potential movement.

SUMMARY /

In summary, this article has attempted to demonstrate the use of the "unpacking method" in an analysis of the complex concept of confluent education. The P.I.R.S.G. factors listed above, and the working definition, are the outcome of this kind of "subjective factor analysis." These are merely the components for a model of confluent education which will need to be tested for clarity, comprehensiveness, and usefulness to teachers in the field. In addition, much empirically based research (cf. Shiflett,[12] and Shapiro and Shiflett [13]) will be helpful in validating the concepts.

REFERENCE NOTES /

1. G. I. Brown, *Human Teaching for Human Learning: An Introduction to Confluent Education* (New York: Viking, 1971).

2. R. Jamgochian, "A Tentative Operating Model of Confluent Education." Unpublished paper, Graduate School of Education, University of California, Santa Barbara, California, 1971.

3. J. M. Shiflett, "Beyond Vibration Teaching: Research and Curriculum Development in Confluent Education." Occasional Paper no. 11, DRICE, Development and Research in Confluent Education, University of California, Santa Barbara, California, 1971. This article also appears as a chapter in *The Live Classroom*.

4. G. A. Weinstein and M. F. Fantini, *Toward Humanistic Education: A Curriculum of Affect* (New York: Praeger, 1970).

5. J. Wilson, *Thinking with Concepts* (Cambridge, England: Cambridge University Press, 1963).

6. P. H. Phenix, *Realms of Meaning: A Philosophy of the Curriculum for General Education* (New York: McGraw-Hill, 1964).

7. E. P. Torrance, *Encouraging Creativity in the Classroom* (Dubuque, Iowa: William C. Brown Co., 1970).

8. Weinstein and Fantini, op. cit.

9. J. Piaget and B. Inhelder, *The Psychology of the Child* (New York: Basic Books, 1969).

10. S. B. Shapiro, "Patient Wisdom: An Anthology of Creative Insights in Psychotherapy," *Journal of Psychology*, 1952, vol. 54, pp. 285–291.

11. H. Jackins, *The Human Side of Human Beings* (Seattle, Wash.: Rational Island Publishers, 1965).

12. J. M. Shiflett, "An Examination of the Affective Components of Confluent Teacher Training." Unpublished manuscript, University of California, Santa Barbara, California, Department of Education, 1972.

13. S. B. Shapiro and J. M. Shiflett, "Loss of Connectedness during an Elementary Teacher Training Program." Unpublished manuscript, University of California, Santa Barbara, California, Department of Education, 1972.

13

BEYOND VIBRATION TEACHING: RESEARCH AND CURRICULUM DEVELOPMENT IN CONFLUENT EDUCATION

— *John M. Shiflett*

In reading lots and lots of cookbooks written by white folks it occurred to me that people very casually say Spanish rice, French fries, Italian spaghetti, Chinese cabbage, Mexican beans, Swedish meatballs, Danish pastry, English muffins, and Swiss cheese. And with the exception of black bottom pie and niggertoes, there is no reference to black people's contribution to the culinary arts. White folks act like they invented food and like there is some weird mystique surrounding it — something that only Julia and Jim can get to. There is no mystique. Food is food. Everybody eats!

And when I cook, I never measure or weigh anything. I cook by vibration. I can tell by the look and smell of it. Most of the ingredients in this book are approximate. Some of the recipes that people gave me list the amounts, but for my part, I just do it by vibration. Different strokes for different folks. Do your thing your way.

> HOPPING JOHN
> *Cook black-eyed peas.*
> *When they are almost done add rice.*
> *Mix rice and peas together.*
> *Season and — voilà! — you got it.*

This brief quotation, out of context, does an injustice to Verta Mae's message contained in her book *Vibration Cooking*.[1] She is an exceptionally gifted artist, giving an unreconstructed, backstage account of her art which she labels "vibration cooking," making the point that good cooking does not flow from overly rationalized, slavish adherence to mechanical formulas and recipes.

Cooking, like gardening, learning, and teaching, has a passionate or affective component, and while it can be, and has been, disastrous to lose sight of this simple truth, the overemphasis of the affective, beyond the redress of neglect, is to create an alternative mystique, equally partial and equally unsatisfying. While the emotional dimensions of learning and teaching must enter the purview of those concerned with education, an exclusive focus upon the affective realm has tended to create the mystique of "vibration teaching" where teachers operate on the basis of vibrations in the classroom. There is no reason why good cooking, gardening, and teaching must await the accidents of time, place, and circumstance that yield the rare and gifted practioner of this, or any other, style of teaching.

Though they are admittedly only part of the story, recipes, spoons, tools, trowels, theories, concepts, and other cognitive baggage are there, and must be explored and used if we are to attempt seriously to improve the practice of teaching and to broaden our general understanding of teaching, learning, and the dynamics of schools. As Verta Mae might point out pragmatically, the proof of the pudding is in the eating.

THE CONFLUENT PURPOSE /

Various writers, from different perspectives, have made the central point: "Cognition, feeling, emotion, action, and motivation are easily separated by abstraction, but no single one of these can function independently of the others." [2] From primarily cognitive concerns, Piaget, as quoted by Simpson,[3] notes that "the developing child, moving from the level of concrete cognitive operations toward a capacity for formal or abstract reasoning, may find insecurity a major stumbling block to progress." Finally, Simpson [4] in a fascinatingly broad synthesis of diverse theoretical and empirical studies, states:

For twenty-five hundred years since Plato's analysis, a false schism has divided these domains (and a third, the conative or directive and motivating). "In short, we must learn to remove the intellectual quality from reality if we are to be faithful to it," wrote José Ortega y Gasset in *Historia Como Sistema* (1962), yet this is not possible, for nowhere in nature is reality so separated. Inextricably interwoven, cognitive functioning is not apart from affective responses; one is the counterpart of the other. The two components vary together.

The general proposition which forms the core of the confluent approach (the integration of the cognitive and affective domains), as stressed by Brown,[5] is nothing new.

What is proposed here is common sense, is something we've "known" about for some time, is possible within the present educational establishment, and although possibly eventually leading to considerable modification in school organization and curriculum, can be readily instituted in schools as they are now. "Readily" could be from five to ten years, for a very good beginning — a time period no longer than that of curriculum reforms like the new math.

The change would be simply to be aware that thinking is accompanied by feeling and vice versa, and to begin to take advantage of the fact.

We suspect that gifted teachers have long recognized, consciously or unconsciously, the interrelatedness of these factors and that their practice, drawing upon this recognition, forms one of the dimensions of their gift.

What *is* new is the concern for actual program, curriculum, and research development that will capitalize on the inextricable relation between cognition and affect, a task currently being addressed by the DRICE (Development and Research in Confluent Education) project at the University of California at Santa Barbara. (The term "curriculum" is used in a variety of senses ranging from strictly written documents (lists or outlines of goals, topics, techniques, instructional materials, texts, etc.), to the broad concept of the complete array of learning experiences encountered by students in formal and informal educational settings. While this broader conception, including what has been called the "hidden" curriculum, is sociologically useful, our use of the term here lies between these two extremes. We mean by "curriculum," simply *planned* learning experiences, of whatever form.)

Acceptance of the view that cognition and affect are only analytically separable with regard to *learning* does not imply that they are inseparable for the establishment of *teaching* goals or strategies, curriculum modification, program development, or research. The dominant mode of current educational practice provides ample evidence that one half of the equation, whether we are pleased with the consequences or not, can be underemphasized or denied. To effect the balance that ultimately will be needed, and without losing sight of the larger integrative purpose, it will be necessary in the immediate future to lay principal stress upon the affective. It is in this difficult and neglected domain that knowledge is weakest and where the greatest need for attention to basic research and development exists. Concurrently, and with only slightly less emphasis, the relation between the affective and traditional cognitive concerns needs explication, both in terms of concrete empirical research and tentative total curricular offerings.

In struggling with the problems facing research in confluent education, and attempting to clarify further the relation between the cognitive and the affective, several distinctions have emerged which are implicit in the literature and which, when made explicit, seem to facilitate research concerns and similarly might be useful in curriculum modification and program development. There are, of course, a number of additional distinctions which usefully could be made, but the following are those which appear to be primary and crucial at the present stage of development.

The major distinctions are between affective *concerns and blockages* and affective *loadings*. Let us consider each in turn.

CONCERNS AND BLOCKAGES /

What I now see for the first time is the mechanism by which fear destroys intelligence, the way it affects a child's whole way of looking at, thinking about, and dealing with life. So we have two problems, not one: to stop children from being afraid, and then to break them of the bad thinking habits into which their fears have driven them.

What is most surprising of all is how much fear there is in school. Why is so little said about it? . . . Like good soldiers, they control their fears, live with them, and adjust themselves to them.

But the trouble is, and here is a vital difference between school and war, that the adjustments children make to their fears are almost wholly bad, destructive of their intelligence and capacity. The scared fighter may be the best fighter, but the scared learner is always a poor learner.[6]

By blockages are meant those underlying psychological concerns of the learner, rooted in fundamental human needs, which, if unmet and ungratified, impede learning. These are the affective factors that have thus far received the greatest attention in theoretical and research literature [7] and in the writings of those concerned with problem-learners, the "disadvantaged," curriculum development, and school reorganization.[8] While there is incomplete agreement on what these specific basic needs are — a reflection of the state of our knowledge at present — there are general overlapping and surprisingly few major dimensions that recur in the literature.

Although detailed and sophisticated treatments of the topic of needs are available, considerable consensus is attached to the notions of security, self-worth, positive affiliation, and power, as somehow fundamental, lower in a hierarchy of needs and manifest in educational settings as pervasive underlying concerns.[9] When unmet, these concerns may function as blocks to the development of higher needs and goals such as the aesthetic, the creative, and the intellectual, or the more purely cognitive.

The designation of precisely what these needs are, for the purposes of this article, is secondary to the main points, which are that these factors form a *separable* dimension of the affective domain, are *ever-present* as concerns if not blockages, in any learning situation, are *specifiable* on the theoretical basis of a model of human needs (more generally, a model of man), and may themselves *represent instructional objectives*. With our view of the relation between the cognitive and the affective, our consequent understanding of the dynamics of learning, and the considerable practical experience of confluent teachers themselves in dealing with both so-called "problem" and "normal" learners, the predominantly affective can represent legitimate instructional goals in their own right.

Weinstein and Fantini have devoted much attention to a model of what they call a "curriculum of concerns," where discipline-based concepts are selected on the basis of their linkage with underlying concerns, and the subject matter is used as a content "vehicle" with predominantly affective objectives. One of the examples cited by them and used with a "slow" fifth-grade group, many of whom were labeling themselves as failures, was designed to strengthen a positive self-image.[10] The students prepared booklets with the theme "I Am Special," including photographs, poems, and essays. The lesson is not only active and a source of pride for the students but, as Weinstein and Fantini emphasize, may include subsidiary objectives of basic skill development such as writing and verbal communication.

Several cautions have been urged concerning affective objectives. First, the larger purpose is not therapeutic in a narrow sense, although addressing blockages and concerns can be remedial in outcome, but is more concerned with enhancing the development of human potential — a positive, nonpathological emphasis. To consider this point more carefully, a healthy corrective is offered by Brown in posing and answering the question of "how does the teacher draw a distinction between being a therapist and being a teacher?"

> The distinction Richard M. Jones makes between insight and "outsight" is helpful here. Insight is described as the consequence of an introspective act; in therapy the emphasis is often on discovering what is going on or has gone on in relation to the patient's pathological feelings about himself, and is primarily concerned with his history. Outsight is much more existential, and relates instead to how one responds emotionally to the portion of the universe one encounters at a given moment. Within the principles of Gestalt therapy — a contemporary approach in which the use of the term "therapy" is an exception — an individual defines himself in terms of the environment in which he finds himself, the environment including other human beings if they are present. The defining is not limited exclusively to how the environment responds to the individual but includes how the individual feels as he interacts with that particular environment at that particular moment.
> If the teacher focuses on the outsight of his students, there is immediate justification for confluent education: (1) the cognitive content of the curriculum and the skills related to that content represent the environment, and (2) the affective dimension is the student's response to that environment.[11]

Second, the broad issue of the integration with conventional curricula of affective techniques and objectives, dealing with blockages and concerns or with the affective "loadings" to be distinguished below, should proceed within a total perspective. The random, piecemeal development or adoption of technique, with little regard for associated philosophical and ethical issues, in isolation from the objectives of the total curriculum, would be pointless. The stress here is that, even though components of the total curriculum could have predominantly cognitive, affective, or dual objectives, the intent is not to broaden the mission of schools to include the pathological or therapeutic. Rather, it is to recognize the legitimacy of affective goals, principally those stemming from fundamental human concerns, and to place these goals within the disciplined context of a total curriculum, "soundly constructed, effectively taught, properly sequenced, and carefully evaluated." [12] The expectation, however, based upon experience thus far, is that within a confluent approach, difficulties of "problem-learners" which have been labeled "pathological" are dramatically reduced when content is focused or based upon positive affective growth.

LOADINGS /

To repeat the central proposition, there is no action or learning devoid either of cognitive or affective dimensions. There is no topic or goal within conventional curricula which does not have an integral affective component. Loadings are those affective aspects of all learning tasks, stemming from basic concerns or not, which, if taken into account, may enrich personal meaning, increase relevance, and broaden understanding in a manner not possible, or only haphazardly done, by focusing on the cognitive dimensions alone.

It is useful at the present stage of our knowledge to skirt the issue of whether, or in what way, loadings stem directly or indirectly from fundamental concerns, or are associated with the emergence of yet higher needs, or are meaningfully related to specific models of human needs at all. We need not await the resolution of these theoretical and research issues to recognize the utility, for research and curriculum modification and development, of distinguishing between loadings and what we have been discussing in the previous section as concerns and blockages.

Concerns and blockages are specifiable theoretically from panhuman characteristics of the *learner* and are pervasive underlying considerations. In contrast, loadings are less categorical, beyond their affective character rooted in human experience, and are defined by characteristics of the subject matter, topic, or *learning task*.

With predominant, although by no means exclusive, *cognitive* objectives, confluent modification, with respect to loadings, would mean inserting into the curriculum, where appropriate, the *human experience* associated with the curricular objectives or topic.

> . . . because much of the curriculum is founded on human experience, human dimensions can be reintroduced into classroom learning. And this is where there is hope. The aspect of what and how the learner feels can be integrated with what schools believe he should know. This integration can not only increase his desire to know but also assure that his continuing learning will be a rich, meaningful, and emotionally healthful personal experience.
>
> For a long time we have known the importance of personal involvement in learning. Educational psychologists have, however, expressed this negatively: "If learning has no personal meaning, it will not change behavior." Seldom has the converse been stated: "If we add an emotional dimension to learning, the learner will become personally involved and, as a consequence, there will be change in the learner's behavior." [13]

The following diagram illustrates the relation between concerns and blockages originating with the learner, and loadings associated with subject matter as mediated by a confluent curriculum:

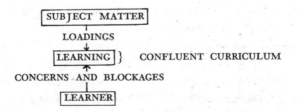

Drawing on the definition of the affective provided by Brown,[14] loadings can be divided analytically into affect concerning wanting to learn (*orientation loadings*), affect associated with learning itself (*engagement loadings*), and affect associated with the completion of a learning task (*accomplishment loadings*). Loadings could vary by type and degree as a topic ranged from the empirical (e.g., social studies, history, or literature, with rather clear related human experiences), through increasing abstraction (social forces, or historical "trends"), to the formal (abstract or formal models, or to the biographical or social dimensions of the same topic. The particular constellation or mix of concerns and loadings could vary, naturally, from course to course, unit to unit, topic to topic, or as the focus shifts within each of these.

Interestingly, one technique described by Weinstein and Fantini was considered theoretically deficient by them in spite of its obvious success in the classroom. Entitled "Chairs," the technique was designed to improve the teaching of literature by broadening the student's understanding through personal exploration of the affective dimensions of clearly defined characters.

> Unlike role-playing, in which several students play different characters, "Chairs" is played by one person — preferably a volunteer — taking all the subparts within a single individual. He begins by sitting in a chair and talking like the character in a story. When he reaches some discrepancy or conflict in the character, he sets up another chair and has a dialogue with it. This discussion among an individual's subparts can become a trio, a quartet, and so on, and can even include contributions from other chairs representing forces outside the character which impinge on his behavior.[15]

> This particular episode, specifically designed to teach literature, seems to offer an excellent approach to that subject and helps students to get inside a character. It stops short, however, of making the connection between the subselves of the literary characters and the students' own committee of subselves. In that respect, it fails the model's objective to deal with the students' concerns for self-identity.[16]

In our view, this technique deals with engagement loadings with confluent (both cognitive *and* affective) objectives and needs no further theoretical justification, although it is clearly difficult to place within the framework of the curriculum of concerns proposed by Weinstein and Fantini.

Mathematics or the study of other formal systems, for example, may involve primarily orientation loadings (apprehension, etc.) and accomplishment loadings (mastery of the system, satisfaction of solution within the system, etc.), but even here, it is easy to see that the thoughtful blending of practical considerations or biographical materials, as is often done, could lend a human dimension to an otherwise purely formal topic.

Some of the innovative techniques used by experienced confluent teachers illustrate other mixes of loadings. Improvisational acting has been used by Montz [17] to deal successfully with what appear to be orientation and engagement loadings in an English unit on *Julius Caesar*. The unit was introduced by a discussion of contemporary events, with parallels drawn to the play.

> We could see a lot of comparisons and similarities between Julius Caesar and President Kennedy, so we showed scenes of Kennedy's assassination and read lines from the play. We brought it into a little closer context with what they were doing, where they were.[18]

Major themes were drawn from the play by the instructor, and acted with different roles played by different students, unlike the "chair" technique described above. Scenes, such as Marullus' rage at the celebration of Pompey's death, and Caesar's assassination, were discussed and acted with dialogue from the play following improvisational sessions cast in modern and personal terms. What otherwise had been expected to be a poorly received and boring unit was transformed into one with greater depth and understanding.

The distinctions which we have proposed here appear to lend added conceptual clarity to these and numerous other examples of innovative affective techniques and help to place these efforts more clearly within the context of systematic curriculum modification. A general strategy of maximally effective confluent teaching would, to oversimplify, need to deal with affective dimensions in the order in which we have discussed them: concerns and blockages, orientation loadings, engagement loadings, and accomplishment loadings.

The affective domain is an exceedingly complex aspect of learning and it yields reluctantly to analytic exercises such as this. The preliminary work has begun, though, and the initial and most important steps have been taken by simply recognizing the importance of the integration of the affective and the cognitive within a total confluent curriculum. The distinctions drawn here have facilitated our research in some small measure, and if they prove useful for confluent curriculum development, we shall be able to move that much further beyond vibration teaching.

REFERENCE NOTES /

1. Verta Mae, *Vibration Cooking* (New York: Doubleday, 1970).
2. Nevitt Sanford, "The Development of Cognitive-Affective Processes through Education." In Eli M. Bower and William G. Hollister (eds.), *Behavioral Science Frontiers in Education* (New York: John Wiley, 1967), p. 79.
3. Elizabeth L. Simpson, *Democracy's Stepchildren* (San Francisco: Jossey-Bass, 1971), p. 40.
4. Ibid., p. 71.
5. George I. Brown, *Human Teaching for Human Learning* (New York: Viking Press, 1971), p. 9.
6. John Holt, *How Children Fail* (New York: Dell, 1964), p. 49.
7. Simpson, chaps. 2–6.
8. Gerald Weinstein and Mario D. Fantini, *Toward Humanistic Education: A Curriculum of Affect* (New York: Praeger, 1970).
9. Abraham Maslow, "Some Theoretical Consequences of Basic Need Gratifications." *Journal of Personality*, vol. 16 (1948), pp. 402–416.
10. Weinstein and Fantini, pp. 61–63.
11. Brown, pp. 248–249.
12. Weinstein and Fantini, pp. 219–220.
13. Brown, p. 16.
14. Ibid., p. 4.
15. Weinstein and Fantini, p. 119.
16. Ibid., p. 118.
17. Ibid., chap. 3.
18. Ibid., p. 285.

14

SEARCH FOR A WORKING MODEL: GESTALT, PSYCHOSYNTHESIS, AND CONFLUENT EDUCATION

— *Thomas Yeomans*

This article addresses itself to one basic question: What is confluent education? It does not purport to give a complete or final answer, but rather it attempts to clarify one central and important aspect of the concept, namely, what happens inside a person as a result of a confluent education experience. To do this it builds a psychological model for confluent education based on the central concepts of Gestalt therapy and Psychosynthesis. The article's nature is exploratory; its findings are not as yet empirically verified. It pulls together hitherto unconnected ideas into a coherent scheme which, hopefully, will provide a clear focus for further work in this field.

CONFLUENT EDUCATION /

As is stated elsewhere in this book confluent education has been defined as the integration or flowing together of the affective and cognitive elements in individual and group learning. Its proponents seek an education that will attend to the emotional as well as the intellectual experience and growth of students, an education that helps them make connections between these two and so integrates their thoughts and feelings in their lives. This integration, it is held, reduces and then overcomes many basic psychological conflicts within a person, particularly during adolescence, leading to learning which is significant to the learner and which will produce intelligent behavior in him as he matures. "Significant learning" is defined as that learning which has relevance to a person's existence; "intelligent behavior" is defined as behavior which is reality-based and which manifests clear and sound use of the intelligence in guiding one's existence. For the most part, formal schooling has not encouraged the integration of the two, with the result that many students do not consider the school experience as being a vital part of their lives, even though they may choose to stay on, or are forced by law to stay on, to suffer and endure the boredom and meaninglessness they experience there. This sorry state of affairs has been widely documented in educational literature such as Kohl's *36 Children,* Kozol's *Death at an Early Age,* Herndon's *The Way It Spozed to Be,* and books by John Holt.

Further, the proponents of confluent education argue that acceptance of, and work with, the emotions in classrooms not only produce healthier persons, but as important, also increase intellectual achievement. Children who are involved in and excited about their learning are going to learn more and better, and what they learn is going "to stick" and be useful and relevant to them. Confluent education sees the emotions as central to motivation for learning, and seeks to find ways (1) to excite children about the possibilities of learning, and (2) to help them structure this excitement into learning experiences that lead to intellectual as well as emotional growth. A large body of practice has been built around this basic concept, both in teacher education and in the teaching of various subject matter at all levels, and the results are proving both impressive and heartening.

Now, however, it is time to look more closely at the concept itself, and particularly, to examine systematically what it is exactly that confluent education does, i.e., how this integration of thought and feeling actually happens within a person. To do this, I have found it helpful first to shift the term's focus slightly, moving from "confluent education" to "education for confluence." (I am indebted to Dr. Stewart Shapiro who led a DRICE (Development and Research in Confluent Education) group during the academic year 1970–71 for this turn of phrase.) This allows a shift of emphasis from an external to an internal orientation and a concentration on the experience of confluence itself rather than on the pedagogical practices of confluent education. The experience of confluence lies at the core of the educative process, and if we can better understand exactly what it is, the broader concept of confluent education will, I believe, gain depth and clarity.

CONFLUENCE /

What then is confluence? First of all, it is an *experience* and not just a concept. It is something that actually happens in a person, and as such, it has psychological and physiological correlates that can be identified and described.

As a process taken in its root meaning, confluence is a merging of formerly separate elements — quite literally a "flowing together." The flowing together may take several forms. If, for example, we consider the literal image of a "confluence," we might see two or more streams of water which converge to form one flow. As they do this, the bodies of water at first flow side by side, then intermingle, and then finally become one new body of water. Drawing on this image symbolically we can call these three stages interaction, integration, and synthesis, confluence being the general principle behind all three. Now, in a person, the elements that combine in this way may be a thought and a feeling, several thoughts, several feelings, two or more colors in the imagination, two or more movements in the body, two aspects of one's personality, or whatever. The point is that whereas before they were separate and unconnected, now they are joined through the process of confluence in some relationship which leads to union. So, first I take "confluence" as a term which includes "interaction" (mutual or reciprocal action or influence), "integration" (the combining of two formerly separate elements), and "synthesis" (the joining of two or more elements to form a new, third whole).

However, confluence can also be defined, again using our physical image, as the "flowing together" of the stream and its banks. Drawing on this image, we are dealing symbolically with the confluence, specifically, of cognition and affect. An important difference in this kind of confluence is that rather than a blending of elements we get an alignment wherein neither element loses its identity as such, but becomes part of a higher level of organization (e.g., banks plus water make a river). In terms of the mind (the banks) and feeling (the water), as these become aligned in a person, that which is seen as reasonable to do is also increasingly felt as desirable to do; what is thought about is loved, and what is loved is thought about, and this leads to a smooth flow of emotional energy through the forms of the mind. On the other hand, where there is little or no alignment, there is conflict between mind and feelings (the banks overflow or are empty; the water has no direction or is forced uphill), and much energy and effort in teaching and learning is misspent or simply wasted.

Confluence, then, occurs in both the ways described above, and is the principle which underlies several related processes, these being: interaction, integration, synthesis, and alignment.

Confluence is also a psychological process and phenomenon that can be affected by external events, i.e., its occurrence is correlated with the nature of external stimuli, structures, and environments, and its happening can be increased or diminished by changes in that realm. In this respect, although it is "internal," its process often involves interaction with the environment and others, and it is affected by "external" events. As such, although confluence is an unconscious ongoing process in every person to some degree, its effect can be inhibited or enhanced by conscious choices and directions taken in education — a fact sadly overlooked by most educators — and it is a psychological process that is particularly vulnerable and therefore in need of care, evocation, and education.

"Internal" and "external" need some clarification. Obviously the two realms are inextricably related, and each reflects and affects the other. However, here I take the person's skin as the rough dividing line — for clarity, take other people, chairs, buildings, etc., as external, and thoughts, sensations, feelings, intuitions, imagination, etc., as internal.

Confluence is an experience that we all have in varying degrees of intensity, sometimes in learning situations, sometimes in relationships with other people, and sometimes when we least expect it. Always it yields new meaning and understanding that arise from seeing a hitherto hidden connection or relationship, and is accompanied by a release of energy, often manifested by excitement on the feeling level, a sense of significance and involvement, and on the mental level by increased concentration and mental functioning. It is very much akin to what in "creativity theory" is called the "aha" experience, the moment of insight and recognition when, after the collection of experiences and a period of incubation or brooding over unrelated data, a pattern of organization suddenly is seen, often in a "flash," and a new idea or poem or invention is conceived and then elaborated into final form.[1]

Confluence, in fact, is merely a new name for a natural, very ancient, and familiar psychological process that has been valued under other names by many peoples. Yet, sadly, much has been done and is being done in schools that prevents it from happening as much as it might. It is central to the realization of a better, more balanced, and whole education for ourselves and our children, for it is the key to the growth and development of young persons into alive, mature, intelligent, and creative adults who can function well both as individuals and as members of society. Therefore, an understanding of confluence is of the utmost importance.

ENERGY /

Another very useful way to define the experience of confluence is through the metaphor of energy. It is beyond the scope of this article to go into the complexities of physiological and psychological energy systems but, generally speaking, each of us has a measure or level of energy available for use at any particular time, and this energy we employ in a number of ways — to meet our needs, to create, to cope, whatever. Further, in most of us there exist psychological blocks and conflicts which absorb energy unproductively, thereby considerably lessening the amount of energy available with which to work. In some cases these blocks and conflicts lead to severe disability, but in most cases they produce mild malfunction and a nonutilization of potential resources within each of us. And in all cases valuable energy is lost or wasted through our inability to channel it properly and efficiently and by our not having control over how it is used.

Now, as was said above, the experience of confluence is defined as being accompanied by a release of energy, either emotional or mental — usually both — a release which is also experienced in some way in the body, i.e., it has physiological correlates. This release results from (1) the removal of some block that was keeping two elements of the personality apart, (2) the simple interaction or integration or synthesis (confluence) of two previously separate elements, or (3) the attainment of an alignment of mind and feelings. In the first case both the energy used in blocking *and* the energy generated from the confluence of the two elements is now available to the person. In the latter two cases energy is generated from the confluence itself. In all cases more energy is made available to the organism. This energy release can be manifested on the emotional level in excitement, enthusiasm, laughter, and ecstasy, and on the mental level in concentration, prolonged attention, intense thought, etc. Most often it is manifested in some combination of the two. The point is, however, that the experience of confluence provides both more energy for a person than he formerly had available and creates a more efficient utilization of that energy in that he is more "together," i.e., less blocked.

Note that this experiencing of energy release may lead to the learning of a mathematical concept, to the writing of a poem, to the winning of a footrace, or to making love; and, clearly, the energy released needs to be channeled in new structures so as not to be lost or "burnt up" needlessly. Confluent education addresses itself to this related problem, and works to create structures through which this released energy can flow. Unless this happens the energy not rightly utilized, after creating a feeling of euphoria, will flow away again, leaving the person merely tired. Ideally, the energy (at least part of it) can be directed toward nourishing and sustaining the process of confluence, thus creating a chain reaction or snowball effect in the person's development. As this experience of confluence proceeds, it can energize a person and give him more "power" to do what he chooses to do. This "power" is experienced in two ways: as awareness and as activity. When, as the result of confluence, mind and feelings are aligned, they act to correct, balance, and deepen a person's awareness of himself and his world. Like two eyes rather than one, they give two distinct vantage points from which to view the world and these merge into one tri-depth perception. This leads, for example, to far superior and more realistic work in planning something than that done by a primarily emotional or mental person.

All of us at one time or another have had the experience of being suddenly flooded with energy. This can occur in moments of darkest personal tragedy, when the deep meaning of events suddenly strikes and restores us, or it can occur sometimes at moments of great joy and peace. The point is that, as at these peak moments, so too at the daily moments of insight, discovery, expansion of knowledge, understanding, or consciousness, energy is released into our systems as a result of what is here defined as "confluence" — the combining, in some form, of formerly disparate and unconnected or malaligned elements so as to produce a newly experienced whole. There is an interesting connection here with Weinstein and Fantini's concepts of identity, connectedness, and power.[2] Confluence gives a person more "power" and control in his life. It also confirms him in who he is at that moment ("identity") and it works to link him more surely with others and generally with the universe ("connectedness"). Thus, confluence can be seen as the means by which a person's identity, connectedness, and power are assured and strengthened.

Now, given these two concepts, confluence and energy, let us turn to the building of our model. Here I plan a brief retracing of the steps in my thinking in order to make clear just how Gestalt therapy and Psychosynthesis each makes its contribution, and then I shall present a final version which represents a synthesis of the two.

GESTALT THERAPY /

Gestalt therapy, which was developed by Frederick Perls as a reaction to traditional psychoanalysis, draws upon existential phenomenology for its philosophical bases, and works to develop a person's awareness of his present experience. It holds that all clues to a patient's cure lie in here-and-now behavior, and that by accepting, exaggerating, and exploring this behavior and experience, a person can get in touch with, and work through, emotional conflicts or blocks that are preventing his growth and further development. A wide range of awareness techniques are used in this work [3] and its basic aim is to restore to a person his potentially "whole" or integrated personality, unassailed by severe emotional conflicts or splits. The basic intent of Gestalt is to enable a person to live as rich an emotional life as possible, and to help him allow emotional experience to occur without trying to control and/or avoid it through fantasy, intellectualization, muscle contraction, or projection. It conceives of the personality basically as a flow of life energy through the organism which, when it becomes blocked, can be freed again through the use of awareness, present-experiencing, and working with projections, introjections, and retroflections.[4] The basic aim of Gestalt therapy is emotional growth.

PSYCHOSYNTHESIS /

Psychosynthesis is an approach to growth, developed over the last sixty years by Dr. Roberto Assagioli, a psychiatrist. It has recently become known in this country as a comprehensive and effective therapeutic theory and practice, based on a conception of man as being in the process of personal growth, whose personality can be organized around a center of awareness and energy — first in the personal self and then in the transpersonal self. This center is conceived of, and can be experienced by man, as a focal point from which, through the identification of an awareness of it and the disidentification from any other aspect of the personality, we can regulate, direct, harmonize, and integrate the many elements within our psyche. This, in turn, leads to a more highly integrated and effective life activity and experience.

In this approach, transpersonal experience and spiritual development are considered legitimate and natural directions of growth, and can be conceived of as a "vertical" dimension, along with physical, emotional, and mental development, which proceeds along the "horizontal" or personal dimension. An integration is worked for in both dimensions, between the many aspects and elements in each and between these levels, in order, finally, for the personality not only to be integrated within itself, but also with others and within the universe.[5]

The "work" of Psychosynthesis is directed toward facilitating a process already inherent and ongoing in the human organism — the process of synthesis. It is beyond the scope of this article to treat this matter fully. Suffice it to say that it is clear that the natural sciences have already demonstrated the existence of synthesis on the biological and physiological levels. Synthesis is the basic process by which all living things grow and achieve higher, more complex, and more efficient structure and organization.[6] What is less well known is that this same process occurs on the psychological level, and it is the means by which we, as living organisms, develop and grow. It is always happening to some degree, for the dynamic is built in, so to speak; but once we become aware of it and understand it, it can be facilitated and any impediments can be removed, thus making the journey smoother and perhaps quicker. This, then, is the central aim of Psychosynthesis.

The techniques used in Psychosynthesis are many and wide-ranging. It incorporates techniques from such related therapeutic practices as guided imagery, creative movement, Gestalt, meditation, symbolic art, writing, and journal-keeping as well. In each existential situation the specific technique selected is the one most effective in fostering growth, but all have as the ultimate goal the facilitating of this basic process of synthesis within the psyche.

Psychosynthesis conceives of the personality as having three interpenetrating fundamental aspects — body, feelings, and mind — which develop in that order in a person's growth, each interpenetrating the previous one(s). These are considered the bases of personality. Psychosynthesis posits the existence of "subpersonalities," psychological entities that are built up out of these three major aspects. The subpersonalities may consist of roles, combinations of character traits, complexes, patterned behaviors, or essential qualities, manifested in each person. At any one time only a limited number of these subpersonalities will be active within the personality, and in time these may grow and change themselves — combine, split, etc. — but they are constellations of attitudes and behaviors which contain enough energy to play a semi-independent role in the person's life. This formulation is similar to that propounded in ego therapy and subself theory.[7]

These three major aspects of the personality, and the many subpersonalities that arise from them, make up what I have, and will, refer to as the "elements" of the personality — the entities involved in the processes of interaction, integration, synthesis, and alignment I have described above. "Elements" also will refer to parts of the external environment (e.g., another person's behavior, a poem, an equation, or a tree or plant), but here I restrict the discussion to the internal environment.

It is important to realize that we are dealing with a developmental sequence, and that the aspects of the personality and subpersonalities do not exist at the same level of psychological organization. Of the three aspects, the physical is the first to develop, the emotional second, and the mental third. This is not to say that at any time all three may not be present, but generally, in childhood, our focus and awareness is on the physical aspect, on action and doing, with the other two subsidiary to that. In early adolescence the focus shifts to our emotional aspect, and we tend to do, or think, in order to feel. Then, in the late teens and early twenties, if we have not become stuck somewhere along the way, our focus shifts again, this time to the mental aspect, and we then tend to subordinate our physical and emotional experience to the mental. "Mental" here does not mean intellectual only. Rather, it is a broader concept which includes all activities of consciousness as directed and experienced by the brain and the nervous system. The intellect is an important part of the mental aspect, but it is only a part.

Often there is conflict between the aspects of personality, particularly between the emotional and mental, but for the moment what is important is that, as we develop in this way, because of the existence of the basic ongoing process of synthesis, subpersonalities begin to develop around temporary centers, which, depending on when in the sequence they are "born," will draw on one, two, or all three of the fundamental aspects. Some experience — say the loss of a limb, a mother's deep love, or being taught chess at the age of four — will be sufficiently powerful and magnetic to become a temporary center around which a subpersonality forms (e.g., "the cripple," "mama's boy," "brains"). As a person lives his life, many subpersonalities are born and grow with him, some in one or another aspect, some in combination, but all to a degree rigid and limited. The aspects of personality provide the material for the subpersonalities, and are the ground in which they grow. So, implicitly, when we work with the elements, the subpersonalities, we are also always working with the major aspects of body, feelings, and mind.

The personality in Psychosynthesis is therefore seen as composed of many elements, mostly in the form of subpersonalities. If we were to draw a diagram of this, we would get something like Figure 1, each circle representing a subpersonality.

FIGURE 1

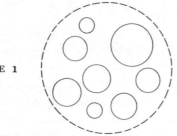

First, note that the circles are of different sizes. This is done deliberately to indicate the amount of energy invested or encapsulated in each element, i.e., some elements are more "powerful" than others. And though obviously these elements would vary from person to person and would shift within each person from period to period of one's life, the amount of energy in each determines the "shape" of the personality at any one time.

Second, note that the lines around the elements are unbroken. This need not be so, but here it indicates that energy is trapped there, that it is not readily available for other uses. I could have drawn broken lines (permeable boundaries) which would have indicated that energy could flow freely in and out of the element. But, for the moment, let us leave them unbroken, as that describes the situation most of us are in.

Third, note that the outer circle is formed by a broken line. This, too, is intentional, in that a person who is identified with whatever elements he ascribes to himself (self-identity) leaves out many others (often the opposites) which he also "is," and thus his personality is to some degree partial. The broken line, therefore, indicates only a potential, not a fact, for the personality as experienced is not so whole.

The elements themselves are seen as related and relating within the personality, but in somewhat random and haphazard ways, and they are often in conflict or at odds because of the rigidity of their structure and the lack of any means to structure their relationships.

The diagram, then, provides us with our first simplistic view of the human personality as seen through Psychosynthesis, but it lacks an important distinction between the elements viewed by a person as "him" and those he sees as "not-him," even though, in fact, they are. It is here that the Gestalt concept of ego boundaries comes to our aid.

EGO BOUNDARIES /

Perls never formulates an explicit definition of an ego boundary, but his use of the term implies a definition as "a constantly shifting boundary encompassing whatever a person thinks to be 'him' at any particular moment." [8] An ego boundary, therefore, in our terms, encompasses a partial personality, and bounds those elements with which a person identifies. As a person grows, and particularly as he integrates new experience into his personality, his ego boundary will expand. If for some reason he fails to take in new experiences, his ego boundary may not expand and may, in fact, contract or rigidify.

Coupled with this concept are the related concepts of projection and introjection. [9] Both are psychological processes which directly affect the ego boundary. In the first process, a person "disowns," i.e., sees as not a part of himself an element of his personality which is in fact his, and projects it onto another person, thereby putting it outside his ego boundary, which results in shrinkage of the boundary. An example of this would be a person who, having difficulty in expressing his anger, will imagine others to be angry with him; i.e., he projects his anger onto them rather than accepting it as his own and expressing it.

In the second concept, introjection, a person may accept an element of personality from another which he then comes to view as his own when, in fact, it is not. In this case he has introjected the element and placed it within his ego boundary. This leads to an expansion of the ego boundary, but it is an overexpansion, for the element remains foreign inside him and may cause a good deal of confusion and stress in its relation to the other elements. Freud's "super ego" is a classic example of an introject.

In both cases the ego boundary is altered by either shrinkage or overextension, and the person loses touch with who he really is. Ideally, he would neither project nor introject, so that whatever elements the ego boundary encompassed at any one time would be truly him. Unfortunately, this seldom is the case.

ASSIMILATION /

How, then, does a person deal with new experience and grow from it so that the ego boundaries do not change? In Gestalt parlance, he assimilates it. This means that he experiences something, takes it into his ego boundary and, metaphorically, chews it up and digests what is useful to him, discarding as waste what is not.[10] In our terms, when he encounters a new experience (element), he absorbs any energy encapsulated in the experience, and then assimilates the energy into his system to use as he sees fit. Assimilation thus is achieved by means of our interaction — integration — synthesis process (confluence). It is the general process by which an organism grows, and can work on both new experience (outside the ego boundary, and either truly new or a projection), and familiar but compulsive experience (inside the ego boundary — an introjection or retroflection). Clearly, this is a complex matter involving more than I have discussed here, but what we have now is sufficient for us to draw another diagram (Figure 2).

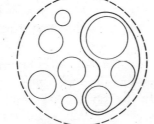

FIGURE 2

Here I have taken Figure 1 and added an ego boundary to indicate that some elements are "disowned" (outside the ego boundary) and probably projected, while others are "owned" (inside the ego boundary) and accepted as "self." Some of these latter elements may be introjects, but for the moment let us put that issue aside and focus on the fact that the personality is only partially fulfilled when some of its elements lie outside the ego boundary and are construed as alien or unknown to the personality.

To go back now to our metaphor of energy — this means that the energy in projected elements is not available to the personality. The person has given the "power" inherent in them to someone else, and consequently his own power is diminished. Even in the case of the introject, the energy is still not available since it is still encapsulated and under the control of the "other," so that though a person uses it as "him," he has no control over what it does, but must follow powerlessly its dictates, for he has failed to break it open and to assimilate its energy.

Further, within this ego boundary a person may still have energy encapsulated in elements which are really "him," as well as conflicts or blocks between elements which again drain off energy. So, all in all, he is very lopsided and partial in his development.

In Gestalt terms, what this personality needs is the re-owning and assimilation of projections and introjections, and perhaps, also some work with retroflection — the introjection of a projection. Basically, each of these elements needs to be accepted and broken down to release its energy, which can then be used in rebuilding the personality into healthier functioning elements and patterns. At any one time a person will only work with one or two elements, but eventually, to complete the process, all elements will need to be dealt with in this way.

Gestalt sees introjects as basically unhealthy. Psychosynthesis would agree if the introject is controlling the personality. However, if through disidentification, the person controls and uses the introject for his own growth, as in the case of the ideal-model introject, then this would be considered healthy and useful.

AWARENESS /

Before going further, it is important to discuss and define the concept of awareness as it is understood in Gestalt therapy and Psychosynthesis. In Gestalt, awareness is a kind of psychological searchlight which can be pointed, within limits, as a person chooses. I say within limits because at any one time a person is aware of only so much, depending on how well he uses his senses, and how he blocks their uses, and how he conceives of who he is. A person can usually "be aware of" whatever he considers himself to be (that which is inside the ego boundary), although he most likely cannot do this all at once; thus the play of the searchlight. He will experience great difficulty being aware of parts of himself which he does not consider "him" (that which is outside the ego boundary), those parts which for some reason he has disowned. Much of Gestalt therapy works precisely with this problem, by attempting, through the focusing of awareness (the therapist "stating the obvious and making the implicit explicit"), to break open ego boundaries and encapsulated elements in order to reintegrate disowned elements and to clear out or assimilate introjected or rigidified elements. Awareness is a capacity which is used as a tool in this task. As mentioned earlier, a Gestalt therapist concentrates on helping a person become aware of what is happening at the moment, in the "now," for almost immediately the most pressing problems (blocks, conflicts, etc.) will appear, and the therapist then can help the patient deal with whatever he is avoiding. Lack of awareness is actually lack of access to oneself and to one's potential for growth.

In Psychosynthesis, awareness is seen more explicitly as a function of energy. It is the energy of consciousness that can be focused at will, and which also plays like a searchlight across the personality. As in Gestalt, awareness is a tool in facilitating growth and it is used in the same way, but here it has an added function expressed in the phrase "energy follows thought." This means that the object of one's focus will grow, so that awareness can be used as an energizer in and of itself. It thus becomes an instrument for building up, balancing, directing, and harmonizing, as well as breaking down, elements in the personality. In terms of our model, it plays on the elements and can be used to nourish those which a person considers important to develop, either in themselves or in combination with others.

Awareness is the foreground of consciousness — consciousness being the field in which it exists. It is a major tool for expanding this field. If used properly, it can constantly "bring to light" new elements of the personality, both inside and outside the ego boundaries, and in their assimilation.

By putting these two concepts — awareness and ego boundaries — together, we have four levels of personality identification over which awareness plays. On the first level are those elements which a person identifies as himself, as "me" (inside ego boundaries). On the second level are those elements he "owns" but does not identify with (also inside ego boundaries). On the third level are those elements he does not like and avoids whenever possible, elements which he is conscious of but disowns (outside ego boundaries). On the fourth level are those elements which are unconscious and of which he has no awareness (also outside ego boundaries), either because he is severely blocked against them, or simply because of where he is in his development.

As we have seen already, much trouble and pain, and loss of energy and potential can accrue on this spectrum, a further complication can arise, in that development and identification will often be out of kilter. A person — for example, an intelligent woman — because of her sex role, may identify with her feelings even though these are actually not as developed as her mind, which she may ignore. For true harmony and synthesis within the personality, this misidentification must be corrected, both by proper identification with the mental and emotional aspects, and an alignment (confluence) of the two.

THE CENTER /

How, then, is this chaos, consisting of many elements and levels of awareness, to be harmonized? This is particularly difficult when the relationship between the elements of the personality in our model is random and potentially full of conflict, and there is no place from which to direct the awareness one might have — a situation which creates the possibility of the awareness, like energy, becoming trapped or encapsulated in a particular element.

Let us return to Psychosynthesis to pick up the concept of a "center" around which these elements can be organized. This concept is very important. It holds that there exists an experience from which all personality elements can be seen "as if at a distance." Another term sometimes used for this point is the "observer," and it is similar to what Perls calls "the point of creative indifference" in his discussion of organismic balance. [11] Basically, from this point, one is able to "disidentify" from any other personality element while still remaining centered (identified) with one's personality as a whole. From this point, one is able to be aware of, for example, both sides of a polarity (opposites) — a conflict, a relationship between other elements — and to work with these toward their resolution and integration by accepting both (becoming them), yet remaining apart and drawing on both to create the resolution. It is a point from which one can direct and control one's growth, rather than letting oneself be controlled by certain partial identifications; given this center, the personality can be organized around it, its growth can be directed from there, and from there awareness can be focused wherever necessary to foster this process.

Disidentification is the liberating process by which a person comes to experience this center after having freed himself from the control of other elements. It is not to be confused with "disowning," for here, rather than rejecting an undesirable element, a person accepts it but says also that "though I have it ("own" it), I am not it." As this is done, with more and more elements, a person ceases to be rigidly identified with, and locked into, any particular elements of his personality and begins to experience his center. From the center he is free to enter fully into any one aspect (element) of his experience if he chooses, for he does not fear it will engulf him and define or limit him and, in short, he has control over the directions he takes.

Ironically, a person often disowns a part of himself because he is fearful of its taking over, or because he is afraid he cannot change it. But, with a center, this fear is no longer a factor, because the process of disidentification allows him not only to know he will not become overwhelmed and that he can control and change the element, but also to know that it allows him to go further into whatever element he chooses and to experience it most fully, for he always knows that he has it, but is not it. Therefore, the center is a great help in growth, for disowning is no longer necessary and fear of change is considerably reduced.

If we accept this concept of a center, we have the altered diagram of Figure 3.

FIGURE 3

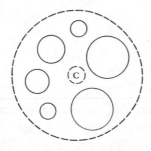

An interesting phenomenon occurs here in relation to the ego boundary. With the existence of a center, the ego boundary both contracts around it through disidentification, and simultaneously expands to include all elements of personality through ceasing to disown any quality; i.e., from the vantage point of the center one can be aware of them all. Thus, paradoxically, the personality becomes both center and circumference. Further, it now has access to all parts of itself as these exist at any one time, and it experiences a tremendous expansion of awareness and consciousness.

In terms of energy, the organism, by having a center, has much greater access to its own energy through ceasing to struggle with partial identification, and so can focus on freeing the energy which is still encapsulated in particular elements, through the use of awareness and whatever Gestalt or Psychosynthesis techniques are useful. Gradually, as more elements are assimilated and their energy freed into the system, increasing amounts of energy are available for this work, so that further interaction-integration-synthesis (confluence) is facilitated and the personality achieves higher and higher levels of integration and organization around this center. Also, in terms of alignment, the center provides a point through which mind and feelings can become aligned, so it is central to this particular kind of confluence.

Thus, given all of the foregoing, we get a final diagram representing the ideal personality toward which it may be said we are all growing (Figure 4).

FIGURE 4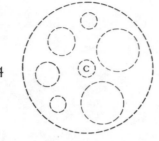

This drawing represents a personality largely whole and without conflicts, which, as it expands, is able to assimilate new experience and resolve any conflicts that arise both within and without. This personality does not waste energy through projection, introjection, or retroflection, and its ego boundary is permeable, as are the boundaries of its elements. It manifests a high degree of integration and an ample amount of freely flowing energy over which it has control and with which it can direct its further growth. Clearly, it is the most vital and efficient of possible systems.

Actually, this personality would best be represented in four dimensions so that the movement through time and space and the flow of energy could be shown. We could construct it as a sphere in which the elements revolve around the center. Then, if the ego boundary were to shrink or be indented for any reason, it would look like a punched-in ball and would have "holes" in it. If a high degree of integration existed, it would be a full sphere and energy would flow freely within it.

Further, this personality sphere could be part of a larger whole, including the subconscious and superconscious, which would connect it more explicitly with Freudian and Jungian theory; but for the moment this is not necessary and it could be somewhat distracting. (For a discussion of this connection the reader is referred to Assagioli's book *Psychosynthesis*.) The sphere can be seen as moving through a sea of elements most of which, at first, are experienced as foreign, but which gradually, as the sphere grows, are assimilated; the personality and the sea (universe) become as one, and a complete correspondence (confluence) is established.

EDUCATIONAL IMPLICATIONS /

The Process of Confluence: The Student

We now have a functioning model of the human personality and an image of its process of growth. We have a sense of what prevents growth and what wastes energy in the personality; we have a technology for facilitating growth, for increasing the amount of energy available to the person, and for healing splits, conflicts, or blocks within the personality.

In terms of education, how do we work with this model? How does this personality function in the classroom? The main lines of this process have been implied, but let us go over them now more explicitly.

First of all, if we reconceive education in terms of what we have said here, it becomes a "leading out" of an individual's capacities, talents, uniqueness, person, into his whole possibilities, and its aim becomes the balanced development of the personality toward intellectual, emotional, social, and moral maturity. As such, education clearly becomes person-centered, rather than oriented to the teaching of subject matter, skills, or disciplines, per se — which is not to say we are abandoning these disciplines, but only that we are putting them in a secondary position to the learner himself.

The student's experience is primary, the foundation on which he builds his education. Questions such as "Who am I?" "What do I want?" "What has meaning?" become vitally important and central to the process of education and must be dealt with fully and directly. In order to do this a student needs to find and experience his center, become aware of his personality aspects and subpersonalities and how they operate, assess his blocks, conflicts, and polarities, and then begin the work of growing, using the processes of awareness, energy, assimilation, and confluence.

In doing this he must work first with the "internal" elements of his psyche as he considers the central question of identity, "Who am I?" He also asks such questions as "With whom am I?" (others), and "Where am I?" (environment), but the primary thrust here is toward self-awareness and understanding, for this is the foundation on which his education will be built.

The confluence sought for here is the first kind (interaction-integration-synthesis) and its aim is to increase self-knowledge and achieve as much "wholeness" as possible. Also, as a person becomes more aware he can begin to choose his own directions for growth and experience and take responsibility for these choices. Thus awareness-choice-responsibility is another sequence which confluence generates as it occurs in persons.

The second kind of confluence (alignment) is also of utmost importance, for without it there is no energy (motivation) for learning and, as we have seen, the organism is paralyzed by conflict, ambivalence, etc. If, on the other hand, this confluence is occurring in learners, then increasing energy is available and the person experiences greater capacity for introspection, expansion of awareness, choice, responsibility, or whatever, as he directs his own growth and education.

All this can happen only if a student's experience is put first and foremost (in everyone's mind) and is valued by teachers, peers, and individuals as legitimate and the basis of all educational growth.

If the primacy of this position is given, the student may work from his center, using his awareness, to enlarge an underdeveloped element of his personality, or to break open an overdeveloped element in order to use some of its energy elsewhere. Or he may explore a block or conflict with the aim of removing or resolving it through the energy of his awareness and the process of assimilation and confluence. Or he may explore one element that particularly interests him. In all cases, he is clearly in charge of his own learning.

Inner and Outer Worlds

A distinction must be made here between internal and external elements, recognizing all the while that the boundary between the two is constantly shifting and somewhat arbitrary. Internal elements are those such as subpersonalities; external elements might be a poem, a concept, a fact. The former are constantly being dealt with and expressed; the latter, which were someone else's internal elements, moments or years before, are constantly being encountered and impressed (either by introjection or assimilation). The point is that though we started with the "internal" world, actually the student constantly works on himself *and* his world, educating each through the other, focusing sometimes on internal elements, sometimes on external, and increasingly making the two worlds one.

As the student turns toward the external world and begins to expand his internal world through interaction with it, basically what he is doing is building a sensibility. By this I mean he is linking his inner world with the outer world, connecting his experience with that of others, relating his personal knowledge to interpersonal and public knowledge.[12] This sensibility is a kind of mediator between the inner and outer worlds and an interpreter of one to the other. Therefore, its existence is crucial to the development of mature, informed, and original persons, for it is where the two worlds join and are integrated with each other. The sensibility created may be literary, historical, mathematical, scientific, religious, economic, whatever. Any number of "subjects" (external elements) may be used. But the point is that a sensibility, of whatever kind, is both person and world. It is the coupling which connects inner and outer; and again, both kinds of confluence are central and instrumental here, for it is by their occurrences that a harmonious and sure connection is made and a sensibility fully developed.

Note that again the reins are in the hands of the student. As with his "insides" so with his "outsides"; he chooses, directs and takes responsibility for his education. He assesses his needs, faces his blocks and limitations, and focuses his energy and awareness on the problems that are important and meaningful to him.

The Teacher

The student still needs the teacher. Indeed, a teacher may become even more vital to a student than he was before (if he was vital at all). But always the teacher exists as a resource and facilitator for the student's growth, not as an imposer or giver of knowledge and meaning. Happily this arrangement frees the teacher to become a student again, to pursue his own growth; so the two become fellow travelers and learners, sharing their resources to their mutual benefit.

Also, the disciplines no longer have the authoritarian hold over both teacher and student that they once had, but exist rather as open studies, more easily added to and reshaped by the creative intelligences working in them. As with the internal elements, these external elements are broken open by this approach, and their energy freed for new use.

And finally, the energy that is released by the process of confluence can be used to further the same process in other areas and with new elements. In other words, once the process is started it accelerates, and excitement in one area will lead to excitement and learning in another. The student experiences greater power (also connectedness and identity) and ability to make his own choices and to lead a creative life. In still other words, confluence begets more confluence. Increasingly, the student wants to direct his own learning, is excited and involved, builds his sensibilities, and explores the world within and around him, thereby growing in a harmonious and balanced way toward actualizing his full human potential.

A Model

Now, if we draw a diagram of this process, we have Figure 5.

 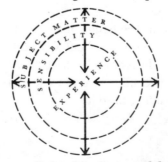

FIGURE 5

At the core of this learning model is the individual student's experience and his encounter with his internal elements. On this is built his sensibility, a sensibility constructed from the center outward through the expansion of the inner circle and consciousness (inside world), and through external elements (outside world), be they concepts, poems, formulae, or whatever.

There are two dynamics of this model. One is the constant shuttling (indicated by the two-way arrows) between inner and outer circles as the learning process progresses. The other is the gradual expansion of all the circles as experience and sensibility grow and new areas of subject matter are encountered and dealt with. Obviously, there is no end to the process — education is a lifelong activity — and the expansion allows for increasingly sophisticated ideas, skills, and meanings to be encompassed and mastered by the learner.

Clearly, our two models (Figures 4 and 5) are closely related. Figure 4 is what we need in order for Figure 5 to work as smoothly and richly as it can; i.e., if we have confluence in the person who is learning, he will be able to master all of the knowledge of importance to him, overcome whatever blockages there are, while maintaining a creative, generative, confident center based on his experience *and* drawing on all the available resources others can offer. In fact, if we have confluence within a person, then gradually confluence will occur between inner and outer worlds via the confluent sensibility, which can lead at least to a productive, integrated life in the world and at most to an experience of total unity with the universe. Admittedly, this is a tall order, but anything short of it will give us less than we can have and deserve.

Clearly, the experience of confluence, both within the person and between self, sensibility, and world, is central to all this. The models we have built are of a confluent person (Figure 4) and of confluent education (Figure 5). Now only one question remains: practically, how do we get all this going?

CONFLUENT EDUCATION /

We are back to where we started, asking, "What is confluent education?" My answer is: It is any educational practice that fosters the experience of confluence (as defined here) in learners, and helps them to develop along the lines I have laid out above.

In saying this, however, it would be foolish to claim that confluence is only happening in classrooms where confluent education techniques are being used, for, as has been stated several times, this process is universal and ongoing in all living situations and, in respect to schools, it often occurs in situations that are seemingly "unconfluent"; e.g., in a packed lecture hall a great deal of confluence is occurring in speaker and audience alike, which results in much energy being released and available, and much significant learning is occurring on everyone's part. Indeed, most of us have had, in our educational career, one or two "good" teachers who have had a profound effect on us even though he or she knew nothing of Gestalt, Psychosynthesis, or other practices of the human potential movement. Yet, clearly, those teachers were facilitating confluence in us, so that what we learned had meaning and stuck; it was relevant to our lives and concerns at that time, and perhaps even now.

Nevertheless, it is equally important to say that some practices and structures for learning greatly increase the probability of confluence and some decrease it — a point that goes back to our initial definition, in which I indicated that external circumstances can effect the occurrence of confluence. Some structures for education inhibit and stunt; some encourage and nourish. Thus it is useful to spend time and energy developing ways to break open inhibiting, disintegrative modes of pedagogy, and to create more integrative, facilitating modes to take their place.

Confluent education, drawing largely on humanistic psychology and the human potential movement for its theory and practice, has begun to develop ways in which to increase the probability of confluence happening in classrooms and within the structure of subject matter. This may take the form of the interaction-integration-synthesis of elements or, more particularly, of the alignment of the mind and the feelings in learning. And to do this workers in the field are designing new ways to educate teachers at all levels, and curriculum is being written that works both with thought and feeling and their integration, using the subject matter as media. Pedagogical practice is being developed and tested with the goal of finding the means by which a confluent education can occur and young people can grow into the riches that are theirs by birthright, but which so often they never receive. Much of the material in this book is the result of these efforts.

CONCLUSION /

In this article I have tried to create a background for such work by defining confluence as it exists as an outcome of confluent education. Using the personality theories of Gestalt therapy and Psychosynthesis, I have formulated a model for personal growth. My hope is that this conceptualization will inform future work in the field.

Clearly, in seeking to foster confluence in education, we are dealing with huge problems that exist not only in schools, but in our culture generally. What progress we make will be slow, for nothing less than a complete evolution of theory and practice is required to move toward an education which develops the "whole" person as we have described him here — an education in which cognition and effect are fully integrated, and all the elements of the personality and person are integrated with environment. Yet there is no reason for discouragement; on all sides, increasingly, young and old, teacher and student, are demanding this "wholeness" for themselves and for others. If we have the perspective, patience, and wisdom to see behind the confusion and turmoil in ourselves and in our world, we can build on this demand and actualize it in education.

Confluent education is a new concept, and we have only begun to mine its implications. Hopefully it will be of use for years to come, and through it we will move closer to an education that is truly and fully humane.

REFERENCE NOTES /

1. Frank Barron, *Creative Person and Creative Process* (New York: Holt, Rinehart & Winston, 1969); E. Hammer, *Creativity* (New York: Random House, 1961); George Kueller, *The Art and Science*

of Creativity (New York: Holt, Rinehart & Winston, 1965).

2. G. A. Weinstein and M. F. Fantini, *Toward Humanistic Education: A Curriculum of Affect* (New York: Praeger, 1970).

3. F. S. Perls, *Gestalt Therapy Verbatim* (Lafayette, Calif.: Real People Press, 1969); John O. Stephens, *Awareness* (Lafayette, Calif.: Real People Press, 1971).

4. F. S. Perls, *Ego, Hunger and Aggression* (New York: Random House, 1969).

5. R. Assagioli, *Psychosynthesis* (New York: Viking, 1971); R. Assagioli, *The Act of Will* (New York: Viking, 1973).

6. A. Szent-Gyorgyi, "Drive in Living Matter to Perfect Itself," *Journal of Individual Psychology*, vol. 22, no. 2 (Nov. 1966) pp. 153–162.

7. S. Shapiro, "A Theory of Ego Pathology and Ego Therapy," *Journal of Psychology* (Sept. 1962), pp. 81–90.

8. Perls, *Ego, Hunger and Aggression*, chap. 7.

9. Ibid., chap. 5.

10. Ibid.

11. Ibid., chap. 1.

12. M. Levin and N. Newberg, "The Self, Others, and Public Knowledge," *Humanist* (May/June, 1972).

15

PROCESS IN THE CLASSROOM

— Steven R. Bogad

Let me begin by stating that I do not believe that by simply introducing affective components into the standard curriculum we will achieve the goals we are seeking in terms of the fully alive and integrated person. At best this tactic may serve only to provide new motivational techniques to teachers who are attempting to teach the same subject matter in basically the same way. It is not surprising that I have been approached by teachers who have had little real training in confluent education, asking for more "turn-on" games and affective exercises to excite their students about prepositional phrases or Latin American culture. I do not believe that this is the end we are seeking, nor do I think that much change actually takes place with these teachers in their classrooms. (I feel that it is indeed unfortunate that some of the attempts to "spread the word" of confluent education to teachers in the field have focused almost totally on developing affective techniques for current curricula.) What we may end up with are new sets of written, prepackaged curricula, complete with cognitive and affective goals and techniques to be used in a school or classroom setting, that do very little to promote the actual objectives of the material. I believe that confluent education entails much more than that.

For me, the most crucial factor in providing confluent learning opportunities is the concept of *process*. Process, as defined by Webster, is a "continuing development involving many changes." It is obvious to me that this definition of process is synonymous with education and growth. As students, we are all continuously developing — learning, growing, changing. We don't just learn instantaneously; we don't change in hourly or weekly segments; we don't just grow up each time we have a birthday. We are always becoming.

Our educational system has typically avoided dealing with process and has been most concerned with the end result — accomplished by almost any means necessary and demonstrated and measured in statistical terms. By ignoring process we fail to acknowledge that there is a continuous development, a growing up, that involves many changes, and that learning takes place regardless of the person the student is dealing with or the kind of institution he attends.

By paying attention to the process, to what's actually happening in the classroom, we are acknowledging what's real. And in order for a student to own his successes and failures and to accept responsibility for his own growth (personal, social, and academic), he must be able to believe that the environment he is working in is a *real* one. By real, I mean that if we're playing a game, it's called a game; that if we say something important, we're not kidding; and that our feelings as well as our thoughts are significant and important, even if they don't always make sense. Acknowledging reality, then, is actually awareness — awareness of the ongoing process, of what is going on in the here and now of the classroom experience.

The here-and-now curriculum that I have sought to develop has been grounded in the experiences and class climate I provided in three basic areas. First, as we began to *distinguish between fantasy and reality,* between what's real and what's imagined, we found that we were able to operate more fully in these areas. We learned how to play games and how to be real; we learned to distinguish between what we saw and what we imagined we saw. We were able to see more clearly the uniqueness of each individual and the similarities we shared. Secondly, as more of the *implicit messages became explicit* we saw a value in direct and honest communication. Our communication skills improved immensely and were used more creatively as our statements became explicit. The frequency of "I don't get it" statements decreased. We learned about listening while we learned about talking. We began to truly own our written expressions as they began to flow out of our learning process. Thirdly, as the children began to realize that their own *thoughts, feelings, concerns, and values were legitimate,* they began to consider themselves as much a part of the curriculum as the teacher who guided them or the books and papers they read. They began to see that what was being studied was very much a part of their own lives. School soon became more than just a fragmented aspect of their lives — it became another experience in the totality of their reality.

As the children began to grow in this curriculum, I, too, became involved in a process. I saw children experiencing, learning, reevaluating — becoming aware of themselves, of others, and of their environment. Once I began to be aware of the here and now, of what was happening, I could respond to what emerged out of the present. What emerges may be a student wanting to understand how to solve a math problem; it may be my desire to start a discussion about a story we read; or it may be a demand to "help me find a book about volcanoes." As I exist in the here and now, I can choose what to focus on and what to let pass; which concerns must be dealt with immediately and which ones can wait. I can choose to respond to where the children are and they can choose to respond to where I am. We begin to develop that ability to respond: responsibility. Responsibility is the ability to respond to what emerges, to a need; to see what has to be done and to do it. I become responsible as I learn to provide various kinds of learning opportunities for the differing needs of different children, as I learn to accept the uniqueness and integrity of each individual.

One of the ways I sought to develop my own responsibility in the classroom was to reduce the instances of mindlessness in my own teaching experience. I interpreted mindlessness as meaning anything obsolete, anything not real. This meant that I had to reduce the obsolete responses I had been using. *"Can this room be available to you before 8:15 a.m. and after 2:30 p.m.?"* It meant taking a close look at what was actually happening in my classroom. *"Can you learn from each other besides listening to me?"* It meant exploring all reasonable alternatives in trying to solve the problems that arose. *"Can you eat when you're hungry if you're only allowed to be hungry at lunch time?"* It meant looking at the children as individuals who have thoughts, feelings, and concern — who are capable of being responsible. *"Can you be responsible for deciding when to walk out of this room and where you go during school time?"* It meant learning how to stop doing the things for the children that they are capable of doing by themselves. *"Can you decide what the appropriate noise level is in this room and how and where you are going to sit?"* It meant being honest with the students and demanding that they be honest with me. *"Can we share our genius, our fool, our devil, our angel, our master, our slave?"* It meant looking at what it is in me that my students *really* need. *"I am here. I am strong. I have real limits and I expect a lot from you!"*

THREE

The Practice of Confluent Education

In this part we enter the live classroom, and through each article we are given a glimpse of what this classroom looks like at different levels and in different subject matter.

The first two articles deal with the early years and contain, as well as vivid portrayals of the use of Gestalt awareness work, a number of descriptions of the ways in which subject matter can be handled so that the integration of feeling and thought is effected.

The third article provides insight into how confluent education can be useful in working with a special group of students — the emotionally handicapped.

The next three articles deal more specifically with the teaching of different subject matter confluently — mathematics, English, and French. The focus here shifts to somewhat older children and, again, working from a Gestalt base, all three teachers are able to educate their students both to a greater awareness of their own internal reality and to the reality of the subject matter under examination, thus nicely affecting the confluence of affective and cognitive experience.

The last article is a very personal and vivid report of one teacher's involvement with a class of "difficult" students and her own search for a way to work with them. What she came up with is another good example of confluent education, and, since many teachers will recognize themselves in her, they may find this report a good place to start their own search.

All the articles are intensely individual and reflect a passionate concern for both student and subject matter.

This last is extremely important, for confluent education seeks to include both person and subject in the learning experience rather than to concentrate on one to the exclusion of the other. When this happens, as it does in the experiences presented in these articles, learning then can be both joyful and enlightening.

16

GESTALT IN THE FIRST GRADE:
TEACHING ALIVE — BEING ALIVE

— Sherry Carty

I am writing on the board and I tell you to listen
because the lesson is important. I see you sitting on
the rug patiently. You are quiet and looking at the
words on the board. The recess bell rings and I see
your face light up and your whole body is full of
energy and moves freely towards the door. You are
talking excitedly to a friend about building a tunnel
in the sand. As you leave, the classroom becomes
silent and I feel lonely. What I am teaching is irrelevant to your world.

Recently in education notable work has been done on curriculum
reform and in reconsidering what a child can learn in school. Richard
Jones says, "Corresponding experimentation with new instructional
methods, which the new materials often vaguely demand but cannot themselves supply, has not been proceeding apace. In this, the
discipline of 'educational psychology' has proved embarrassingly
sterile, due to its traditional emphasis on achievement rather than
on process, on the practical rather than on the possible." [1] Fritz Perls
says, "Learning is nothing but discovery that something is possible.
To teach means to show a person that something is possible." [2] It is
with these possibilities that I wish to deal in this article.

In my teaching I deal with more than just a child's rational faculties. Many situations occur where a child expresses his joy, anger,
frustration, and love. I can maximize these occasions and enable
the child to discover his feelings and to accept them as a part of himself and to deal with them. The child's identification of these parts of
his experience increases his knowledge about himself, the others
around him, and his world. The split in education between learn-

ing what is practical as opposed to learning what is possible has deprived the child of attaining a balance in his development.

Gestalt therapy offers some possible approaches to help the learner fill the holes in his development and to coordinate what he is with what he has available.

The Gestalt process stresses two basic areas for growth: (1) *sensibility*, the ability to use one's senses, and (2) *responsibility*, the ability to respond. The level of sensibility means awareness through our senses — what we hear, see, touch, smell, taste — the obvious. Awareness is the basis of knowledge and communication, and enables the learner to stay in the "now." The "now" of Gestalt covers everything that is structure and behavior, all that is actually happening — the ongoing process. Awareness is accompanied by individual responsibility to accept and integrate whatever is being learned. Responsibility, the ability to be what one is, is expressed by using the word "I." Getting the child to use "I" means that I have to ask him questions. Each time I refuse to answer his questions he must do the work and develop his own resources. For without some frustration, there is no learning. Here is a typical classroom encounter which illustrates the kinds of questions I ask a child. These questions help the child take responsibility for what he is doing now.

> I see two boys, Larry and Chester, coming in from recess. Their faces are red and their bodies are tense and rigid. They are intensely aware of each other's space. Larry tells me that Chester socked him. Larry waits to see if I will punish Chester. Then I see Larry sock Chester. I ask some questions: "Larry, what are you doing?" He says, "He hit me first." I ask him again. He says, "I hit Chester." "Chester, how do you feel when Larry hits you?" "I feel mad and I wanna hit him back." "Where do you feel angry?" "I feel mad in my arm." "Can you make your arm be madder?" I see Chester clench his fist. "How do you feel now?" "I feel strong." "Is there anything else you want to say to each other?" "No!" They come to the rug and the fight is over.

This is a beginning step in developing a child's awareness of his anger and strength. By accepting their feelings and not placing any value judgment on them, I let the two boys experience a frustrating situation, and they take the responsibility for dealing with it.

Before Larry and Chester came to a situation like this, I had given many lessons in readiness. In presenting any new skill, the children need to be ready or the experience will be meaningless. At the beginning of the year I have the class do numerous awareness exercises, literally to "wake up" their senses. Many teachers have been using these types of lessons without realizing their full potential. Here are a few examples of readiness lessons.

1. Passing different objects and becoming aware of their weight, size, shape, texture, etc.
2. Imitating animals sounds and movements and comparing how we are alike or different from animals.
3. Keeping a musical rhythm to a person's name by using hands, feet, arms, etc.
4. Classifying objects by smell, color, or other characteristics.
5. Role-playing human situations.
6. Discovering how we control ourselves by acting like robots.
7. Taking imaginary trips to explore fantasy.

As in all curricula, one experience tends to build on the next. This establishes a climate in the classroom that is receptive to Gestalt techniques. Learning becomes relevant and the experiences involve the child in simultaneously developing a knowledge about himself and his world. With this knowledge he is aware of the possibilities and can discover more as his awareness expands.

In applying Gestalt techniques in the classroom, I find that it broadens the present curriculum. The learning is complete, in that we not only study about a subject but also learn how we feel about it. This internalizes knowledge and it flows into other areas of learning.

When I teach a lesson and somebody is not listening or raises an unexpected question, I deal with what is happening in the now. I change, substitute, and innovate, however the lesson is flowing. The flow depends on how the children are reacting and as I observe what they are doing, I respond appropriately. This is nothing new. The art of teaching has always demanded these skills. I find that I shuttle back and forth as I flow with a class. For me Gestalt techniques are physically and mentally exhausting. At times I see a good learning situation evolve, and I realize that I don't have the energy to do anything about it. This occurs when I get feedback from the children on what has happened to them as a result of the previous lessons. For example, Kim was involved in a writing lesson. The girl sitting next to her, aware of her efforts, said, "Oh, your writing is so messy!" Another girl overheard the conversation and said, "How would you feel if someone said that to you? She's trying her best."

Since Gestalt is relevant, it carries over into many learning experiences that the child encounters. It gives him the skills to confront real-life situations. It is not bound by grade levels or curriculum. Gestalt techniques enable the child to become stronger and to grow. He can stand on his own two feet without someone else doing all his work for him. His strength comes from knowing that he can do his work by himself and that he has the ability to choose to learn.

APPLICATIONS /

I find that with each year of teaching I become more confident in trying various Gestalt techniques. Here are a few examples of lessons that evolved from my classes in Gestalt training. I will describe them under basic subject areas to show how these techniques can be applied to any curriculum no matter what the grade level.

Social Studies — Communications Unit

"MAKE ME"

In this lesson we discuss how people make contracts with each other concerning their expectations of the relationship. I start a sentence which the children are to finish. I have them tell me what they want from me. The sentence begins, "I want to make you . . . ." Here are some of the responses:

. . . take us to the bowl and play.
. . . let us go home.
. . . have more free activities.
. . . like me.
. . . stop asking me questions.

. . . let us do math.

. . . read to me.

The next sentence deals with the child's expectations of himself. "Mrs. Carty, make me . . . ."

. . . listen.

. . . be good.

. . . be quiet.

. . . do my math.

. . . learn to read.

. . . be smart.

The third sentence concerns their responsibility and what they can realistically accomplish. "I can make myself . . ." (do my work, listen, be good, stop being silly, etc.). In this part they re-own what they themselves have control over.

TALKING TO A SECRET

We discuss how people feel when hearing and telling secrets. We then play a game called "Telephone." We all sit in a circle and I tell the child next to me a secret. He passes it on to the next and so on around the circle. When the secret reaches the last person, he tells it aloud. Some children become very frustrated and angry with themselves and with the other children for passing the secret incorrectly. Other children will pass on a made-up secret even if they don't understand what they hear. I then ask one child at a time to step into the circle, where there are two chairs facing each other. When the child sits in one chair he is the sender or receiver of the secret. When he sits in the other chair, he becomes the secret. A dialogue is carried on, with the child changing roles. This dialogue helps the child become aware of his power to include and exclude people from his world.

BODY ENGLISH, OR NONVERBAL COMMUNICATION

This lesson deals with how our bodies send messages. The class is divided into two circles with a teacher in charge of each group. A child is chosen to assume a pose that indicates a feeling, such as crossed arms, a tapping foot, a hand on the hip, etc. The group guesses what the implicit message is. The child then picks a partner and sends his body messages to that person. The partner reacts non-verbally to the messages he receives thus creating a nonverbal dialogue. The child spontaneously expresses his resentments and appreciations. Some children will engage in aggressive activities such as clapping, pushing, and wrestling, with one child controlling the situation and the other being controlled and manipulated. The child who does the choosing usually selects a weaker partner so that he may control the situation. A child may refuse to be chosen at any time during the activity, so if he is being controlled, it is by his own choice.

In doing this lesson every child is anxious to have a turn. To allow for this, I end the activity by saying, "If there is anything you want to say to someone, you may say it now." When I have given this lesson, I have been pleased with the children's responses. Several children confronted some unfinished situations with their classmates. When I was chosen as a partner, I felt so warm and close to the group that I was reluctant to end the lesson; this feeling was shared by other members of the group.

SAYING GOOD-BYE

During the week a lot of things happen and I may not be able to respond to each child. The final minutes of school on Fridays are a good time to spend a few moments with each child individually. We begin by having a short evaluation period on what has happened during the week and how we might make improvements in the coming week. Each child comes up to me individually and says good-bye using "hand talk." If we feel good about each other, we touch gently. If one of us is angry and has unfinished business, this is the time to express it. Using this technique helps clear the air and gives us a fresh start for Monday.

Art — Man Expresses Himself through Art

I read a story called "Going for a Walk with a Line" by Douglas and Elizabeth MacAgy and then show the class some drawings by Klee, Miró, and Picasso. I divide the class into five groups and have each group sit around a long piece of butcher paper on the floor. They draw imaginary lines in the air to various drumbeats. I then tell them to use their crayons to draw lines that express the rhythmic pattern, with the color of the crayon corresponding to the intensity of the beat. Some of the lines the children say they want to draw to the beat of the drum are: sharp, wiggly, soft, gooey, bumpy, jagged, crazy, scribbly, curly, anxious, fuzzy, happy, warm, angry, dancing, steep, fast, tired, etc. After this initial experience the children go to their desks and, with their own paper and paints, draw some of their favorite lines. They write on their papers, "I made a (wiggly, gooey) line."

Science — Waves, Tides

Our class goes on a field trip to the beach and watches the action of the waves. We discuss the effect of the moon on the tides and the power of waves. To illustrate the action of the waves on the beach, I have the class act out what they have seen at the beach. The class is divided into two groups — one group representing the waves, the other representing the beach. Each member of the wave group is given a sheet and the group is formed into three rows representing the incoming waves. The children discover that one wave follows another and crashes on the sand according to the contour of the beach. Each receding wave carries out bits of sand. A drumbeat is used to guide the children through the activity. The roles are switched and repeated so that each group can experience the power of the waves and how they have control over the beach. At the end of the activity I asked them which role they like best and how they feel about being the controller or being controlled.

Math — Cuisenaire Rods, Size Relationships

The child works with ten rods of different colors and sizes. He discovers through manipulating them that he can build a "staircase" with the graduated lengths from the smallest to the largest. In becoming aware of the different sizes, I let ten children make a staircase with their bodies. We talk about the smallest white rod and its square shape and how it feels to be so small at the bottom of the staircase.

We discuss how it feels to be each successively bigger rod until we reach the largest orange rod. We relate these feelings to being a part of a family and how the middle child feels being in his place. What does it feel like being the oldest? What responsibilities does the oldest have that the youngest doesn't have? Using family relationships helps the child to act out family problems and to get in touch with the feelings of others. This shows how a lesson on mathematical relationships can also teach social relationships.

Movement Exploration — Body Rhythms

Each child has his own space. The child sits and listens to his inner-body rhythms, his breathing, his heart. As I play the drum, he develops a corresponding rhythm. First he moves his head, then his neck, shoulders, arms, and so on, until his whole body is in motion. As more of the body becomes involved he will find it necessary to stand and move about the room. The child then chooses a partner who he feels has a similar body rhythm and they develop a rhythm together. He then chooses a partner who has an opposite rhythm. He tries his partner's rhythm and vice versa. I ask awareness questions during the experience. "How does it feel when your partner has an identical rhythm? Can you let yourself try a different rhythm? Do you like your partner's following your rhythm? Can you find a rhythm that is comfortable for both of you?"

Other activities may be added like "Magic Slides." "Look into your partner's eyes and slide across the floor holding hands as if you were one person." Or like "Sensitivity Jumps." "Stand side by side, and without looking at your partner, be aware of his rhythm and see if you can jump together, moving across the room."

A Spontaneous Lesson — Boundary Lines

After lunch the children come to the rug to listen to a story. Some of them come right away while others linger. I start the story and the children are inattentive and squirmy. I keep reading and I am aware of how useless it is. I stop and ask the class if they have noticed what is happening. Their answers are very accurate. "I hear talking." "I see Tom out of bounds." "I am wiggling."

I decide to try a shuttling exercise that I had seen George Brown do at a workshop. I tell the children the rules. "You find a place that is out of bounds during story time. I will give you time to get there and stay a while. When I count to five, return to the rug."

The children scurry around and go to places they want to be in. Some children stand in trash cans, on top of chairs, under counters, in closets, in the playhouse, behind the rocking chair. I am really surprised to see them all come back quickly when I begin counting. We repeat the activity several times. Each time I add more ground rules. "If you chose a high place, this time find a low place — if dark, find a light place — if closed, find an open place," etc.

Exploring the boundaries gives the children an opportunity to discover the extreme poles of being in and out of the group. We talk about how they felt and which places they liked. Story time is over, and the class moves into writing without hesitation.

SUMMARY /

The techniques in the activities I have described are not used for the sake of technique alone. The purpose of using Gestalt in the classroom is to promote the growth process and to develop human potential. There is no "instant joy, instant sensory awareness, instant cure. The growth process is a process that takes time to grow." The lessons help create an excitement that flows immediately into an ongoing spontaneous activity. "If you are in the now, you are creative, you are inventive. If you have your senses ready, if you have your eyes and ears open, like every small child, you find a solution." [3]

REFERENCE NOTES /

1. Richard M. Jones, *Fantasy and Feeling in Education* (New York: New York University Press, 1968), p. 3.
2. Frederick Perls, *Gestalt Therapy Verbatim* (Lafayette, Calif.: Real People Press, 1969).
3. Ibid., pp. 2, 3.

17

GESTALT IN THE SECOND GRADE: MERGING OF THE INNER AND OUTER WORLDS

— Anita Cassarino

Educating the total individual consists neither of applying a lacquer of information nor of unleashing a geyser of knowledge. Rather, it is developing a fluidity between the outer-human world and the inner-human world. Education, if it is to be relevant to life, must approach knowledge in a very human way — through the human faculties of the mind, the senses, and the emotions.

Presenting knowledge through the vehicle of Gestalt awareness training is one means at a teacher's disposal to achieve a human classroom environment. In my experiences with Gestalt-tempered lessons, I have seen the children in my classroom enthusiastic about what they were doing. I have seen them learning about the outside world from the inside.

Following are some of the "experiments" I have tried in my teaching.

I. SCIENCE — SOIL /

In science we have been studying soil, including its formation. We had seen a movie and talked about the action of water on rocks — how it wears them away, making them smaller. I divided the class into groups of four or five each. One or two people were to be water and the rest were to form one big rock. The members of each group were to act out in their own way the phenomenon of the wearing away. I reminded them that they must think of how they would make their rock smaller. After brief intervals, I suggested that they trade places so that each could have a turn being water and rock.

Then I had the groups come back together to discuss what happened.

Each group reported on how they had shown the action of the water on the rock. Their methods were:

1. Some children shrank to make themselves smaller.
2. Some children broke off from the rest to show the rock breaking up.
3. Some pretended they were "cloud bombers" breaking up the rocks with rain.
4. Others sat on each other to make the rock "collapse."

Then I asked them questions about the experience as relating to themselves:

How did you feel when you were the rock?
How did you feel when you were the water?
Which one made you feel stronger?
Which one did you like being?

It seemed that more liked being the water because they could break up the rocks. One boy liked being the rock because as a rock he didn't have to wear a raincoat in the rain. One girl felt "strong" as the rock, but didn't know why. One boy liked being the rock because he could get smaller and smaller until he wouldn't be seen and then he would be (as a boy) only legs and arms and could really play well in football. A couple of children favored being water because they liked water and wetness.

Other possible questions: Are there times when you feel as if you are being worn away like the rock? How did you feel as the rock when it was whole? As the rock coming apart?

Goal for next time: Get more of the quiet ones to talk.

II. SCIENCE — SEEDS /

Since we were studying seeds, I wanted to use Gloria Castillo's (a fellow teacher) idea of acting out plant growth with sheets. To give the children a basis for their acting, I gave each one a presoaked lima bean seed. I told them to see what they could find out about it. I hinted that there was a surprise inside.

Amid much talking and excitement, they discovered the seed coat, the baby plant, and the plant food. I told them the names of the parts of the seed that they had discovered. We talked about what the baby plant needed in order to grow and how its existence changed when it began to move out from the seed.

Then we went to a multipurpose room, each child had his own sheet. Since we hadn't used sheets before, I gave them a little free time to experiment. Then we began. I told them to find a way to use their sheets to become baby plants inside the seeds, and that the sheets would be their seed coats. After allowing them some time in their seeds, I went around and tapped each one as a signal to begin growing.

When our garden was completed, I called all the children together and we talked about the experience. I asked, "How did you feel being under the seed coat? How did you feel growing from a baby plant to a big plant?" Here are some responses:

ALICE: "I liked the food that was in the seed. I ate too much and I felt like a pig."

HARRY: "I liked growing out so I could be king of the plants."

BILL: "I wanted to grow into a big plant so all the other plants would look at me."

Many agreed that it had been warm under the sheet and the cool air felt good.

It was apparent that the children enjoyed this activity. It was delightful to watch the way they eagerly and aptly assumed their roles, moving slowly and gracefully.

III. SCIENCE — PLANTS /

Continuing our unit on plants, our next lesson dealt with plants that live off other plants, in this case mushrooms and molds. I began with a discussion of how green plants make their own food and introduced the dependent kinds of plants.

The children then rotated to one of three areas to draw mushrooms, to view mold under a microscope and draw it, or to view and discuss mold growing in a jar. The first two activities were self-directed; I participated in the third.

In the third activity we discussed the fact that mold did not grow from seeds but that pieces of it floated in the air, and when they settled under favorable conditions, mold began to grow. I then asked for volunteers to think of a conversation that might occur between the food in the jar and the mold. Here are some examples:

FOOD: You get off of me.
MOLD: No, I won't.
F: I'm going to tell my mother.
M: You go ahead and tell.

F: You're not going to get on me, mold.
M: Yes, I am.
F: When you get on food, you look ugly.

F: You can't get me! You can't get me!
M: Yes, I can. Gotcha!
F: Ugh.

An interesting thing happened when I introduced the conversation exercise with the first group that came to the jar. As one child was talking, a number of children working at other activities stopped what they were doing to come over and listen. A hush fell over the room.

I felt that through the conversation between mold and food the children could grasp the dependency relationship better than if I had just stuck with scientific explanation. It also reinforced the idea that mold develops from something outside the plant.

IV. SOCIAL STUDIES — BUILDING A HOUSE /

In Gestalt therapy the patient assumes the role of the elements of his dream for the purpose of making those elements a part of himself. Similarly, when a student can assume the role of what he is studying, the knowledge can more readily become a part of him. This idea is incorporated in the following lesson.

I explained to the children that they were going to act out a story about building a house. To give them background for their task, I read a little to them from a basic social studies book to familiarize them with job titles, tools, and the sequence of construction.

Then they listened to a Young People's Record selection entitled "Build Me a House." It is a musical story about a family who wants a new house. Then enlist the help of a contractor who gathers the necessary workers to make the house.

Everyone in class was given a role: family members, contractor, electricians, plumbers, steam shovel operators, cement workers, carpenters. They devised their own makeshift props. Each child became involved in his own part. The steam shovel operators used yardsticks as the arms of the shovels and scooped up "dirt" as they regulated the operation with levers made of rulers. Sound effects were also added. Electricians busily put up old wire, while plumbers laid out a pattern of rulers which served as pipes.

After we enjoyed going through the story a couple of times, the children began work on booklets that explained the jobs and people involved in building a house.

It was interesting to note that the record was the major source of information for their booklets rather than the information I had read to them.

V. LANGUAGE ARTS — PANTOMIME
AND SELF-EXPRESSION /

I began the lesson with a short movie entitled, "A Place in the Sun." It is an animated cartoon without narration about two men who fight for the most comfortable place to enjoy the sun. After playing tricks in an attempt to outwit each other, they both end up without any sun. They then begin to warm each other — the message thus being that people must learn to understand and cooperate with one another.

I saw this movie as a good introduction to the exploration of the feelings behind the type of struggle portrayed by the two characters. This activity also served as a basis for experiencing the polarities of human interaction: total conflict and total cooperation.

After a very brief discussion of what happened in the movie, we launched into pantomiming other situations:

1. Two participants want to write, but there is only one piece of paper.
2. Two participants both want to read the same book.
3. Two participants both want to play with the same deck of flash cards.

I asked the children to enact both "no cooperation" and "total cooperation" in their situations, as they had seen in the movie.

I was truly amazed how each set of participants got into their task. Joe and Bruce took the first situation. Of the three pairs, they were the most gentle with each other. They resolved their conflict by drawing a line down the middle of the paper so each could write on half. I asked them, as with the other pairs, to pay attention to how they were feeling while pantomiming. When they finished, as with the other pairs, I asked, "How did you feel when your partner had the object and you couldn't get it? How did you feel when you had the object and your partner couldn't get it? How did you feel when you and your partner began working together?" Bruce's and Joe's answers were the habitual "good, bad, sad, happy" variety. I couldn't get them to be more explicit. So, to get the rest to be more definitive, I banned the use of those four words.

The next situation was handled by Lucy and Ellen. They were physically more aggressive and emotionally more involved than Bruce and Joe. When I asked Lucy how she felt when she succeeded in keeping the book from Ellen, she replied with a self-satisfied look, "Pleased!"

Bill and Harry took the last situation. They were the most aggressive and involved of all. These two never resolved their conflict because Bill spurned every one of Harry's conciliatory advances. This really aggravated Harry. When Bill was in possession of the cards, he said he felt "like a hero." Harry, when in the same position, said he felt "like a king."

I regret not having discussed with the children how body movements and facial expressions give messages. But time ran out.

VI. LANGUAGE ARTS — WRITING STORIES /

I read the book *A Little House of Your Own* by B. S. Regnievs and I. Haas to the class. It is all about secret hiding places children can have. Next I gave them the following instructions.

> Now, get comfortable and close your eyes. Do not speak. Just think in your head about the questions I will ask. Later we will talk about it. Think about a place you like to go to when you want to be alone. I want you to put yourself in your secret place. Pretend you are in it now. Does your place have a lot of space or a little bit? Is your space high or low or right on the ground? Are you alone in your hideaway or is there something or someone with you? How do you feel inside your own place? How does your face feel? What are you doing with your hands and arms? With your legs and feet? Do you see anything or anybody while you are in your own little house? Do you hear anything or anybody? What does it smell like in your place? Are you doing anything in your secret spot? Stay in your hideaway a little longer. How are you feeling now? When you feel like coming out of your own little house and coming back to our classroom, you can open your eyes. But remember, if someone else is still in his or her little house, be very polite and quiet.

When everyone returned, we sat in a large circle and some children told about their secret place. Then the children wrote stories about their hideaways, and those who wanted to read their stories to the others.

I was very pleased with the results. Some children wrote more involved stories than had usually been their habit.

With a couple of spelling corrections, here is Alice's story — one of the best she had done all year.

My Place

My place is in the family room. The family room has a closet. The closet has a light. I am happy when I am in my place. My family never saw me in my place. My dog visits me sometimes. Sometimes I come out and scare my mother when she is sewing me a dress.

VII. LANGUAGE ARTS — USING QUOTATION MARKS /

We had been learning the mechanics of quotation marks and today's lesson was to give the children an imaginative way to put them to use.

I asked the children to freeze in their sitting positions. I asked them to note two parts of their bodies that were touching, like a hand on a neck. I asked them to make up a conversation between these two parts and write it down. Again I briefly reviewed the mechanics. (Jean could not find two touching parts so I told her to make up a conversation between her pencil and paper.) Here are some results:

The toes said to the foot, "Get off my toes. It hurts."
The foot said, "My foot is comfortable on your toes."

The knee said to the leg, "Stop laying on me."
The leg said, "No, I like it here."
The knee said, "Please?"

The children were very enthusiastic about writing and reading their conversations. Next time, I will precede this lesson with some verbal experience in composing conversations and really help them get into the feelings and images behind them.

VIII. BEHAVIOR — SWITCHING IDENTITIES /

I instructed the class not to disturb the adjustment of the microscope through which we were viewing mold. Not long after we began our work Harry and Bruce began accusing one another of poking a pencil at the slide and disturbing the focus. Each one told exactly the opposite story about what had happened. I have difficulty coping with such situations.

During lunch an idea came to me. I had both boys come into the empty room. I explained to them that I wanted them to tell me again what happened, but this time Harry was to tell it pretending that he was Bruce and Bruce pretending to be Harry.

Both boys' stories pointed to Harry as the instigator. I talked with Harry about his behavior. I knew from the way he responded that I had gotten at the truth. I wish now that I had proceeded further with the role-playing so that Harry could have gotten a feeling of how it was to be in Bruce's shoes in that incident.

The next three lessons have not yet been "classroom tested" because we have either completed the topic or have not yet come to it.

IX. SOCIAL STUDIES — TRANSPORTATION /

Cognitive Area

Simple machines: pulley, wheel, lever, inclined plane.

Methods of transportation: trucks, trains, planes, cars, buses, ships, etc. Machines composed of parts functioning together.

Simple machines we can observe in use in the various transportation modes; types of cargo; transportation in other lands; unusual and new modes of transportation.

Affective Area

The interfunctioning of parts: Begin with small groups of four or five working together to form their own human machine with distinctive movements and sounds. When mastered at this level, larger groups can be formed.

Questions for exploration: How did you feel as part of a machine? How did you feel when you did not blend in with the rest of the parts, or when someone else in your machine did not blend? Have you ever experienced being part of a group of people who seemed to work together like a machine?

X. SCIENCE — THE SOLAR SYSTEM /

Have the children assume the planet positions — one child per planet. Have the sun be represented by a circle of three or four children. Have the "planets" orbit the "sun." Remind the children to be aware of how they feel in their positions.

Possible subjects for discussion or writing: What or who is the most important "sun" in your life? How do you feel when you are close to your "sun"? When you are distant from it? How do you feel when you want to be with others and can't be? How do you feel about having a pattern to your life — doing the same things in the same way?

XI. SCIENCE — SOIL FORMATION /

Activity: To demonstrate that rocks may be worn into smaller particles that help make up soil. Each child should be given two soft rocks to rub together and observe the results. Point out that the rubbing action by the hands is taking the place of the wind blowing sand against rocks or of water carrying pebbles that rub against other rocks. Ask each child to choose which situation is occurring with his two rocks. Ask the children to compose a conversation between their own rocks.

For me, experimenting with Gestalt in the classroom has been an exciting move away from the *occupation* of teaching and toward the *artistry* of teaching.

18

CONFLUENT EDUCATION FOR THE EMOTIONALLY HANDICAPPED

— *Jane Brody Spira*

I work with a class of ten emotionally disturbed children. My role as an aide consists mainly of working with children individually, and working and playing with smaller groups. The curriculum is determined by the teacher. Actually, there is very little planning, and the basic academic skills are taught by programmed instruction. Often I bring in things for the whole group to do — imagination exercises, synectics games, group fantasies, Gestalt games. Most important to me, however, is the development of my attitude toward the children. I have learned that I can support them while not taking responsibility for them.

In my individual work with the children, I try to liven up their reading and phonics work by relating the material to whatever is happening now, in reality or in our imaginations. I read with Anthony each morning. He doesn't understand the meaning of many of the words he is learning to pronounce. "What does 'have' mean, Miss Brody?" I place my hand on his head: "Now I have my hand on your head." "Now I have my hand on your eyes." "Now . . ." He completes the sentence according to where I put my hand. "Now, you try it, Anthony. Like, 'Now I have the book in my hands.'" "O.K. Now I have my feet on the floor." And so on. This brings in many things: He is letting me touch him, he is enjoying our game, he is learning a new word, he is making sentences, and he is aware of what he is doing at the moment. "What's this word, Miss Brody?" "Hamburger. Do you like hamburgers?" "Mmmm." "What are your other favorite foods?" (He sounds them out, I write them down, and we pronounce them again, reading them.) "What are the foods you hate?" (Another list.) "Let's make believe you can have anything from the good-food list. What is it?" "Ice cream." "O.K. How does it feel to have a huge dish of ice cream in your hands?" "Mmmm." (He eats the ice cream with gusto.) "O.K. Now you must have a dish from the hate-food list. Which one?" "Uh-uh." (Grimaces.) Anthony has a vivid imagination. By relating new words to enjoyable imagination games, I think he will retain them more clearly.

I want the children to feel responsible for their learning. I feel very strongly that answers should not be given to them. Often they plead, but I will help them only if I feel the question is too difficult, and then only after they've done some thinking. When a child asks me for an answer, I will reply with another question, so that he can eventually solve it himself. I want children to realize their potential, to discover for themselves, so that they will value the *process* of learning, and not just the product. I want them to be aware of the good feeling that comes from solving a problem independently.

At first, I would justify my stubbornness to them: "It's important that you think for yourself." "I know you can do it." "Isn't it a good feeling?" Now, when they solve a problem by themselves with my guidance, I ask, "How do you feel, getting it right?" I realize it is better for them to *experience* the discovery and the good feeling of accomplishment, rather than to have me *tell* them it's a good feeling.

Their resentment at this treatment has decreased. When I returned from a week's absence, they told me that the substitute was stupid because she gave them all the answers! (I suppose that in many regular elementary classrooms, children are encouraged to discover on their own, but in Emotionally Handicapped classes, at least those I have seen, most of the teachers' energy is devoted to discipline and control, and little to the quality of the learning process.) When a child asks an academic question, it's so much easier to give the answer than to face a resentful look or the possibility of another outburst.

Six months ago Anthony couldn't read a word; now he is using a second-grade reader. He has built up so much frustration over the years that I felt we would go nowhere if I didn't tell him each word he didn't know. But he has become dependent on me, so much so that he hardly reads unless I'm with him. So now I make him attempt to sound out words, and more often than not, he gets them. If he tries and doesn't get them, I tell him right away so that he doesn't get discouraged. But if he doesn't try, I won't tell him. The other day he slammed his book, screamed he would never read with me again, and then sat by himself until he figured out the word and ran to me shouting, "I got it, Miss Brody — train! train!"

My attempting to encourage the children to become aware of what they are doing and to take responsibility for themselves does seem to alleviate many types of problems — fights, cheating, daily encounters. During the quarter I kept a journal of some of these incidents in which I felt "Gestalt Awareness" was pervasive. Here are a few of them.

JANUARY 15 — I checked Dorothy's math work and found she had copied her arithmetic page from the answer sheet in the back of the book. *Dorothy, I must let you know you don't have to cheat. There are no grades. You're too afraid to ask for help, and all you want is to get through the morning's work unnoticed. I want you to know you needn't be afraid of me. I want to prove this to you. I want you to tell me you cheated, and to see that I won't hurt you.*

ME: Dorothy, how did you get the answers?

DOROTHY: I worked them out the same as I did the other paper you gave me.

ME: But it's weird that you got one whole row wrong here, and all else perfect.

DOR (*not really listening. Assumes loud, whining voice I had never heard her use before*): Honest, Miss Brody, I did them. I'll get the paper I worked them on. (*Fumbles.*) I threw it out. (*Looks miserable.*)

ME: How do you feel now?

(*Tears begin.*)

ME: What are you doing with your hand?

(*Rubbing her eyes violently. Won't answer.*)

ME: Can you look at me?

DOR (*looks at me and blurts out*): Susie [little sister, of whom she is extremely jealous] broke the dish and I had to stand in the corner all day. She lies and I get in trouble. My mother punishes me.

ME: Would you like to pretend your mother is sitting right here and tell her what you're mad about?

DOR: No. (*Pause.*)

ME: Dorothy, I'm not your mother. I won't hurt you or punish you, no matter what you do. Can you look at me? How did you get the answers?

DOR: I didn't do it, honest. (*Looks away.*)

ME: I'd like you to try something. Just say the words, even if you didn't — just to pretend. Say, "I got the answers from the back of the book."

DOR (*struggle, inability to talk*): Wait a second. I can't say it yet. (*Pause.*) O.K. (*Looks at me.*) I got the answers from the back of the book. (*Breathes deeply.*) (*We smile at each other.*)

ME: Did you?

DOR: Well. . . .

ME: Can you look at me?

(*Nods her head to tell me that she did copy.*)

ME: When I was in junior high, I cheated in math all the time. It was my worst subject. I was too scared or bored to tell the teacher I I didn't understand anything. I want to help you in arithmetic. Will you accept my help?

(*Nods her head yes.*)

ME: How do you feel now?

DOR: Good. (*Smiles broadly.*) (*I put my arm around her.*)

ME: Let's go outside.

JANUARY 20 — Many fights, crying during recess. I had the children re-enact scenes on the playground. Very hard — they kept telling me what happened.

ME: Alan, you're fighting with Jim. Tell him.

ALAN: Jim, you're so stupid!

JIM: You are!

ME: Alan, can you tell Jim he's an idiot in a serious, angry tone of voice?

ALAN (*tries, laughs*): I'm just playing

ME: Lots of times I see you hurting people when I know you're just kidding. Do you know when you're kidding?

ALAN: Yeah.

ME: Well, how can you show how you feel to others?

ALAN: I know if I'm kidding.

ME: But how can you let others know?

ALAN: By telling them.

ME: Can you go around the room and tell each person that you're kidding?

ALAN (*goes up to each, smiles, and says*): I'm just kidding. . . . I'm only kidding. (*Gets playful and goes into his comedy routines — whole class in uproar.*)

This led into a discussion about feelings. The children described feelings that they had had and I wrote them down. Then we went around the circle and each of us gave an example of the feeling. "I get frustrated when I can't play the piano." "I get angry at the chair when I bump into it." And so on. Dorothy hasn't responded in the discussion. She has never shown anger or frustration. She shows embarrassment constantly — she often stuffs her hand into her mouth.

ME: Dorothy, are you ever angry?

(*No response.*)

ME: How about the time I made you do your math over?

(*Nods yes.*)

ME: Are you ever angry?

DOR: Yes.

ME: How can you show us?

(*Silence.*)

GAIL: Punch 'em in the mouth.

(*Dorothy laughs.*)

ME: Why don't the two of you figure out a way for Dorothy to show everyone when she's angry?

(*A few minutes later Gail speaks for Dorothy.*)
    GAIL: She could raise her hand.
    ME: Try it, Dorothy.
(*Hesitantly raises her hand. End of class.*)

Since then Dorothy has become much more outgoing and expressive of her feelings.

There are perpetual conflicts occurring in the classroom. Most of them settle themselves, but many times the children reach a pitch that could cause someone to be hurt. I then take the children aside and have them confront each other. So far I've used only verbal encounters. I'm a little afraid to use physical encounters. I try to move the encounter past the name-calling stage into a more constructive dialogue. "What are you angry at?" "Now tell her what you do like." "How would you like her to change?"

I engage in one internal activity throughout the day — getting in touch with my own feelings toward the children, be it love, anger, hurt, or frustration. Often I share these feelings with them. But sometimes sharing my feelings would be inappropriate, considering what the child is going through at that moment. By being *aware* of my own feelings, though, I can refrain from acting out of my own needs — exploding, judging, manipulating — instead, I can try to get the child to be aware of his actions through constructive criticism.

19

CONFLUENCE IN MATHEMATICS: CAN 1 + 1 BE A CREATIVE EXPERIENCE?

— Steven R. Bogad

Mathematics has long been considered the most rigidly sequential subject in the curriculum, and for a long time it has enjoyed the position of being immune to changes in curriculum design or in teaching techniques. One of the major attitudes underlying this was the belief that while the problem of "Why Johnny Can't Read" was a serious one, the problem of "Why Johnny Can't Count" could be easily explained by saying that Johnny just didn't have "a head for numbers." This attitude is now manifest throughout our lives in the housewife who can't balance her checkbook, the bridge partner who can't keep score, etc. — all with the explicit rationalization of "I just never did catch on to arithmetic," and the implicit message of "I have a fault, and that makes me more human." (The emphasis on raising reading scores, and the like, has reached panic proportions, with many teachers often disregarding all other aspects of the curriculum — cognitive as well as affective areas.)

Certainly, if the average person had little need for numbers beyond grocery-store/income-tax arithmetic, then why provide education beyond that, except for students in various technical fields? We were long satisfied with a mathematics curriculum which stressed memorization of the facts, lock-step presentation of topics, textbooks designed to be "covered" in one school year, and a whole series of experiences to promote right-wrong thinking, to reward noncreative responses, and to build failure upon failure. More recently, the "new math" has arrived with new prescriptions, new curricula, and new approaches — achieving many of the same goals of the old math, but retaining many of the same problems. The attempt to make people into mathematical computers is still not realized. So the question to be answered is: Why not educate for first-rate human beings, rather than second-rate computers? Here I would like to examine some of the wider aims of mathematics education in terms of some of the basic concepts of confluent education.

THEORY /

Without going into a detailed justification, let me state five basic goals, or directions, for education based on the implications of Gestalt therapy.

1. The student moves from environmental support to self-support.
2. The student differentiates between awareness and fantasy.
3. The student develops and practices differential thinking skills.
4. The student recognizes the difference between understanding and explaining — between awareness and conceptualization — and is aware of which procedure he is using.
5. The student constantly works toward wholeness, toward Gestalt formation and integrated functioning as a whole person, and he recognizes and accepts responsibility for all the parts of himself and for all of his actions.[1]

What I propose to show is that the aims of an active, creative mathematics program can be directly related to these overall confluent goals. Such aims revolve around three specific areas. First, the program is designed "to free students, however young or old, to think for themselves." Second, the curriculum is set up to provide opportunities for the students to discover the order, pattern, and relations which are the very essence of mathematics, as well as being the basis of the natural world. The third area involves the training of students in the necessary skills.[2]

In order to realize these aims we must first see the benefit of the shift in the curriculum from an emphasis on content to an emphasis on experience. This shift is beginning to take place in many curriculum areas. It involves, partially, the old Dewey adage of "learning by doing." But this in itself is only a half-step, for we must make provisions for the wide variations of abilities and interests that are present in every classroom. We might gain more insight if we look at this problem in terms of three variables: the materials used by the children, the rate at which these are used, and the goals the children achieve.

	MATERIALS	RATE	GOALS
1.	same	same	same
2.	same	different	same
3.	different	different	same
4.	different	different	different

Looking at the above scheme, we can see many classroom patterns. Number one might represent a traditional or even "levels-program" classroom, where all the children use the same materials at more or less the same rate to achieve the same goals. Numbers two and three represent, in varied degrees, more recent attempts at individualizing curriculum, although each is limited in the sense that the goals achieved remain constant. Number four represents a new level, which I will call the "optimum learning situation." Here we find different children working with various materials at a speed which is appropriate for them in order to achieve goals which have been individualized. This is one of the crucial points at which much of the "new" curriculum fails, for no matter how advanced and relevant our teaching tools may be, often we still expect all of our classes to accomplish the same minimum goals which *we* have set up. Can we as teachers accept the fact that not all of our fifth graders will learn fractions at this point in their lives? Can we accept the capabilities of students who can make use of advanced algebra for the situations they encounter? Can we move on from that point and still provide an exciting, creative, and relevant learning program involving everyone, without judging good and bad students — without hierarchies of teacher approval? I believe that this is possible, although not easily accomplished.

The emphasis on experience also implies viewing education as a process, a dynamic flow of situations. This process includes the child and the teacher as thinking and feeling human beings — not simply as people assuming roles when they enter the classroom.

What most of this points to is a learning environment — a class-room attitude which acknowledges the thoughts, feelings, and con-cerns of everyone. It embodies trust, openness, freedom, and re-sponsibility. It is not a series of techniques or a body of curricula. Each teacher will develop his own methods to identify and meet the needs of his own students.

APPLICATION /

The first thing we might look for in specific classroom activities is a child-centered program. This involves situations which are built around the children, not around the curriculum and the teacher. The emphasis is on learning, not on teaching. "The image of the teacher as the fountain of all knowledge, occupying the front-and-center of the classroom, dominating and directing all activity, must disappear." [3] The teacher can serve as a guide, as a facilitator, as an important resource in the class, but certainly not the only one. An important fundamental here is using the natural curiosity of the children to stimulate and structure learning experiences. This does not mean *no* structure; rather, the teacher focuses on the children as the primary source for structuring learning experiences. It also does not imply that there is no place for learning certain facts. Memori-zation of specific facts will always have some place in education, but it need not always result in boredom and irrelevancy. A simple ex-ample is the student who is given the task of learning the multiples of two. He is given brief instructions by the teacher and sufficient examples of how this skill might be of use to him. (It would be better if the student could experience a need for the skill before he is given the task.) Once he feels he has mastered this operation, he demonstrates the skill to the teacher, who then records it. Practice may be needed periodically, but hopefully this will occur in specific situations in which the student is involved. It is very important that we begin to use the student's own evaluation of himself. First of all, this will be a valuable start in evaluating his own accomplish-ments without the proverbial gold star. And, second, it will stimulate an atmosphere of mutual trust and respect.

Relating this back to confluent goals and the specific aims of a creative math program, we can begin to see that when the student is more involved in his own learning, he can be expected to take responsibility for that learning more easily. Concurrently, he is learning to think for himself and to depend less on the teacher — gaining self-support.

Another activity in the classroom is based on the theory that the more senses a student uses, the more efficient the learning will become. Concrete materials, man-made as well as natural, are crucial learning tools in their own right, as well as steps toward gaining abstractions. We can't just say that hearing and seeing are the only valid ways to pass on, or to gain, information. Touch is a sense that is often overlooked, once the child finishes the primary grades; thus playing with blocks becomes a "baby game." The result of this is that we not only cut off the student from valuable learning tools, but we also cut him off from parts of himself — we keep him from experiencing his totality, keep him from being a whole person. We find many situations, common to the intermediate grades, where boys won't touch girls (or other boys) and vice versa. We proceed to dismiss this as adolescence. The point here is *not* that by providing more touch experiences in the classroom we will eliminate adolescent behavior; the point is, that by providing opportunities where the child can use and be aware of more of what he has available, the more he will be able to be in touch with his own reality as a whole person.

The development and use of differential-thinking skills occupies another aspect of this math program. Loosely defined, this involves "remaining alert in the center" and "avoiding a one-sided outlook." [4] In a sense we're talking about objectivity, and although it may be only relative, "one can attain clearer understanding if he can see both sides of a situation rather than only one." [5] I may be stretching this point a bit in its application to mathematics, but I feel that I am justified. In traditional mathematics education we are taught that there is a problem and a single solution to that problem. I will admit that in some instances precision might mean that there is a single answer, but the emphasis on right-wrong thinking is highly overdone. For, what actually happens is that this attitude carries over into other mathematical areas, as well as into other curriculum areas. An example of the use of differential thinking in this context is the use of open, rather than closed, questions. Here are some simple examples:

CLOSED: Count out three red beads and five green beads. How many have you altogether? Take away four beads. How many are left?

OPEN: Count out eight beads. Arrange these in patterns in more than one way. Compare your patterns with those of your partner.

CLOSED: Measure the length and width of the hall, giving your answer to the nearest inch.

OPEN: Without using a ruler, find the ratio of the length and width of the hall in as many ways as you can. Compare your results and comment on them.[6]

The open question gives the child the advantage of being in the "middle of the problem" — he can seek a single solution or he can look at the situation from various aspects. Thus he gains perspective and possibly arrives at important understandings through his experiences.

This leads directly into learning as discovery, understanding rather than explaining. As Perls states:

To me, learning is *discovery*. . . . There is another kind of learning which is the feeding of information into your computer, so you can accumulate knowledge, and as you know, knowledge begets more knowledge until you want to fly to the moon. This knowledge, this secondary information, might be useful whenever you have lost your senses . . . as long as you can see and hear, and realize what's going on, then you *understand*. If you learn concepts, if you work for information, then you don't understand. You only *explain*.[7]

Those who favor "new math" might easily take issue here with Perls, for they have actually switched from a fact-centered base to a concept-centered base. However, the "new math" is still wholly cognitive; the affective dimension is ignored. Thus, in a sense, the new curriculum has taken only a half-step. It has, to a great extent, neglected Perls' distinction between understanding and explanation. As Montz puts it:

In order to understand what Perls means, we must realize that he is contrasting *awareness* as learning through discovery with *conceptualization* as learning through accumulation of knowledge. Discovery of something involves for Perls the discovery of meaning, which results in understanding. Understanding he defines as "coincidence with your real life." Accumulating knowledge, on the other hand, results not in undertaking, but in "explaining." It is possible to be able to master terminology, to explain an idea, or to communicate a concept that has no existential meaning for you, no coincidence with your real life.[8]

Thus, it is a primary aim of a creative mathematics program to provide situations where the student can experience an idea or its consequences and, thereby, the concepts can take on existential meaning for him — real understanding can occur.

I believe that it is the open situation which leads to understanding and the closed situation which leads to explanation. The closed question is not of great interest to children, but if it is framed in a different way so that they are challenged to think and to become involved, they may become interested in the results. Specifically, the open assignment might embody these two requirements:

1. The children must do something: go out and measure, design experiments, organize tables of facts, improvise techniques for comparing weight, volume, capacity, etc.
2. The children must record their findings in some way that will communicate their procedures and conclusions.[9]

It is important that the open assignment not be ambiguous. It can challenge the child to think, but it should not be too difficult for him to execute. (The appropriate level of frustration is significant.) Closing a situation too soon may well give a child the clue he did not need and thereby deprive him of making a discovery himself. Most important, the child should be made aware that he is taking the final step on his own, however small that step may be.[10]

The use of the open assignment can be viewed as a transitional period in the development of a program that is child-centered rather than subject-centered. "It is a firm and quite lengthy bridge between the exclusive use of a textbook and the ultimate goal of using real life experiences of children to provide the necessary stimuli for learning." [11]

There is a real joy — an excitement — in the process of discovery which can be experienced by both the teacher and the student. Removing from our society the notion that learning is hard work and, by its nature, usually unpleasant, is a large task for anyone, as most of us know. This is just one of the challenges facing teachers who attempt to create an atmosphere for creative learning.

REFERENCE NOTES /

1. Robin D. Montz, "Five Ultimate Goals for Education: A New Approach Based on the Implications of Gestalt Therapy." Unpublished paper, 1969. University of California, Santa Barbara.
2. Edith E. Biggs and James R. MacLean, *Freedom to Learn* (Toronto, Ontario, Canada: Addison-Wesley, Ltd., 1969).
3. Ibid., p. 7.
4. Frederick S. Perls, *Ego, Hunger and Aggression* (New York: Random House, 1969).
5. Montz, op. cit.
6. Biggs and MacLean, op. cit.
7. Frederick S. Perls, *Gestalt Therapy Verbatim* (Lafayette, Calif.: Real People Press, 1969), p. 25.
8. Montz, op. cit., p. 21.
9. Biggs and MacLean, op. cit., p. 14.
10. Ibid.
11. Ibid., p. 15.

20

GETTING AT RESPONSIBILITY IN A NINTH-GRADE ENGLISH CLASS

— Sandra Newby

This article is written about a real situation. However, I want readers to know that I don't believe in "ninth-grade English." I want to see learning centers where learners range from the age of one week to one hundred years old, and where learners freely choose their classes and teachers (fellow learners). There would be no compulsory attendance and no grades as they presently are used. Classes might meet every day, but most would meet for several hours or days at a time — months sometimes, for example, a trip to Mexico.

I'm thinking about you as students in the ninth-grade English classes long before I meet you. I'm concerned about you now, and I'm concerned about how you will fare with the future. Mainly because I'm seeking to get my own thoughts into better perspective, I felt that reading Alvin Toffler's *Future Shock* would help me gain insights I hadn't even considered. Knowing that changes occur at an ever-increasing exponential rate, I'm concerned as a teacher about how you and I will "adapt — or fail to adapt — to the future." [1] *Future Shock* is partly "a book about what happens to people when they are overwhelmed by change." [2] If we are not prepared, "the future will have arrived too soon." [3] If you and I ignore the realities of the future and live with the "mental opium" [4] of idealism that everything will turn out all right, we are not being responsible to ourselves individually and as a society. Consider several of Toffler's statements: [5]

> *Future Shock* is about those who seem to thrive on change, who crest its waves joyfully, as well as those multitudes of others who resist it or seek flight from it. (p. 11)

Even among the young we find an incomprehension of change: students so ignorant of the past that they see nothing unusual about the present. (p. 21)

To survive . . . the individual must become infinitely more adaptable and capable than ever before. (p. 34)

(Quoting three sociologists, Seeley, Sim, and Loosley): "The rapidity with which the transition (of frequent changes of residence) has to be accomplished, and the depth to which change must penetrate the personality are such as to call for the greatest flexibility of behavior and stability of personality." (pp. 80–1)

Change, roaring through society, widens the gap between what we believe and what really is. (p. 154)

We are creating a new society. Not a changed society. Not an extended, larger-than-life version of our present society. But a new society. (p. 165)

Changes will alter work, play, and education beyond recognition. (p. 166)

The commitment to one style of life over another is thus a super-decision. (p. 279)

We are not asked . . . to adapt to a new culture, but to a binding succession of new temporary cultures. (p. 330)

Thus we need neither blind acceptance nor blind resistance, but an array of creative strategies for shaping, deflecting, accelerating, or decelerating selectively. (p. 331)

In the past, culture emerged without premeditation. Today for the first time, we can raise the process to awareness. (p. 384)

Where do we begin? Where we are, here and now. How do we live now and yet prepare for the future? By taking individual responsibility for our actions.

One day I will have you sit in groups of five or six. (The size of the group is significant in that participation and interaction drop below a desirable level when groups consist of larger numbers.) I will ask each of you to list the things that were bad in your previous English class, the things that were good, and suggestions you have for this class. That will be all for the first class period. I want you to know right away that talking is all right and I want you to have the opportunity to establish relationships immediately. I will begin typing up your responses, because I believe students should write to be read by other students as well as the teacher.

On the following day I will again have you sit in groups of your own choice. Each group will work on producing at least twenty questions in response to the questions: "What's worth knowing?" "What questions do I need to ask myself about living now and in the future?"

We will use the next several days to discuss, as a large group, the questions you raised about "What's worth knowing?" and your reactions to the questions about your English classes. Reason: As soon as a teacher doesn't demand your attention, the first thing you do is to talk madly. Perhaps if you can talk madly for a few days in a class, you won't feel so repressed. My one request is that you try hard to let only one person speak at a time.

As we begin the days of talking madly, I will also ask you to keep a journal and to write in it for about ten minutes each day. I want you to learn to let your writing flow according to whatever thoughts are in your head. I will try to respond to your writing almost every day for about two weeks. However, I won't be able to keep up the pace of responding to 120 students each day. It's impossible for me to spend two or three hours after school to respond to your journal writing when I also need time to plan for each day's work. But I hope that my limited number of responses will encourage you to write freely about the numerous thoughts you have.

Sometime during the second week I will begin asking you questions about responsibility:

At what point in your life will you take total responsibility for how you are living, and not blame teachers, parents, friends, or society in general?

At what point in your life will you take total responsibility for your learning?

What would you do if no adults came to school for a month and the school was all yours?

Then I will explain my plans for the next month. We will have three kinds of class sessions — ours, yours, mine.

OURS: One day a week we will meet as a large group to talk about whatever might be of concern or interest to any member of the class. Since some students are shy or embarrassed about bringing up certain topics, we will have a box for submitting ideas anonymously.

Yours: Two days a week you will decide how you want to spend your time. Reason: The only way one learns responsibility is to have the opportunity to be responsible. George Brown expands what I believe about responsibility:

> For a democratic society to flourish . . . its members must learn how to combine freedom with responsibility and responsibility with freedom.[6]
>
> Each time we deprive an individual, whether adult or child, of the opportunity to make a decision that he could make himself, we negate the democratic process. Psychologically, we learn to assume responsibility by successfully assuming responsibility. As we learn to assume responsibility, we become aware that we can.[7]

You may choose to work by yourself or to join other students, depending upon the needs of your plans. I encourage students to work together because you can make friendships and learn from one another. To begin, you might sit and think, read, talk, play games, organize a newspaper, record imaginary or real conversations on tape or in writing or both, produce a videotape, arrange to visit a certain person or place, create experiences for the rest of us to try — go with your imagination. You will write up a mini-contract to help you carry out your responsibility in taking action for your own learning. Evaluation will be a part of our large group discussions. Reasons for wide choice of activities: "Whatever concerns language behavior is the language teacher's domain." [8] "We may even go so far as to say the reality which matters is the reality of interests — the *internal* and not the *external* reality." [9]

Mine: Two days a week I will ask you to trust me to provide experiences that will enrich your learning in ways you might not encounter by yourself. I want to offer you experiences that you probably can't get from watching TV or from being with your family. Gaining your trust will take a while, but I'll be patient. Carl Rogers says:

> The student has been "conned" for so long that a teacher who is real with him is usually seen for the first time simply exhibiting a

new brand of phoniness. To have a teacher prize him in a non-judgmental way arouses the deepest disbelief. To have a teacher truly and warmly understand his private world is so unbelievable that he must not have heard correctly. Yet, it is this last, the emphatic response, which is probably the first element to get through, the first reaction which begins to convince the student that this *is* a new experience.[10]

I will ask you to ask questions. If you are going to be actively involved in learning, I believe question-asking is of paramount importance. I will not give you many answers nor will I expect you to have all the answers for your questions. Brown quotes Paul Tillich's statement about the teacher's "fatal error": "To throw answers like stones at the heads of those who have not yet asked the questions." [11]

I will also ask you many questions. Usually I will want you to respond to your own questions and mine because I want you to express what your thoughts and feelings are now. I will often be impatient with "I don't know" answers. Sometimes I will ask you questions that leave you hanging — questions that require heavy thinking and take a long time to answer, if ever.

I want you to concentrate on the *here* and *now*. Through various experiences I will be asking you to get in touch with yourself and "regain the feel of yourself." [12] You are often embarrassed to think or act freely, or you respond with an "I don't know" because in the socialization process you've lost much of your trust in yourself. Rogers says:

> In an attempt to gain or hold love, approval, esteem, the individual relinquishes the focus of evaluation which was his in infancy, and places it in others. He learns to have a basic *dis*trust for his own experiencing as a guide to his behavior. He learns from others a large number of conceived values, and he adopts them as his own, even though they may be widely discrepant from what he is experiencing. Because these concepts are not based on his own valuing, they tend to be fixed and rigid, rather than fluid and changing.[13]

> Like the infant, too, the psychologically mature adult trusts and uses the wisdom of his organism, with the difference that he is able to do so knowingly. He realizes that if he can trust all of himself, his feelings and his intuitions may be wiser than his mind, that as a total person he can be more sensitive and accurate than his

thoughts alone. Hence, he is not afraid to say — "I feel that this experience (or this thing, or this direction) is good. Later I will probably know *why* I feel it is good." He trusts the totality of himself.[14]

Part of getting in touch with yourself will involve accepting your "unwanted emotions." [15] Some exercises will seem disconnected and others will come from the literature you read and write. As I ask you to try experiencing innumerable feelings, actions, and ideas, I must continually remind myself to let you take baby steps in encountering what might seem strange and unusual in an English class. I have heard you say, "This is dumb. Why are we doing this? This is stupid. Is this an English class?"

I will try to listen to you as much as I can. Normally I will limit my talking to five per cent of the time so that you will have much opportunity to express yourselves.

I will confront you about occurrences in the class. You will be able to improvise situations and feel what other students might be feeling. Ramón Morales said to me one day, "They don't want us." A few days later he was throwing seed pods at his classmates. I hear many students say, "I'm not prejudiced," but what have you done to interact with the Mexican-speaking students? Do they have the right to the education you expect?

During the first month I will ask you to write every day. Many of you are afraid of writing and some of you don't know that you can express yourselves in writing. I'd like you to gain that confidence by training your will to write. After twenty or so sessions, you will be able to concentrate more and more on *what* you want to communicate. Assagioli says: "As the repeated habitual actions are taken over by the unconscious, the conscious is freed for other and higher activities." [16]

After the warm-up month, we will dig into more questions:

What would happen if you told me what you really think about class?

Why do you let some kids do all of the talking?

Have I been honest with you?

What are your real goals in school, in this class?
How will you be ready for the future?

In summary, I want to create a student-centered classroom. I want you to be actively involved in deciding what's important in your life and what you want to learn. I resent my often stereotyped role as a teacher — I want to be a human resource for you. I want to give to all of you, but I hope that you will gradually want to bring your "gifts" to our group. I want you to share the responsibility for creating a meaningful time together. I'm here because I believe in you. I believe that you young people will have much opportunity for personal growth if you *now* accept the challenge of assuming more and more responsibility for how you live and learn.

REFERENCE NOTES /

1. Alvin Toffler, *Future Shock* (New York: Random House, 1970), p. 3.
2. Ibid., p. 3.
3. Ibid., p. 11.
4. Ibid., p. 272.
5. All following quotes and page numbers are from Toffler, op. cit.
6. George I. Brown, *Human Teaching for Human Learning* (New York: Viking, 1971), pp. 228–229.
7. Ibid., p. 241.
8. James Moffet, *A Student-Centered Language Arts Curriculum K–13: A Handbook for Teachers* (Boston: Houghton Mifflin, 1968), p. 314.
9. F. S. Perls, *Ego, Hunger and Aggression* (New York: Random House, 1969), p. 40.
10. Carl R. Rogers, "Bringing Together the Cognitive and the Affective-Experiential." Unpublished manuscript, Center for Studies of the Person, La Jolla, Calif., 1971, p. 1.
11. Brown, op. cit., pp. 15–16.
12. Perls, op. cit., p. 185.
13. Carl R. Rogers, "Toward a Modern Approach to Values: The Valuing Process in the Mature Person." In *Moral Problems in Contemporary Society: Essays in Humanistic Ethics* (Englewood Cliffs, N.J.: Prentice-Hall, 1969), p. 83.

14. Ibid., p. 89.
15. Perls, op. cit., p. 179.
16. Roberto Assagioli, *The Training of the Will* (New York: Psycho-synthesis Research Foundation, P.R.F. Reprint 17, 1966), p. 15.

21

GESTALT THERAPY:
NEW WINE IN OLD SKINS

— Beverly Galyean

Gestalt, experienced even in the short period of a single-quarter class, makes for tremendous growth, both as a person and as a teacher. New wine in old skins really won't burst the skins at all. Rather, the skins become mellow, soft, flexible, expanding and, consequently, able to hold more and more wine. The more the wine, the stronger the growth of the skins. And we all know the delicacies of bacchanalian wine feasts. Okay. This is Gestalt. New wine in old skins.

My own skin has stretched and grown, expanding in amoebic fashion to draw in much more of the world around me. In this article I will refer specifically to the world of the school — to its people and to its events. What has happened to me as a teacher/person, and how my own experiences with Gestalt have helped me — as well as the kids and the class environment — to grow, lead me to believe that even a very limited experience with Gestalt makes a great difference in both the teacher and her students.

In journalistic fashion, I will report some interesting events in connection with various persons I have worked with during the past two months. These particular events leap out at me as being more significant than others in that they exemplify more momentous breakthroughs in my awareness of the other person's "internal what's going on" as well as my awareness of my own "what's going on." And in each event cited, there is a definite growth in the region of choosing self-support rather than environmental support. This awareness and "response-ability" as well as growth toward personal support are central to the entire Gestalt approach. The ingredients of the wine, you might say.

MARCH 6—FIRST PERIOD FRENCH 1 /

It is raining. The kids are droopy, tired, drugged, right in tune with the monotony of the rain. Plink . . . plink . . . plink—the rain rhythm is hypnotizing them. Doesn't seem to be affecting me though.

I put the kids into groups to work on exercises. They start to come alive. They're involved, talking, challenging—having fun, too! I withdraw from the activity to watch them work. I am becoming mesmerized by the rain. Plink . . . plink . . . plink . . . sleepy, sleepy, sleepy. My attention wanders from them to the rain . . . to rhythm . . . to me.

Insight: At the beginning of class when I was talking, involved, presenting a lesson, the kids were sleepy, hypnotized, and I was alive. In group work they came alive and I, having withdrawn momentarily from the activity, became progressively sleepy. Involvement seems to be the key. Our own involvement in our own activity.

SAME DAY — SECOND PERIOD FRENCH 2 /

Having just experienced the rain/sleep syndrome in first period, I'm more aware of the possibility of the same situation occurring in this class. Class begins. Sure enough, the kids look tired, droopy, listless. I notice that they are making a decided effort to work despite the weather. I wonder what would happen if we all got in touch with our own rhythm and shared this with each other? Would this bring more energy to all of us?

Class dialogue originally in French:
BEVERLY: What's the weather like today?
CLASS PEOPLE: Rainy, cold, muggy.
BEV: How do you feel today?
C P: Tired, depressed, weary, bored. Life is monotonous, sleepy.
BEV: Does anyone see a similarity between the rain and their feelings?

c p: (Several yesses.)

BEV: It's interesting how many of us cited depressing adjectives to describe ourselves. In French the words "rain" and "cry" are quite similar — *il pleut* and *je pleure.*

c p: Yeah, they go together.

(Class interest is really picking up at this time. Good time for sharing feelings.)

BEV: Let's try a fun exercise! Listen to the rain and really hear it. Tap your fingers to the rhythm.

(The kids really get into it. Energy is coming to the class.)

BEV: Great! Let me show you my rhythm right now.

(With both hands and fingers I start snapping how I feel. As I do it, I go from a rapid to a very drowsy rhythm, then rapid again. I tell the kids how I actually hypnotized myself, the further I got into my own feelings, but when I thought of the class, I again became energized.)

BEV: Okay, now you try it!

(They're all doing it, even the shyer ones. Some are keeping the same rhythm, others are changing rhythm midway, others are more erratic.)

BEV: Okay, let's share what happened.

GRACE: I feel kind of bored today so I snapped in monotone fashion. I almost put myself to sleep.

ROBERTA: I was thinking about an activity after school which will be lots of fun, so I tapped with excitement.

MIRIAM: I started off really slow and then my mind wandered to this friend. As I thought about her, my snapping became more enthusiastic.

JUNE: My snapping was mechanical. I feel like a robot — no life.

It is interesting how even those who claim to be "dead" are really alive in this exercise. The class is now energized so I think we can get into some grammar work. But I don't want to deviate from the experience too much, so I think I'll have them use their experiences and the necessary vocabulary as an oral/written exercise. Then we can launch into the paragraph work.

Insight: Getting all of us in touch with our feelings definitely energized the class, and me too. I'm not sure whether the energy came from getting in touch, or from the fun interaction. This question I will try to pursue in continuing experiences. As for working on skills in language, the kids seemed sharper and more able to work on new concepts. I seemed sharper, too.

MARCH 6 — SEVENTH PERIOD FRENCH 1 — ABBY /

During this year, Abby has rarely turned in an assignment and frequently tries to do her homework in class. On occasion, however, she's really "turned on" to French and works very well in class. She's bright, enthusiastic, and "right on" when she has these rare moments of life. Up to this time we have talked about her work and on each occasion I have sensed a verbal goodwill on her part, but no real breakthrough as to commitment either to her work or to an understanding and acceptance of the consequences of nonpresence in the class.

For today's class, the kids have each made mystery maps of the school and are sharing them in groups. They are having fun trying to guess the various routes. I see Abby is again not sharing anything.

BEV: Abby, where is your map?

ABBY (head down, whispering) : I don't have it.

B: Would you please come outside with me for a moment?

(Since the groups are all involved in their activity, I can afford to leave the class. I am also fairly certain that Abby will not be unduly embarrassed.)

BEV: Abby, you are rarely prepared for class. I've noticed that when I give an assignment to be prepared at home you almost never do it. Very often you attempt to do it during class while the others are already sharing their work. Are you aware of this?

ABBY (head bowed) : Yes.

B: I feel it is unfair for you to arrive in class without doing your part. You take from others, but don't give. How do you feel?

A: I don't take from others.

B: If you don't take from others, where have you learned your French?

(Her head is still bowed. She is silent and seems trapped by my questioning.)

B: It seems to me you've learned from the people in the class as well as from me. What have you given?

A (long silence): Nothing.

B: Is that fair?

A: (Silence.)

B: Abby, you are silent. What's going on inside you now?

A: (Still looks at ground.)

B: You are rubbing your hands together quite vigorously. Something seems to be going on.

(At this point I noticed that Abby really seemed trapped. I am wondering if my manner of questioning was really helping her. I felt that I was asking questions which were "loaded" with value judgments on my part. By asking value-loaded questions, I am preventing Abby from answering honestly. I decided to work with the idea of being trapped. I am acting on intuition in choosing "trapped" as a focal point for continuing.)

BEV: Abby, you seem trapped. Are you?

ABBY: Yes.

B: Who is trapping you?

A: (Silence.)

B: Are you trapped by the class?

A: I'm trapped by lots of problems in my life right now.

B: You have many problems that are trapping you?

A: Yes, lots!

B: How are you trapped by them?

A: (Long silence.)

B: Your hands are showing lots of activity. Something is going on inside you. Do you know what's happening?

A: (Silence.)

(Abby really seemed stuck. I respected her silence and gave her long pauses in which to answer if she wished. Perhaps she's not yet willing to talk about the problem. But I'm not sure yet.)

BEV: Do you like being trapped?

ABBY: No.

B: Do you want a way out?

A: Yes, but I don't know how.

B: Okay, how do you trap yourself?

A: By conforming.

B: By conforming you trap yourself?

A: Yes.

B: How do you conform?

A: (Silence.)

B: Do you conform in my class?

A: No.

B: Are you trapped in French class?

A: (Silence.)

B: Abby, again you look trapped. You've said you want a way out. I can't give this to you. Only you know the answer because only you really know what's going on inside of you. You're sort of an "Abby" expert, and that's kind of neat.

(Abby begins to show signs of interest, as if she might like to talk some more.)

BEV: Would you like some more time to think about how you trap yourself?

ABBY (relieved): Yes!

B: Is there some time when we can meet again and see if you can come up with a plan to help yourself, to get out of that trap?

A: Lunch on Thursday.

B: Okay, lunch on Thursday. See you then.

Insight: Abby traps herself by fantasizing her problems. This is typical of freshmen. Abby and her friends seem to share the same syndrome: lethargy for classwork, using problems as excuses, withdrawing from activities. Although there are many academic explanations for this behavior, I would like to see if Abby can really help herself grow deeper in the knowledge of what she is doing, and how she either takes or refuses responsibility for herself. As for myself, I'm becoming more aware of value-loaded questions such as: "Do you think that is fair?" My value is that it be fair. Although shared learning is a value in my classes, and I believe it is also necessary for learning with others and in the presence of others, it may not be an individual's value at the moment. The key to conversation seems to be to allow an individual to express oneself freely and trustingly, and then to admit acceptance or rejection (and responsibility for) various value systems, whether those systems be in a class, a school, or a home.

MARCH 8 — LUNCH TIME — ABBY /

Abby looks bouncy, cheery, happy, and wanting to talk.

BEV: Hi! Have you thought much about our conversation on Tuesday?

ABBY: Yes.

B: You really seemed trapped that day and I felt it was useless to pursue the conversation at that point. How do you feel now?

A: Better. I can talk about it now.

B: Okay. Let's begin again with my first concern. How do you feel about your lack of preparation?

A: It's unfair. I'll try to do better.

(Abby has said this to me before, but it doesn't seem to carry any weight with her.)

BEV: You'll try to come more prepared. What do you usually do at home, after school and in the evening?

ABBY: Homework, TV, phone calls.

B: You do homework every night?

A: No. Just sometimes.

B: Oh, sometimes you do homework. Does that say anything to you about your classwork?

A: Yes. I'm sometimes not prepared in class.

B: What are you doing when you're not tuned in?

A: Thinking about problems.

B: You're thinking about problems. Do you have anyone with whom you can discuss these problems?

A: The counselors.

B: Do you see them regularly?

A: Yes.

B: Do they help you?

A: Yes.

B: But even though they help you, you still need more time on your own to think about problems.

A: Yes.

(At this point I sense in Abby a commitment to spend much time fantasizing her problems. She likes what she's doing. Perhaps the most growing experience for her at this point is to understand and own her commitment. In this way she will feel accepted for whatever is happening to her, and also be able to take responsibility for herself.)

BEV: Okay, you use class time to spend on your problems. Are you aware of the consequences?

A: Yes.

B: Do you like the consequences?

A: No, I don't want low grades.

B: It seems like you're trapping yourself again. You are caught between wanting good grades and wanting the freedom to spend on yourself.

A: Yes, and I don't know what to do about it.

B: Abby, every one of us gets caught between choices. We have to set up our own priorities, and then take full responsibility for what we choose. We are our own experts. The important thing is to be aware of what we're choosing and the consequences accompanying a particular choice. Okay, you don't want low grades, but you are choosing not to do the work necessary for grades. Are you willing to accept the consequences?

A: Right now, yes. But I still think I spend too much time daydreaming. I think I can stop it though.

B: Yes, and neither I nor anyone else have given you any solution as to how to stop daydreaming. Do you remember what I told you Tuesday about this?

A: You mean when you said I'm the only one who knows?

B: Yes. Do you believe that?

A: Yes. When I'm ready I'll move on.

B: Great! You are already making honest choices. By the way, have you figured out how you trap yourself?

A (huge grin): Yes, by avoiding certain things.

B: By avoiding certain things? I don't understand.

A: I try to do two conflicting things, and by choosing one I can avoid the other. Then I can just tell myself that the other was impossible, and that's a cop-out. I really don't think I have to avoid so much.

B: Very often we do avoid unpleasant situations by involving ourselves in conflicting tasks. I'm glad you recognize how you handle avoidance.

A: Yes. I'm going to try to work out some things.

B: Okay, I'd be interested in knowing how you do work things out. If you feel like keeping me posted, I'd like to hear. And remember, you're the expert on you.

A (huge grin): Thank you! Bye.

It is incredible to me how Abby arrived at the idea of avoidance. All of a sudden she seemed to have an insight into what she does. The truth leaped out. I would like to do more work with her, but will wait for her to come to see me.

Insight: This work with Abby enabled me to see many things about myself that both help and hinder self-awareness. I tend to ask too many value questions, use too many words, and come on too strongly. I also lead too much. I need to let the other person work more on his own, and to value the moments of silence. Also, I may be encouraging the person too much by using exclamatory phrases. Young people especially are impressionable, and too much affirmation may lead them to act in order to please me. With Abby, I noticed that even though she seemed very passive, whenever I mentioned the idea of her own expertise about herself, she showed an interest. This statement seemed to energize her and reinforce her.

MARCH 15 — FRENCH 3 INDEPENDENT STUDY — KAREN /

Karen has chosen to work with the play *La Leçon* by Ionesco. She understands the vocabulary but is having a difficult time understanding the ideas or seeing any relationship between Ionesco's presentation of the material and contemporary society. The play presents itself to her only on the level of factual comprehension.

BEV: Karen, do you see any relationship between the professor and the student in the play and the classrooms of today?

KAREN: Not really.

B: Okay, at the end of the play Ionesco refers to the professor as the murderer and the student as the victim. Does that say anything to you?

K: I guess he's calling teachers murderers and students victims.

B: How are teachers murderers and students victims?

K (long pause): I don't know.

B: Okay, let's talk for a moment about stripping someone of his humanity, which is a kind of murder. Karen, what makes a person be a person and not some sort of a robot?

K: Creativity, thinking, individualism, questioning.

B: Let's write them on the board. I'm going to play a game with you for a moment. I want you to react in any way you'd like — angry, complying, happy, bored, or whatever. Don't worry about what you say. I won't tell.

K (laughing): Okay.

B: Karen, scratch your knee!

K: No.

B: Yes.

K: I don't want to.

B: Do it.

K (progressively louder and more agitated): No!

B: I said to scratch your knee. Do what I say.

K: I don't have to do what you say.

B: Scratch your knee!

K: Why?

B: Doesn't matter, just do it.

K: No.

B (stopping the activity): How do you feel?

K: Like I'm not gonna move.

B: Yeah! I felt we were really separated, no contact. How'd you feel about me?

K: Like you were trying to control me.

B: Yeah, and you resisted me.

K: I thought your demands were stupid.

B (laughing): So did I.

(Now I point to the board again, to Karen's words.)

BEV: See any connection between your observations here and what just happened between you and me?

KAREN (coming alive): Yes, you were denying all those things in me and I was refusing to meet you.

B: You see how the professor does the same to the student?

K: Yes, dehumanizes her.

B: Right. Even if he hadn't killed her with the knife there was a symbolic murder.

K: He sort of killed her humanity.

(I try another game with Karen to find out if she will discuss even deeper elements of the play.)

BEV: Karen, since we still have enough time, let's try to work a little more on some of these ideas.

KAREN: Fine with me.

B: This time again I want you to react to me in any way you wish.

K: All right.

B: Karen, mathematics is really an important subject.

K: I know.

B: You know?

K: Yes, I'm going to be a doctor.

B: What kind of a doctor?

K: Medical doctor.

B: Medical doctor! Hmm, that's interesting.

K: I want to study at a medical school in Germany.

B: You know German, then.

K: Pretty much.

B: Then you will need to brush up a little.

K (smiling): Yes.

B: Good luck! (End of game.) Karen, when we began I had no idea how you would react when I said so strongly that math is important. I might have been forcing my opinion on you.

K: I never sensed a conflict because I need math.

B: But I still came on very strong with that statement. You didn't feel manipulated?

K: Well, at first a little. But you seemed to agree with everything I said.

B: I really didn't agree, just commented.

K: But that still affirmed me. I felt you were with me.

B: I took the conversation from you and continued trying at every moment to stay where you were.

K: And you let me lead with what I wanted to say.

B (referring again to the words on the board): You mean I treated you as an individual, let you create your own conversation, and do your own thinking.

κ (laughing) : The opposite of killing me.

B: Now, does this say anything to you about school?

κ: Teachers kill students by forcing them to learn stuff that doesn't relate to them. Very often this kind of learning calls for repetition, memorization, and lots of testing.

B: How do students allow themselves to be killed?

κ: By not questioning, not demanding that their ideas be heard, by not saying when they're bored and frustrated, by sitting there.

B: Remember the end of the play when the professor drives the student mad by having her repeat nonsensical words? The last word she repeated was "knife," the instrument with which she was killed. It seems to me Ionesco is showing a cooperative effort between the two in the student's death.

κ: Yeah, the two sort of worked together on it.

B: Cooperative effort. That's what's needed in school. But it can work both ways.

κ: I see better now what Ionesco is talking about and how some of these same situations exist here at school.

After this session, Karen seemed much more alive and involved with the play. She invested something of herself in the work. Up to this time she had mostly limited herself to working with factual information. She seems to have a renewed interest in the work and chose the next play with enthusiasm. I'm going to do some more experiential work with her, as she has chosen Ionesco's "The Bald Soprano," a play rich in language-communication experience.

Insight: Karen, although appearing to be highly motivated and hardworking, usually deals only with material on the surface level of facts. She is also reluctant to discuss ideas for fear of making a mistake either in comprehension of material or in oral expression. By gently leading her into two experiential treatments of the subject matter she (1) made a personal investment, (2) talked on the level of experience rather than cognition, and (3) showed signs of enthusiasm for her work. I am interested in determining how the experiential treatment of further literary selections helps her grow in the areas of personal investment in learning.

In each of these examples, as well as in several not cited, a definite vocabulary of attitudes emerges. Even without in-depth Gestalt training, the interested teacher can help both herself and her students by practicing this vocabulary. It is important, however, that she continually attempt to grow in her own insights into the deeper implications of the words and expressions common to Gestalt. Gestalt "wine" is never stale. Gestalt "wine" continually refreshes itself through progressive refermentation. Even though it may be stored for a long time in "old bottles or skins," the mellowness remains.

The following is a list of questions and expressions which have emerged from my own experience with Gestalt. In each case responsibility is placed on the individual to elicit personally felt responses.

What's going on *now?*
How are you feeling *now?*
What are you doing?
How do you do that?
Are *you* saying that? Or is someone else speaking?
What do you want to do?
What are the consequences of that choice?
Are you willing to take the risks?
How do you hurt yourself?
How do you sabotage yourself?
How do you help yourself?
Only *you* know.
You can resolve it.
I will not do it for you, because you are your own expert.
You are responsible.
I only know what you tell me.

I find that this vocabulary gives me a framework in which to work. It is low-risk and involves the student in his own processes. I have not yet had a negative reaction from a high-school student. On the contrary, my observations show that students become energized, more willing to work or talk about themselves. There is also a marked feeling of satisfaction after working with Gestalt. The kids feel better about themselves and their work. Even the highly intellectual "heady" achievers have been able to get into the activities and appreciate their work.

Working in such a manner also creates a trusting climate in the classroom. I theorize from experiences that individuals, having been respected and appreciated for their own statements about themselves or their work, tend to give the same respect and appreciation to others. It's all right to talk about oneself, and good things happen when we do. Relating a personal experience to cognitive material also helps to learn the material itself.

One word of caution, however, for teachers like myself, who tend to be overly directive and who favor much class dialogue. Gestalt experiences take time for reflection and digestion. This means there is need for more quiet time, and time for the students to speak. I have learned to allow for many moments of silence and reflection, realizing that in silence action and involvement is taking place. Dealing with people on the level of their own experience means that we must give individuals the time to touch their own experiences. The class may appear to be slow-moving at first but, in reality, involvement is taking place on other levels. Gradually, the involvement becomes more lively and verbal.

As for myself as teacher-person, I feel a constant and rather surprising growth in awareness of my own feelings, as well as the students' feelings. I respond to them more on the level of their interest. Even though I have twenty or more students, both my awareness of collective activity and my awareness of individual activity is more acute. I'm more relaxed and, interestingly enough, I'm much more on top of the activity than ever before. And my students are telling me things like: "Hey, class seems to be getting easier. I thought it was supposed to get harder this time of year." "I feel good in here. I have time to learn the stuff in my own way." "I have so much fun I don't feel like I'm working." It was really neat when one of the freshmen came to me and said: "Bev, I hope this doesn't embarrass you but you seem more like a person than a teacher. I mean, you just seem different. How can you hang so loose and still teach us? I mean, you are a teacher. . . ." I could have kissed her.

New wine in old skins does make sense — a lot of sense. Re-creating "old" teachers makes sense too, especially since "old" teachers have had a vast experience with students and with teaching skills. Gestalt is a great and ongoing way of re-creating. And it's fun, too. Our vintage is about eighty proof! And there's always room for more. *Bonne santé!*

22

CHILDREN OF THE UNIVERSE

— Mary Stephens

In *Human Teaching for Human Learning,* George Brown points out that the school, while resistant to change, is the logical place for innovation. Yet he states that while "it is the one institution in our Western civilization outside the family that most profoundly affects the human condition," [1] most schools turn out young people who either have been classified as failures or have been steeped in an idolatrous attitude toward the intellect. In either of these two products of our present educational system, emotion is generally ignored as nonexistent. In those whom the schools reject as failures, emotions, boiling close to the surface, are not allowed to emerge in nondestructive ways; in the other group emotions are repressed as irrelevant to learning. Put thirty-one of these students together in a high-school classroom and you have my ninth-grade, fifth-period English class. Fresh from tracking in the feeder junior high school, they screamed, yelled, shoved, and dragged their way into H32 twelve weeks ago, flopped into the nearest seats, and let all of the life drain from their faces.

Until this year I had not thought I could fail to resolve any problem I might encounter in teaching high-school English — until *this* year, the year of my initial experience with a ninth-grade class of thirty-one boys and girls of mixed abilities and mixed-up attitudes toward their world. I chose to teach this group and a similar one in order to experience their needs and those of the teachers on my staff, who had been working with them ever since they overflowed into our senior high school — temporarily, we were told.

When it appeared that these students would be here indefinitely, I had to make some decisions about how to "integrate" them into a system which had kept them penned in tracked, traditional classes — hoping they would go away as soon as a new junior high school was built. My solutions, I felt, would be invalid and perhaps unworkable if they were based on secondhand experiences.

What were these secondhand experiences? The most disturbing was the physical breakdown of one of our young teachers who, as someone new to the district, was given five ninth grades to teach. That meant meeting with about thirty students a period, five periods a day, every day, five days a week. Three of these classes were categorized as "slow," which, at the time, didn't appear to me to be too threatening a situation. The senior-high students, whom I had taught for several years in slow classes, had been delightful young people whose greatest weakness was their need for directions, which they accepted without question. My goal, which I felt I had achieved when I met them four or five years later, was to change their concept of themselves from "we're dumb" to "we're okay, you're okay." I concluded, therefore, that the teacher who had collapsed had been uptight — surely the problem lay with her.

Another vicarious experience occurred when I offered to substitute for one of my staff in an emergency. Her written instructions said, in effect, that probably no one in class would have read the assigned story, most would pay no attention to me, and the boy in the sixth seat, last row, was to be watched constantly. My experience with the class, however, was exciting, fruitful (for me), and rewarding. When I first entered the room I sat down and we all stared at each other until, uncomfortable with the intense quiet, someone broke the silence with, "Who are you?" I answered him and asked the same question of him. Our question-and-answer session divulged that two people had read the assigned story, one of whom didn't understand it; that this was a dumb class; and please don't make them read aloud.

Glancing quickly through their textbook, I discovered a story involving a white boy who brought his black friend home for lunch and discovered his mother's prejudice. I read the story to them. Some students followed in the text; most watched my face. The discussion that followed took us on journeys of discovery about prejudice, the origin of black people, the building of the pyramids, and, finally, how the students felt _now_ as the period was ending. The boy in the back about whom I had been warned, ceased bouncing a Yo-Yo off the wall almost immediately when the story began and was the most interested and interesting discussant in the group. Yes, I may have been lucky enough to work with them on a "good" day, but I don't think so. When they invited me back with beautifully warm words, I felt honored. How, then, could my experience be so different from that of their regular teacher? And how could five such classes cause such remarks in the teachers' workroom as, "My god, this year's batch is worse than last year's!" Or, "I think we ought to take turns with the ninth grades. It isn't fair that some of us are stuck with them!" Or, wistfully, "When will that new junior high be finished?" (The first shovelful of dirt had yet to be dug.)

Still working from the feedback I was getting from the ninth-grade teachers, or at least from the majority of them, I broke our freshmen out of the tracking they had brought with them from the feeder junior high. The rationale? We had found that nongraded classes (mixtures of tenth, eleventh, and twelfth graders) worked far better for both students and staff. Among our senior-high students, slow students saw, and took part in, learning experiences with which they had been unfamiliar — panel discussions, research for information with which to form new theories, reading for fun as well as wisdom, and mind-stretching. On the other hand, the superior achiever gained firsthand knowledge of those of his peers who hated school and who exhibited all sorts of limitations in dealing with their school world as well as the one outside. Why wouldn't this be a step in the right direction for our ninth-graders?

Pressure by groups with various traditional misgivings about change, especially in regard to students of this age, prevented the more drastic innovation of including them in the elective program enjoyed by the rest of the students. Beginning with our fall semester this year, we allotted freshmen at random to the twenty-two sections of ninth grade. Classes increased in size; teacher hours did not. We saw our neatly defined list of twenty-five students per teacher bulge and give way. The average is now twenty-nine, with some classes of thirty-one and thirty-two. When a group this size, in a too-small room without windows, experienced a sudden release from the tracking they had undergone for three years or more, a new kind of experience awaited our ninth-grade teachers. (I *would* pick this year to learn more about my responsibilities!)

The spread in maturity, size, and ability is startling. From little Patty, who is low in height, academic ability, and self-opinion, to Carol, tall, self-assured, independent, who placed in the top five per cent in a recent nationwide language arts test, and who is turning out her own poetry and short stories; from Carlos without *any* language in which to communicate comfortably, subject to fits of violent temper, expressing his awakening sexuality in drawing giant, erupting penises — to Alex, big, blond, physically enough developed to be taken for a senior, emotionally stunted in his "shoot 'um all" attitude toward Indians, blacks, and hippies, and who verbalizes in spoken and written language his contempt of more gentle boys in the class (he calls them "limp-wrists" and "he-she-its"). Picture these and multiply by eight and you can visualize this one group fairly accurately.

The opening day formalities presented utter chaos. Lost students came wandering in, wide-eyed, embarrased, in all stages of shock. Some didn't arrive in the proper room until the next day. Although many of them knew each other, perhaps slightly, some were strangers who had just arrived in the area. Others had no chance to meet, having been kept in their tracked classes.

For the most part, they sat silently, watching, like unwinking little animals. They offered monosyllabic answers to the necessary questions: "Who are you?" "How do you want to be known? Do you have a special short name?" Shyly, about half indicated nicknames they wanted used. I asked them to sit in alphabetical rows and a large groan arose. I explained that I had a problem remembering names unless I was able to associate them with faces for two weeks or so, and I asked them to bear with my problem. Faces relaxed and they moved to the desks assigned by their last names. Now, more silence. . . . Then I asked a stupid question: "Do you all know each other?" Some glanced quickly toward familiar faces; others either shrugged their shoulders or stared at this dopey teacher who was proving to be in fine form.

How to begin? Begin what? Obviously, I had thirty-one people waiting for something. What does one do at a dull party? Serve drinks? Not here. We all needed to get to know each other a little bit, this first day of a long year to come. From my mental file of "Hillman House Drops" (named for the helpful dittos of a fellow teacher, Aaron Hillman) I extracted something that might work. I asked the students to stand up, move about the room until each came to someone he didn't know, and to sit down beside him. The surprise on their faces told me that I was in green pastures. They jumped up and mixed about, finally settling here and there in pairs. A few stood frozen, but it was no trouble to pair these with each other and soon all were looking at me expectantly. I asked them to speak with each other for five minutes, learning all they could about each other, and at the end of the time limit, to introduce each other to the class by name and by one *good* bit of information each had learned about the other. The uproar must surely have been heard for quite a distance. It made me feel good, this noise and animation with which the dyads worked.

I would like to have formed the rows of desks into a large circle for the introductions, but in my room this was impossible. Two smaller circles, one within the other, sufficed to make a beginning of getting to know one another. The introductions took most of that first fifty-minute period, but I still had a few minutes to make some of the necessary announcements, and I was impressed with the lively faces now turned toward me — friendly faces, I thought.

The week went by swiftly, with three days given, by mandate, to the study of a cleverly humorous handbook devised by upperclassmen for new students. On Friday I issued composition books, calling them journals. Some called out that they had brothers or sisters who used these things. Others stared or asked, "What do we have to write in them?" or "Do we *have* to write?" I told them that they were to write in them every day; occasionally I would tell them what to work with, but mostly they were to write how they felt, or what they thought, or any other kind of ruminating they might indulge in. That day I asked them to write, after one week in high school, how they felt about that week and their experiences during it. Some wrote pages; others, sentences; some just fragments of thoughts; but all communicated clearly how their fears as freshmen were never realized. No one called them names, beat them up, or put them through an initiation ceremony. On the contrary, they found upperclassmen most helpful in giving directions, advice, or a warm "hello." One wrote that he had thrown up the night before in fear of his first day in high school. They praised this best-of-all high schools and were enthusiastic about the months to come. My three boys who understood little or no English responded too. Two of them wrote in Spanish, and the third drew his first three penises. *That* was the week that was!

The traditional curriculum called for more exposure to the various genres of literature. I began with the short story and asked them to ask questions in writing about it. The shallowness of their questions revealed that they had already forgotten everything that the curriculum guide says they had learned in the seventh and eighth grades. One opined that the short story was a novel cut down for those who didn't have time to read. Oh, well — here I was, back in virgin pasture again.

I like to think that my students learn through a process I call "directed discovery." The classes should end, I think, with the students' own definitions and insights, and their heightened awareness of widening horizons. In helping them develop an appreciation of how an author builds a character, I asked each to play God and create a person. I suggested they begin with the known characteristics of themselves, of friends, and of strangers, and mix some of them to create someone new. If uncomfortable with mixing such ingredients, they could create a "paper" person of a real one — that is, try to make someone they know live on paper. This proved successful for those with writing difficulties. I had thirty-one characters, no two alike, some in explicit detail, others sketchy. I then asked the students to exchange their character sketches with each other and to try to "see" the creation. In offering feedback to each other, they explored the phenomenon of how certain words, juxtaposed, can produce a flesh-and-blood human being on paper, and how other words, poorly chosen, form pale shadows difficult to pin down and easily forgotten. From there it was easy to examine the words of our first short story study.

Setting, conflict, and tone were explored in the same way: What words does the author choose to use? Dialogue, as a means of creating a story such as Hemingway's "The Killers," was first encountered in conversations role-played by two students while a third acted as recorder. The laughter as well as the criticism of the "dumb" conversations made the exercise a refreshing experience. And now I can evoke thirty-one different answers when I ask: What is a character? How does Jack London create his nameless man in "To Build a Fire"? What words does he choose to set the Arctic scene? What words does he choose not to use?

Our exploration of point of view proved less rewarding in some ways. The students felt that, since one person wrote the story, one must always "see" things his way. I had read Assagioli's book *Psychosynthesis*,[2] in which he discusses the various selves we encompass: the one we think we see and know; the one others see at varying distances from us; the one we try to become when the way others see us strongly influences us to see ourselves that way. Assagioli, it is true, was discussing these ideas relative to work with therapy patients but, as with many of his suggestions, they can also be used in education and I tried them in the context described here. I suggested that each student write a description of himself as he is physically, referring to himself in either the first person or the third person. Many found this exceedingly difficult to do; others wrote several pages. Some liked the idea of standing off to one side and using a third person pronoun, thus experiencing less discomfort. For example, one girl wrote:

> This person parts her hair down the middle. Her hair is dirty dishwater blond. Her eyes are brown. [There follows a description of clothing.] She always chews gum. She thinks she's real tuff [*sic*], and real smart. I myself don't really like her. She has a habit of hitting herself on the chin with her pencil.

When we discussed this piece of writing, she said she often felt that she didn't like herself but had never actually said it in so many words. We discussed the possibility that this view of herself might be prejudiced. She laughed at such an idea and then, after thinking about it, admitted that it might be so.

Another student who wrote a page of "I am not . . ." took my suggestion that he could deal more economically with what he *is* and took his work home with him. He returned the next day with a poem which he said his father had written because he liked to write poetry and was glad to write about his son. I could get no commitment from the boy that he would write his own description. Later, when the class was asked to take the next step, this particular boy's writing was revealing. I had directed the students to draw names from a box. The person whose name each drew was to be the subject, unknowingly, of a written description. Here the physical description was to be as precise as possible and, besides that, an imaginative description of how the subject thought. Here the writer could project this imaginative writing from perceived action. The papers carried the names of the subject only. The boy who could not write about himself drew my name. He wrote:

> Miss Mary Stephens has Black hair. Drass nice. Whear glass. Age 13. Touth legs. Smat. She nice to people. And to me. And I could tock to her and she could tock to me.

This piece reveals several things. Obviously, he is unable to write well. His penmanship scrawls and jiggles its way across the page, oblivious to lines. He pointed out to me that he wrote my age as thirteen because that day he felt a childlike quality in me (his words!). The line in which he separates himself from people reveals how he feels about himself. And the fact that I talk to him and he to me seems one of the seven wonders of the world to him.

In class discussions that followed these two exercises, I felt that the students were able to perceive the ways in which an author can play about with point of view. I also saw this kind of exercise as a way for students to rediscover themselves in how others see them, whether or not, from these other points of view, the account was accurate. Among the papers handed in were several that were destructive in their coarseness and brutality. I reacted by hastily filing these papers in the wastebasket. I told the class what I had done and explained that we would try this writing again later, perhaps in the spring, when they had all grown more sensitive and perceptive. I referred to some descriptions which had been distortions meant to hurt the one described. The worst (in my judgment) of the lot was written by a boy who, in his self-description, wrote about his bigness, his blondness, and the wonderful way in which he was being reared by understanding parents. The student who in turn wrote about *him* described him as a big, blond ape who traveled with a gang of disruptive boys. I see more uses for this exercise but I must work them out carefully.

This is where I am now, twelve weeks into the year that I will work with these youngsters. I believe what I have written here proves to some degree that I am *aware* of my students. As George Brown points out, "Being aware of a child as he really is is half the battle toward effective and creative teaching, especially in terms of relevant curriculum content and teacher behavior." [3] In the same context, awareness training based on Gestalt therapy, he notes, can help students become more in touch with the Now, and especially that part of the Now which is himself. "As he becomes increasingly aware of the universe . . . the 'person-universe,' . . . the increased awareness of the universe would include that of other humans with whom he lives. . . ." [4] That, it seems to me, is the crux of my problem this year. My ninth-graders, by whatever means at my disposal, must be directed toward a discovery of new and exciting experiences, new wholesome ways of looking at themselves and their immediate human contacts, becoming "aware of the universe as it is . . . and thus realizing their creative potential." [5]

There are already signs of change. Alex brought beautiful cookies to the Christmas party and made sure that everyone had some. Other boys were too embarrassed to carry in their own contributions and sent them with girls. Rick, the student who drew my name and wrote about me, has become more sure of himself and his right to dissent. He wrote of an assignment yesterday: "I not want to do this. I Hade it." He did, however, take attendance, even though it took him the better part of the period to list the few names of absentees in his tortured printing. Carol spent several days talking animatedly with my three bilingual deprived ones. Since she knows no Spanish, they are laboring sincerely to speak to her in English — and doing it well, since she is pretty.

Along with the "directed-discovery" method of helping students to learn, I like to *let* things develop. As Brown notes, one must really listen to see who is there when one works among other human beings. But, coming into my classroom, bearing with them the "undigested rubbish from the past," as Perls labels all the unfinished business of living, how can my students be made aware of the wealth available to them? Certainly not in the world of the traditional schoolroom, where, as Frank Barron has stated, the world of books, words, and classes will produce verbally docile sheep. Rather, through the medium of an aware teacher, awareness of the potential for creative living can be developed in every child. My thirty-one charges, children of the universe, can be shown that universe if I can point out the road that can lead them to its existence.

REFERENCE NOTES /

1. George I. Brown, *Human Teaching for Human Learning* (New York: Viking, 1971), p. 8.
2. Roberto Assagioli, *Psychosynthesis* (New York: Viking, 1971).
3. George I. Brown, "Awareness Training and Creativity Based on Gestalt Therapy," *Journal of Contemporary Psychotherapy*, vol. 2, no. 1 (summer 1969), p. 25. This article also appears as a chapter in *The Live Classroom.*
4. Ibid., p. 27.
5. Ibid., p. 32.

FOUR

Examples of Lessons, Units, and Course Outlines in Confluent Education

This section is, in a sense, self-explanatory. Included here are examples — drawn from one field, English — of specific lessons, units, and course outlines written by a number of teachers who have received confluent training. We have limited the examples to one field in order to give a more substantial view of the possibilities, but clearly the approaches described could be used with other subject matter, and indeed have been.

The writings are the distillation of actual happenings in the live classroom, recorded on paper so that others might have access to them and learn from them. They are written in sufficient detail for a teacher to follow them exactly if he or she should wish to. However, though we do not exclude this possibility, we do not encourage it, and would suggest instead that the interested teacher use these as a concrete resource from which to build his or her own creative "version" — a central theme on which to compose a variation that fits both person and situation. Confluent teaching is, more than anything else, creative teaching, and entails the ability to respond to the immediate situation, be it emotional and/or intellectual, both as a person and as a professional. It is from this response that these units have sprung, and in order to keep them fully alive it is necessary for the teacher who uses them to invest them with his or her own life. The units are included here to offer concrete ideas and support for such work. Confluent education is a reality; this is indicated here and in the previous sections. But what is more important is that it stay alive and growing. This is where you, as teacher, come in.

23

A CONFLUENT
READING LESSON FOR GRADES 1–3

— Victoria Grizzard

The book and worksheet used in this plan would not be my selections for a reading program if I had a choice. I would choose the Bill Martin, Jr., series and use an audio-lingual approach. However, when I am working in a school system that requires a certain reading curriculum (i.e., a California State series or Distar), I modify the reading lesson so that the actual reading *experience* is confluent. When working as a member of a team, I feel obliged to maintain a mutual pace and cognitive end goal, completing a unit or entire book so that the students will not suffer a "knowledge gap" when they go to the next book or level. At the same time I attempt to broaden the reading experience by considering the students' concerns and blockages and developing affective curriculum loadings. I can usually accomplish this within the existing structure and time limit by eliminating the following:

1. The stilted ideas presented in the teacher's manual: "Introduce the following words in the prescribed procedure before reading the story. . . ."

2. The phony motivational strategies: "Remind the children of an exciting event from the previous story. . . ."

3. Drill and practice on known material: "Build the meaning of the word 'frighten' by writing 'fright' on the board. . . ."

All of these destroy the essence, the flow, the beauty, the excitement — the Gestalt *whole* of the reading experience. I replace this with personal contact with the real children.

Text: "Shining Bridges"
Unit: "It's up to them" (leaders and helpers)
Story: "Teacher's Helper"
Materials: Text, worksheet #24, chart paper, paper, pencils

OBJECTIVES /

Affective	Cognitive
1. To enjoy the whole reading experience.	1. To break up parts of the story for development of skills (sequence).
2. To share this enjoyment as well as personal reactions to the story.	2. To appreciate the author's story and ability in relating the story (story analysis).
3. To promote security, give and encourage positive reinforcement, especially during oral reading.	3. To give recognition and support to those who have language and reading skills.
4. To share feelings with the children about their reading ability.	4. To promote realistic judgment of the students' own reading ability.
5. To improve their self-image as readers.	5. To improve reading skills (i.e., difference between conversation and narration).
6. To change right/wrong judgments to familiar/strange.	6. To change words and structures to see how they affect the story.
7. To help the children identify leadership qualities in themselves.	7. To abstract ideas about leadership qualities from the story.
8. To personalize and vitalize the dead drills in the worksheet.	8. To work independently; practice writing and comprehension skills.
9. To express feelings both verbally and nonverbally.	9. To develop verbal communication skills.

PROCEDURES /

1. "Reading" the first picture — discussion, questions.
2. Title — personal reactions.
3. Silent reading.

4. Oral reading — feedback: "James, we enjoyed the way you put so much expression into the reading," etc. Deal with any criticisms (projections?) children may make (e.g., "you read too slow"). Have the critic tell how he feels when he is criticized (e.g., "does it help you to do better?"). "Which would you rather have, encouragement or negative criticism? Would you rather have help or have someone take over?"

5. Discussion/exercises: "Have you ever been in a situation where a group wouldn't listen to you? How did you feel? What did you do? Relate this to the story." "How did the author build excitement?"

6. Worksheet: "Use care in a sentence beginning with 'I.'" "In what ways are you careful of other people's feelings?"

RELATED ACTIVITIES — CHARTS /

1. Discuss other exciting stories about leadership. Children share their resources by printing their contributions on the chart.

2. Feel-Good chart — Each child is assigned a secret word (from the developmental vocabulary) and writes a good sentence using "I" or "me" and the name of another person in the class (e.g., "I feel *wonderful* when *Heather* chooses me."). They pin their sentences to the charts.

3. Sentence completion (verbal or written):
I am a good reader. I can _____.
_____ is a good reader. He can _____.
_____ or _____.
Teacher provides positive feedback: "I like the way you read that paragraph."

SUMMARY /

The objectives of this lesson, both affective and cognitive, are applicable to all reading lessons, although all of them need not be included in any one lesson.

24

A CONFLUENT APPROACH TO TEACHING *BEOWULF*

— *Margaret Harris*

The earliest major poem extant in English is *Beowulf,* an ancient saga of heroism, revenge, victory, and death, composed perhaps four hundred years before the Norman Conquest. These characteristics make *Beowulf* a formidable teaching challenge in high school, yet the aesthetic qualities and the historical interest of the poem merit, it seems to me, inclusion in a standard English literature course.

The problem is to guide students toward an understanding of the social and moral values involved in the poem, and to deepen their experience of an acknowledged masterpiece, while neither boring them to death with ancient history seemingly irrelevant to the twentieth century, nor abandoning the text altogether in search of relevance. To this end, some of the techniques of confluent education may be combined with traditional academic approaches to achieve a better understanding of the poem.

The Beowulf legend was first written down in the language of the Anglo-Saxons, but an excellent translation into modern English by Burton Raffel is available in paperback. Combined with the reading of this, I would include John Gardner's novel *Grendel. Grendel,* used as a supplementary text, can shed additional light on the poem, but the primary emphasis should be placed upon the Burton Raffel translation of the original story. Beowulf is a hero who faces and defeats a monster (Grendel), only to discover that the threat reappears in another form — the monster's mother, with whom Beowulf must fight a return engagement. Triumphant at last, Beowulf returns to his own people, but he is finally defeated when, as an old man, he is obliged by the demands of his position to fight a dragon.

Putting aside for a moment a discussion of the technical excellence and strikingly beautiful imagery of the poem, one good way to begin is to consider the situation of Beowulf about to do battle with a monster who is all the more frightening because he is mysterious. In *Beowulf* the poet never describes Grendel in detail; however, we learn that the monster has claws, that he is huge, that he tears warriors apart and drinks their blood ("blod edrum dranc," the Old English original says), and that all attempts to defeat him have failed. Beowulf is to fight Grendel alone and unarmed. "My hands alone shall fight for me, struggle for life against the monster," Beowulf declares.

Beowulf is an epic hero; that is, he embodies the qualities most admired by his people. He is a figure larger than life, a leader thirsty for glory, honorable, humorless, and stereotyped much in the same way that George Washington is stereotyped in the folklore of America. Yet, in another sense, Beowulf is smaller than life: his human qualities are lessened, because he cannot depart from his role as epic hero.

A deeper understanding of Beowulf's function in the poem might be realized through role-playing: Divide the class into dyads and ask each pair of students to decide who is to be Beowulf and who is to be Grendel. (Often it is useful for students to recall just how the decision was arrived at, to sort out who led, and who acquiesced in the decision.) "Grendel," after a moment's reflection to settle into his role, asks "Beowulf" what it is that he (Grendel) does for him. What would Beowulf be without a monster to fight? In searching for answers to "Beowulf's" question, "Grendel" may be better able to comprehend the function of a hero figure.

After some time has been spent in dyads, ask the students to regroup in a circle and share their responses to the questions. A general discussion can now take place to develop the idea further. Why is it necessary for Beowulf's success, or even his existence, as a hero to have a formidable adversary? Do events shape the man? How often do we allow ourselves to be cast into a rigid mode of behavior by what others seem to expect of us in certain situations? Hopefully, responses can be evoked from students that will be more meaningful to them because they have had a chance to play roles rather than to be told about the situation by the teacher.

A second affective exercise to follow up with is the "Johari Window." Draw a square on the chalkboard, or mark out areas on the floor of the classroom, and work as follows:

1. External appearances	2. Secret inner-self
3. What is seen by others, not by us	4. The unknown

This square may be regarded as a window with four panes. Through the first pane we see ourselves as public persons with the "face" we present to others. Through the second pane, we may see the self which is hidden from others, not revealed unless we are in exceptional circumstances of stress or self-revelation. Through the third pane, perhaps we may perceive some of our blind spots — characteristics visible to others but usually hidden from ourselves by instincts of self-protection. Finally, the fourth pane looks into the unknown, into the future. After explaining this to the class, ask students to become Beowulf — to close their eyes, put themselves inside Beowulf's skin, feel what he feels as much as they can. Beowulf is strong, and his exploits have made him famous; but he is, after all, merely a man. His appearance and reputation are described by the poet, and a reasonably careful reading will enable students to call to mind an image of Beowulf on the eve of battle.

Ask students about external appearances. How does Beowulf look?

How would he walk? What kind of clothing would he wear? (These questions are asked by the teacher, who does not expect an oral response immediately. Allow enough time for an image to form in the students' minds. Additionally, before this exercise takes place, and interspersed with the reading of the two texts, some short lectures ought to be given on Anglo-Saxon life, including illustrations of warriors' battle gear. Slides or pictures of the Sutton Hoo ship burial can be obtained from the British Museum.)

Now, ask students to move (physically or metaphorically) into pane two of the "window." Ask them what secrets Beowulf may have that nobody knows about. Are they (as Beowulf) scared, but keeping up a brave front? Remember that boasting is a pre-battle ritual in this society, and declaring a determination to win or to die trying stiffens a warrior's resolve. What *may* lie beneath the words? What do the role-players imagine may be going on inside Beowulf, where nobody can see?

From here, the role-players should move to pane four and think for a moment about the unknown. As Anglo-Saxons, they believe in "wyrd," the Old English word for fate, or destiny, from which the modern English word "weird" comes, since what is weird is mysterious and other-worldly. Life is harsh, death is ever-present, and no man feels secure or sure of the future; but nobility can be achieved by facing unflinchingly the destiny that lies ahead. How do the role-players feel about what fate has in store for them as Beowulf? (Having read the poem, the students know that Beowulf as an old man must die in killing the dragon.) Ask them to imagine that they are old, facing death, looking into the future. What emotions, what thoughts would pass through their minds at this point in the story?

This experience can be followed by either written or oral feedback, shared with the class if the students wish. A discussion might take place here on the question of free will. Beowulf says, "Fate will unwind as it must." How much control, then, does an Anglo-Saxon think he has over his own life? How large is the area in which he can regulate what happens to him? Do the students themselves feel they can control what happens in their own lives? To what degree?

Beowulf's first adversary, Grendel, is another point of departure in the understanding of the poem. After experiencing what it may have been like to be Beowulf, ask students to repeat the Johari Window exercise, this time in the role of Grendel. Ask them to close their eyes and concentrate silently, getting into the role of the misshapen outcast. What might they, as Grendel, look like to the warriors in the mead-hall? Is this picture different from the one Grendel would see if he looked into a mirror?

Ask students to imagine what secrets Grendel has that others do not know. How might he feel as he creeps up to Hrothgar's hall and listens to the sounds of feasting and merriment inside? Grendel is seemingly unable to communicate with men, but the Beowulf poet makes mention of the hatred Grendel feels when he hears human merrymaking. What does he think of the warriors? Are they, perhaps, as mysterious to him as he is to them?

After a moment to experience whatever it is that the students are imagining, ask them to move on, still in the role of Grendel, to the area in which they consider what aspects of Grendel might be seen by others, but not by Grendel himself. (The Beowulf poet writes about Grendel with a curious mixture of Christian morality and pagan mythology.) Are there other possibilities, other motivations, which the Anglo-Saxons perceive in Grendel, not understood by him? Now, ask the students to continue in the role of Grendel, but to move into the area of the unknown, stretching their imaginations and intuitions, finally creating a fourfold reincarnation of the monster.

A discussion of John Gardner's *Grendel* could follow here. Gardner's book presents the monster from a quite different point of view, since the whole novel is a kind of artistically expanded role-playing. It is written by the monster in the first person, telling his own story from his own point of view. It is an astonishing tour de force of the imagination and a beautiful complement to the study of the original poem.

The point of view from which a story is told correlates (as it must if literature is a valid expression of life) with the way we see ourselves and others in our own lives. To the warriors in *Beowulf*, Grendel is "the other," a nonperson, the devourer of men. We know, for example, that Grendel has arms and claws, that he is powerful enough to burst open the strongest doors, and that he walks upright. Some scholars postulate that Grendel may be the manifestation of a dim racial memory of the bears that ranged the forests of northern Europe where the Beowulf legend originated, and that the monster was later Christianized into a descendant of Cain.

However, Grendel, as created by John Gardner, is rather a pitiful, ridiculous figure. He grieves over his ugliness and his outcast state. "Pointless, ridiculous monster, crouched in the shadows, stinking of dead men, murdered children, martyred cows. I am neither proud nor ashamed," he mutters to himself. "One more dull victim, leering at seasons never meant to be observed." This Grendel is a thinking creature, trying to make sense of the universe. He listens to the scop in the mead-hall, the Shaper spinning tales of heroes and glorious deeds, but he cannot bring himself to believe these stories. He sees the Anglo-Saxons as fools, hypocrites, war-mad men in search of glory. "I'd meant them no harm," he says, "but they attacked me again, as always. They were crazy."

From the exploration of the differing points of view possible, an appreciation of the technical skill of the Beowulf poet should be afforded, and this can best be done by reproducing a few lines in the original Old English. The following are the last three lines of the poem:

> Cwædon thæt he wære wyruldcyninga
> Manna mildust ond monthwærust
> Leodum lithost ond lofgeornost.

Readings on records or tapes are available, but there is probably no substitute for the living presence of a teacher who has taken the trouble to master the pronunciation and cadence of a few lines and can say them to the class. Ask the students if they can spot any words which sound like modern English (for example, *and* and *that* haven't changed much); but in general, Old English is a foreign language, highly inflected and beautifully expressive, structurally more akin to German than to present-day English.

The chanting, in unison, of these or other lines in the ancestral language of modern English can be a good, affective experience, involving both emotions and physical participation. This kind of poetry, more so than most, if brought to life by the voice can have an effect on students. It was meant to be chanted to the rhythmical accompaniment of a harp, and the teacher who can bring to the classroom a guitar or a lute to accompany the chant can perhaps re-create the hypnotic effect of the original poem. Furthermore, chanting in the original language is a sound academic practice; it is a good way to demonstrate the rhythm of the regular four strong beats in each line, and to hear the beauty of the alliteration which ties the words together, in the absence of rhyme — in short, to actually hear how this kind of poetry worked. Students might choose to memorize a few lines, and further, to compose a short poem of their own, using the same poetic devices. Any topic will serve, and what follows is a rendition by John H. Duffin, who uses the Anglo-Saxon poetic technique to comment on President Nixon's problems:

BEETLEWOLF

To Hrichard was given great anguish and grief,
Problems perplexing; with prices and profits
He struggled and strove. Of monies and meanies
His worries grew worse. The dollar devalued drew
Conflict and critics; his game plans and gold ploys
Wrought wrong in all ways. Both merchants and marksmen
With yen and with yearning did wheedle and whine.

Dark days then befell him, for freeze-foes
From far and from near said nix on his notions.
Then Ralph the relentless, the raider crusader
Came quickly to quell. The fearless fraud-foe
Slew the slug-bug; the beetle he blasted
With blistering bane. He had crushed the corvairs
And punished the plunderers, so slaughtered he swiftly
The import important. Then flowed free the fords
And fountains in general; motors took motion once more.

So brave Beetlewolf did save and did solve
Poor Hrichard's infernal inflation affliction.

The foregoing suggestions do not, of course, encompass all that can be done with the Beowulf poem. Like any true masterpiece, it is a rich vein of treasure that can be mined in many ways. What I have suggested is a combination of academic and affective experiences that, with persistence and luck, may serve to enrich and deepen students' appreciation of a traditional part of English literature.

25

WRITING AND THE RED RUBBER BALL
— David N. McCarthy

In Thomas Berger's novel *Little Big Man*, the Cheyenne chief remarks:

> The Human Beings believe that everything is alive: not only men and animals but also water and earth and stones, and also dead things from them, like this hair. . . . But white men believe that everything is dead: stones, earth, animals, and people, even their own people. And if, in spite of that, things persist in trying to live, white men will rub them out. . . . That is the difference between white men and Human Beings.

This difference is manifested in our use of language. Man created language as a symbol system to be used in communicating with other men. It seems certain that the first written language was pictographic. Within such a framework, the symbol and the object or idea it represented were much alike. The formula that picture equals object implied that written language immediately recreated experience. This was especially true before such pictographs became somewhat standardized. Thus, I could tell you about my hunting of the antelope by drawing a symbol of *my* antelope, the animal derived from my own experience.

Man created language to free himself. But as the symbols became more abstract, and also more "efficient," man became frozen into his own words. Language which was initially intended to describe what he saw and experienced, came to limit him to see and experience only what could be described. Generalization and abstraction separate us from the immediacy of experience. Classifying experience into preconceived categories limits perception. Once a child sees a plaything as "red ball," it becomes a *thing* to be used. With this act of "pure" cognition, the child now rolls the ball, not *numerous* times for the spontaneous delight of seeing it roll, but *once*, to confirm his knowledge that balls roll. Thus does abstraction and generalization impede the creative imagination of us all. This "tyranny of language" need not be so; it is the purpose of the following curriculum pieces to suggest ways in which developing the ability to use language can be accompanied by developing the ability to see and feel.

Approaches to teaching writing are generally structural. They begin by describing what elements go into a good sentence, paragraph, and essay. They point out "things," such as topic sentence, paragraph unity, transition, conclusion, etc. Like the definition: "This is a red rubber ball; it bounces and it rolls," they begin by delineating the categories. Rather than encouraging the student to describe what he experiences, they limit him to experiencing only what can be described within the framework outlined. I don't mean to imply that I'm against order and structure in writing, but simply that the traditional approach is essentially backwards. If you will accept my thesis that "learning is a process of self-actualization," you will realize that learning to write, like learning to do anything else, needs to begin with immediate experience in the learner. By starting with the self and moving outward, by starting with an awakening of his own perceptions, the student can use language to articulate his experiences of more and more of the world.

LESSON ONE: FREE WRITING EXERCISE USING ANIMAL FANCY (AARON HILLMAN) /

I. Fantasy

1. Students are asked to assume a relaxed, comfortable, eyes-closed position and, through a standard procedure, encouraged to empty their bodies and minds of resistances.
2. They are asked to imagine, in sequence, the person they hate most, love most, and themselves. They are asked to imagine an animal counterpart for each person, and then asked to write down each animal, preceded by an adjective or two.

3. During three consecutive fantasy exercises, they are asked to imagine a large forest surrounding a field. They are asked to get in touch with the sounds, smells, and touch of forest and field, and then asked to imagine an encounter in the field between:

   a. The animal which is the person they love most and the animal which is the person they hate most.
   b. The animal which is the person they love most and the animal which is themselves.
   c. The animal which is the person they hate most and the animal which is themselves.

II. Writing

After each fantasy students are asked to write freely about whatever experience they have had. They are told that the writing is personal, and not to be handed in.

III. Discussion

1. Small-group or open-class sharing of exercises of this nature depends on the risk level which the class is ready for. After students have had an opportunity to share their fantasies, the instructor might (and again this depends on class readiness) pose questions like, "What did you experience when the animal you loved met the animal you hated?" etc. If the class does not wish to discuss their feelings, such questions might be suggested anyway for private reflection.

2. If the substance of the fantasies are not opened to discussion, the instructor might pose questions like, "How did you experience this writing process? Was it easy or difficult for you? Did you see long or short sentences? Many commas?" etc.

3. This kind of discussion can lead directly to the formal aspects of commas, long sentences, etc.

IV. *Journal*

Students are asked to write in their journals any thoughts related to this exercise. They are asked to focus on the question, "What did I learn about myself?"

Other "free writing" fantasies are similarly useful. For example, the "self now" and "self in ten years" can deal with the questions of "What am I doing now to get to where I would like to be in ten years?" or "How do I prevent myself from becoming my ten-year ideal?"

Pedagogical Significance: Lesson One

1. BLOCKAGES AND CONCERNS

Usually the student comes to his writing experience with blockages such as "I can't write," "I hate writing," or "I don't know what to write about." Traditional answers are (and many times are merely implied): "Maybe you can't write, but that's the object of this course — to teach you." "You may hate writing, but that's because it's difficult, and usually it's the difficult things that are best for us." "Don't worry about having nothing to write about. Read this fascinating and provocative essay about drugs and teenage abortion. It should interest you. Then you will have some ideas. But remember first of all to structure those ideas: paragraph unity, topic sentence. . . ." Notice how these "solutions" not only deride the student, but allow him to manipulate the environment.

In contradistinction, this and other fantasy free-writing exercises channel that energy the student is using to resist into a positive direction. He finds he has something to write about, because he is writing about himself. He not only has something to write about, but he has something that is personally relevant; indeed, a fantasy is purely himself. Finally, the experience of actually writing about something interesting extends the student's ego boundaries to make the strange (writing) familiar. His "hate" will gradually diminish.

2. AFFECTIVE LOADINGS

a. Orientation Loadings

First of all, most people have a positive orientation toward daydreaming, especially in the classroom. By asking them to fantasize, you are asking them to do what they would like to do, but have been discouraged from doing throughout their schooling. By combining whatever energy is being used to resist daydreaming with that energy available for regular classwork, it would seem that the whole student is going in one direction. Secondly, if the fantasy has been a meaningful one, the act of articulating that fantasy will, in itself, engender the flow of words. As the words begin flowing, an incomplete gestalt is created. Thus, the student will have an emotional investment and a positive orientation toward the writing exercise.

b. Engagement Loadings

The student is participating in a writing experience which is personally relevant. He is articulating one of the purest forms of existential messages about himself. Being and knowing are brought together in confluence.

c. Accomplishment Loadings

The student realizes that he can indeed write, and that what he writes has meaning to himself. His diary entry, if it involves insight, will be especially meaningful in this respect. Finally, accomplishment loadings carry over into helping resolve blockages for the next writing he will do. He is discovering that language can be used for self-discovery.

LESSON TWO: SEEING /

I. Slides

1. Students are asked to look at, and react to, a series of stylistically very different paintings: Van Gogh, Turner, Poussin, De Chirico, etc. In each case the discussion centers about what kinds of feelings the slides engender.
2. Students are shown a slide of a modern photograph of perhaps

a ghetto, a battlefield, a party, etc. The photograph should be visually stimulating and lend itself to varied interpretations.

II. *Writing: Pictures to words*

Students are asked to spend five minutes writing their reactions to this photograph, beginning each sentence with "I see" or "I feel."

III. *Discussion*

Students work in small groups, discussing what they saw and felt about the picture. Discussion centers around the question, "How much of what I see is determined by what I am?"

IV. *Writing: Words to pictures to words*

Students are given, orally, a series of emotionally charged and figurative words, phrases and sentences for example: pig and hippie; cool cat; get off my back; the mountain glowered at them and the silent snow dared them to attempt its summit; man, what a set of wheels; she ironed out all the bottlenecks. In each case students are asked to write one or two sentences describing the image which such figurative language created.

V. *Discussion*

Small groups have formed in which students discuss their sentences. Discussion centers around the statement: "How we react to words tells us about who we are."

VI. *Journal*

Journal entries deal with reactions to classwork. Again the question considered is "What have I learned about myself and how I see?"

VII. *Essay*

Students are told to go to some place unfamiliar to them and write about what they see. Sentences must begin with either "I see" or "I feel," and the essay must continue in the present tense.

LESSON THREE: HEARING /

I. Sounds to words: Discussion

1. Students are asked to read slowly to themselves phrases such as the following, and to be aware of what they are hearing: bang, bang, bang; Lucy in the sky with diamonds; everybody must get stoned; ladies and gentlemen; Mary had a little lamb.

2. Small group discussions center around questions: "How did I hear? Could I hear without also seeing? How does what I read and saw tell me about myself?"

II. Sounds to words: Writing

1. Students are asked to assume an eyes-closed, relaxed position, and to concentrate on a piece of music. They are asked simply to let images flow naturally into them. The symphonic poem or other pictorial music is best: Rimski-Korsakov, Smetana, Debussy, Borodin, and others.

2. Students are asked to spend five minutes writing the thoughts and images which came to them during the listening.

3. Discussion: A sharing of experience focuses around the questions "How do we hear?" and "How does what we hear tell us about ourselves?"

III. Words to sounds: Role-playing

1. Students are asked to read silently a set of short public speeches by Malcolm X, George Wallace, Gloria Steinem, and Spiro Agnew.

2. Anyone who wishes may read aloud one or more of the speeches, using the tone of voice and gestures he thinks appropriate. Persons who disagree with readings may do the readings in their own style.

3. Discussion: "How much of what you heard in these speeches was determined by knowing who the writers were? How much was determined by how the words fit together? Is what we hear determined by our preconceptions?"

IV. *Journal*

Students are asked to articulate their reactions and responses to the class exercises, and to focus again on the idea of "What have I learned about myself?"

V. *Essay*

Students are told to go to a place unfamiliar to them, such as a bus depot, and write an essay about what they hear. Each sentence must begin with "I hear" or "I see."

Pedagogical Significance: Lessons Two and Three

Again, as in the case with the free-writing fantasy exercise, we are dealing with the "I hate, I can't, I don't know" blockages by giving the student something to write which is based on personal experience in the now. In fact, the whole term "write about" implies a subject-object split which these exercises undercut. The student is, more correctly, "expressing him*self*." To return to our metaphor of the red rubber ball, the student is not making generalized abstractions; rather, he is expressing his spontaneous involvement with it. Affective loadings are, I think, similar to those of Lesson One.

CONCLUSION /

These lessons can be continued, to include the senses of smelling, tasting, and touching. At appropriate points, as suggested in the first lesson, the instructor can make connections with the more formal aspects of writing such as paragraphing and organization. It is much more meaningful to talk about paragraphs after the student has written some. Then you are discussing *his* paragraphs, not some generalized model. It is similarly necessary to deal with argumentative and other discursive forms of writing, and appropriate affective exercises are useful in these areas, also. But by beginning with the student's personal, imaginative, and emotional responses, and working outward from there, we allow him to endow his language with the immediacy which it deserves. Language becomes a vehicle for self-expression and self-discovery. It widens instead of limits perception.

26

LISTENING TO THE BOOK

— Jean Schleifer

1. Close your eyes. Get into your own private space. Now — from the book you read, try to see the person who means the most to you. Put the person somewhere, either in a place he would naturally be according to the book or a place where you can imagine his being. Try to see every part of the person. What does the hair look like? What color? Length? Curly? Straight? Windblown? Neat? Notice the ears. What kind of nose? Notice the skin. Clear, pimply, tanned? How do you see the mouth? Full? Drooped? Clenched? What is the person doing with the hands? How does the person stand? Walk? What kind of clothes? See them distinctly — the colors, the style, etc.
2. When you are ready, open your eyes. Write a description of your person's appearance.
3. Choose one word from what you have written that is the essence of the description of the person. Write it down.
4. Now write down what to you would be an opposite word — *one* word.
5. Tell your words. Talk about them.
6. Turn your paper over. Draw, in lines or colors, the way you see the person. Don't try to draw a photographic picture. Show the person through shapes, colors, and lines. Talk to others.
7. Close your eyes. Go back to the place where you saw your person. See if you can get into the person's skin. Look around you. From within that person see the place — see every part of it. If you're in a room, lying in bed, for instance, what does your bed look like? The sheets? The blankets? Anything around you? The rug?

Walls? The pin on the table? Be aware of each tiny thing around you.

8. Write what you saw from inside the skin of your person.
9. Write down one word that best fits the description.
10. Write an opposite word.
11. Tell your words.
12. Turn your paper over and show, in lines or colors, how the place feels to you.
13. Talk about the book with people who also read it, or with others if you like.
14. Class feedback.
15. Close your eyes. Get into your own space. Go back to the place you were in as the person you became from your book. Feel yourself in that place. See it. See it as the person. As that person, do whatever you want to. If someone else comes into the picture, fine. Do something with that person.
16. Write what happened.
17. Write one word that describes the action.
18. Write the opposite word.
19. Talk to your group.
20. Use lines or colors to show how you see the action.
21. Talk to your group.
22. Class feedback.
23. Close your eyes. Become that person again. Be in the same place or a different one, if you like. Look like that person. Sit or stand like the person. Make your mouth be like the person's. Feel the way that person feels. Think about some of the things you've done. The people you know. Choose one person. How do you feel about that person? What are you like inside? What is your problem?
24. Write what just happened. How you feel, what you're like inside as that person whose skin you got into.
25. Choose one word that describes you as that person. Write it.
26. Write an opposite word.
27. Use lines or colors to show yourself as that person.
28. Talk to your group.

29. Class feedback.
30. List each one of the words you have written down as the essence of each description you've done. (Eight of them.)
31. Write a poem using the eight words.
32. Write any other thoughts and feelings that come to you about yourself as the person, yourself as you are, etc.
33. Write an evaluation of your writing, drawings, feelings, thinking, talking with your group, and class discussion on this exercise. Do you think you learned more about the person in the book, yourself, and others in the class? Why?
34. Class feedback.

27

THE CANTERBURY TALES FOR HIGH-SCHOOL STUDENTS

— *Susan Wiltsey*

Materials Needed:

The Canterbury Tales:

The Prologue
The Knight's Tale
The Miller's Prologue and Tale
The Reeve's Prologue and Tale
The Prologue to the Monk's Tale
The Nun's Priest's Prologue and Tale
The Wife of Bath's Prologue and Tale
The Clerk's Prologue and Tale
The Pardoner's Prologue and Tale

J. Huizinga, *The Waning of the Middle Ages.* (Suggested for bright students only.)

Journals for everyone in the class

What follows are activities for thirty-eight days for the use of high-school students studying *The Canterbury Tales.* A teacher can follow the activities as outlined, or he can change or omit some, change the suggested order, or use my ideas to create some activities of his own. Hopefully, any teacher using this unit will integrate it with his own teaching style and personality, and adapt it to his particular class of students, thereby coming up with his confluent *The Canterbury Tales.*

FIRST AND SECOND DAYS /

The first two days are spent discovering what the students and teacher know and feel about the Middle Ages. The students are asked what they think of when they hear "Middle Ages." Their answers are put on the board. The teacher then directs discussion about various items such as knights, armor, the Black Death, the church, pilgrimages. The teacher should make sure that most of the main events, feelings, and ideas about the Middle Ages are covered. This will give students a basic introduction to the age. *Note:* If the students are reading *The Canterbury Tales* in Middle English, it is a good idea for the teacher to spend two more days introducing the language so that the students can begin reading the text with some understanding. I am assuming, however, that most high-school students read *The Canterbury Tales* in translation.

Assignment: Read the introduction to *The Canterbury Tales* and begin reading the Prologue.

THIRD DAY /

Have the students sit in circles of ten to fifteen. Ask them to close their eyes and imagine what it was like to live in the Middle Ages. Imagine the corruption, the anxiety. Think of what caused the anxiety. Feel it, if you can. Imagine the highly organized and formalized society — the intense order of things. Imagine yourself a man on top of the scale. What is it like? How do you feel? Imagine yourself a man on the bottom of the scale. Now a woman on the top of the scale. Does it feel different from being a man? Imagine yourself a woman on the bottom of the scale. Imagine and feel the fear of death. The fear of death is with you all the time. If you can, get up out of your chair and move with that fear. How do you move? Can you move? Your life is temporal; it does not last long. Your life may be snuffed out at any time. How will you plan for life after death? What about indulgence? How do you feel about indulgences? Can you show by movement? Now, imagine the Black Death coming. It has hit the town next to you and is coming nearer and nearer to your town. It is sure to come there next. What can you do?

Have the students stop, sit down, and discuss their feelings; or if they wish, have them write in their journal. Stress how all these feelings were with the people of the Middle Ages all the time. There was no escaping them.

FOURTH DAY /

Ask the students if they would like to play "The Killer Game." The game is played as follows: Playing cards or numbered slips are passed to students in a circle of chairs or seated on the floor. One student is identified as "the killer" by a specific playing card or numbered slip (as agreed upon beforehand). If ten or more students are playing, the intensity is increased if two or three "killers" are used. The player who is "the killer" looks into the eyes of the other players and winks, signaling that the one winked at is killed and is out of the game. The rest of the players guess by close observation which player is "the killer." When a player is reasonably certain he knows who "the killer" is, he must gain the support of one other player to make the accusation. If he gains support and his accusation is correct, the "killer" is eliminated. If he is wrong, both he and his supporter are out of the game. If cards are used, any eliminated player turns his card over for all to see, thus enabling players in and out of the game to see who is. If the group playing is large, they may stand and mill around, and when a player is "killed" he sits down.

In playing this game, students look closely at one another, and get to know each other better, as they alternately work with and against each other and enjoy human interaction. Hopefully, too, they will feel the sense of approaching death and the fear and dread of someone being after them. These feelings should be relatively strong if the game is played five or six times in succession.

After they finish the game, ask them whether their feelings were analogous to their feelings yesterday when they closed their eyes and imagined living in the Middle Ages.

FIFTH DAY /

1. In a circle (or circles, if there are more than fifteen students), have students close their eyes and imagine a pilgrimage. What would it be like? Why would you go? Of all the people you know or know about, with whom would you like to go? Just think about it, now — think of all the possible reasons why you might go on a pilgrimage and where you would go, and think of all the people who could go with you. You can write your ideas down if you wish.

Have a discussion on why each person would go, where they would go, and with whom they would like to go. Make a list on the board of the types of people — how many relationships (boyfriends, girl-friends, parents), age groups, professions. Would different kinds of people be advantageous or not? Why might you want a doctor to go along?

2. In the remaining time, the teacher can begin a discussion of the Prologue. (By this time, the students should have finished reading the Prologue, and if not, hopefully today's activities will interest them enough to get to it.) Answer any questions about the Prologue or specific pilgrims. Ask students what they felt about the various pilgrims. Would they include any of them in their own pilgrimages?

Assignment: Finish reading the Prologue.

SIXTH DAY /

The teacher leads a discussion about the Canterbury pilgrims, but before the discussion begins, each student should choose a pilgrim to portray for that day. Each student should try to keep in character and respond to the teacher and other students as if he really were that pilgrim. This exercise can be repeated a few times throughout the course as the tales are discussed.

At the end of the period, ask students to turn to their neighbors and have a conversation in character. The Miller might meet the Wife of Bath for the first time. Have the students talk to as many different people as time permits.

Assignment: Write in journals about today's activities.

SEVENTH DAY /

1. Have a discussion between characters (played by students) on assigned topics. For example: Ask the Monk and the Prioress to discuss freedom; ask the Pardoner and the Miller to discuss love. This should be done with one couple at a time and in the front of the room. Let the students choose their own discussion topics if they wish.

2. Role-Playing Relating Game — Ask one student to choose a character to be and to go to the front of the room and pantomime an activity. Other students choose other characters to be, and go to the front one at a time and relate to the person or persons already there. For example: One student is the Clerk and sits in the front of the room reading; a student playing the Miller goes up to him and slaps him on the back and asks him if he wants a drink of beer; then a student playing the Pardoner goes to the front and tries to sell them both pardons. Another example is to ask a student to play Chaucer and ask other students to play pilgrims. The pilgrims must go up to Chaucer one at a time and tell him why they want to go on the pilgrimage. Chaucer can be very picky if he wants to be.

This "Role-Playing Relating Game" can be repeated with the characters of the tales.

EIGHTH DAY /

With the inner-outer circle technique of observation, one group sits in an inner circle discussing something while a second group sits in an outer circle around them. Each person in the outer circle chooses a person in the inner circle to observe while the discussion is in progress. When the discussion is over, the observers discuss with the observed what they saw.

Using the inner-outer circle, ask students to portray people living in the Middle Ages and have a discussion about their lives. Start with the inner circle as high-class, status people, and individuals in the outer circle watching individuals in the inner circle. After five minutes of discussion, let the observer and the observed from the outer and inner circles get together and talk. Then, ask the circles to change places, with the new inner circles playing middle-class people discussing their lives. If time permits, switch one more time with the inner circle playing low-class people.

The discussion between people of various classes should help the students to understand the class society and the differences and similarities between classes. Tying the discussion in with the inner-outer circle gives the students a chance to become closer to each other, practice close observation, and give their fellow students feedback on how they look, talk, and relate to others.

NINTH DAY /

Journal-writing in class. Use your imagination and answer the following questions: (1) You (each individual student) have just met the Knight on a street corner. How do you feel about him? How do you relate? (2) You have just met the Miller in a field and he has come over to talk to you. He wants to get acquainted. How do you feel? (3) Which character would you most like to travel with? Why? (4) Based on their personalities, what kind of stories do you think the Knight and the Miller might tell? Give some examples.

Assignment: Begin reading The Knight's Tale.

TENTH AND ELEVENTH DAYS — THE KNIGHT'S TALE /

Spend two days discussing The Knight's Tale, chivalry, and the courtly love tradition. Help the students to understand what happens in the story and its relation to chivalry and courtly love.

TWELFTH DAY /

Ask the students to draw a picture showing chivalry or courtly love. What is important is their conception, expressed in any way they desire. When they are finished, have them exchange papers and see if they can find out anything new about chivalry, courtly love, or the person who did the drawing.

THIRTEENTH DAY /

1. There is a game called "You've got it — I want it" in which "it" is never explained. Ask two boys to come to the front of the room and give them the information that one wants it, and the other has it and won't give it away. Have them see what they can do.

Now change the game, making a girl "it." Both boys want to marry her, and she won't marry either of them. Have the three people work it out.

Afterward discuss the games with the class. Ask them what the two games have to do with The Knight's Tale. Discuss frustration and wanting something you cannot have.

2. (a) Ask two boys to act out Arcite's and Palamon's suffering. Have the class decide who is worse off at the end of Part One, and at the end of the story. (b) Ask a girl to portray Emily during the final battle between Arcite and Palamon. Ask her to describe her feelings.

FOURTEENTH DAY /

Have a discussion about freedom in the story. Who was free to do what he or she wanted to do? Who exercised the most freedom? Who the least? Compare freedom then to freedom now.

Assignment: Begin reading The Miller's Prologue and Tale.

FIFTEENTH DAY — THE MILLER'S
PROLOGUE AND TALE /

Introduce The Miller's Tale by talking about the Miller, his state before he began telling his tale, and his conflict with the Reeve. Try to get across the "drama" of the happening. Then, give the students the rest of the class period to finish reading the tale.

SIXTEENTH DAY /

1. Discuss the men in The Miller's Tale. What makes John, Nickolas, and Absolom alike? Different? What kind of comedy does

all their activity remind you of? Which Hollywood actors could play these roles?

2. Ask a boy to play the role of Nickolas and tell the class what he did to John. Have John tell his version of the story.

3. Read the description of Alison. How does she compare to Emily of The Knight's Tale?

4. Ask two girls to play Emily and Alison and to have a discussion about men. Send in Nickolas, then Arcite, to talk to them.

5. Ask a boy to role-play Nickolas and tell a boy playing Arcite all about the great Alison.

SEVENTEENTH DAY /

1. Put the girls in a discussion group and ask them to decide what would be good and bad about being Alison and Emily. Decide who is better off.

2. Put the boys in a discussion group and ask them to decide what would be good and bad about being Arcite, Palamon, Nickolas, Absolom, and John. Decide who is the best off.

3. Or, have the students write in their journals on the above questions.

Assignment: Read The Reeve's Prologue and Tale.

EIGHTEENTH DAY — THE REEVE'S
PROLOGUE AND TALE /

1. Ask a girl to role-play the Prioress and to tell how she reacted to the fight between the Miller and the Reeve. Ask a girl to role-play the Wife of Bath and tell how she reacted.

2. Ask five people to role-play the characters in the story — John, Allen, the Miller, the Wife, the Daughter. Have the rest of the class interview them, asking them questions about themselves.

NINETEENTH DAY /

1. Ask a student to play the Miller and to tell The Reeve's Tale from his own point of view. (Choose the student the day before so he will have time to think it out.)

2. Discuss both tales and tellers, letting the students discover Chaucer's artistry in adapting a story to a particular teller.

3. Talk about how people tell tales that they like. What happens when they're telling a tale they don't like or when they don't like a particular character? What happens when a person tells a tale about himself?

TWENTIETH DAY /

Journal-writing in class. Ask the students to pretend they are different pilgrims and to respond to the three tales read so far. Which tales did they like and which tales did they dislike?

TWENTY-FIRST DAY — THE PROLOGUE
TO THE MONK'S TALE /

1. Read aloud The Prologue to the Monk's Tale. Ask students, "Are you surprised at what the host said about the Monk?"

2. Ask a student to play the Monk and tell the rest of the class how he felt about what the Host said. Have him pretend he is talking to one of his superiors, and then pretend he is just talking to himself.

3. Explain to the student who is role-playing the Monk the Gestalt topdog/underdog concept; i.e., everybody has two sides to his personality — a topdog and an underdog. The topdog is the "should" part, the aggressive, the forceful, the ambitious self. The underdog is the "want to," lazy, "who cares" self which is usually trampled upon by the topdog.

6. Let the Monk talk to his topdog, then to his underdog.

7. If students are interested, have them play the topdog/underdog game with other characters.

8. Briefly talk about The Monk's Tale. It is too long for the class to read, but students should know the type of tale the Monk told.
Assignment: Read The Nun's Priest's Prologue and Tale.

TWENTY-SECOND — THE NUN'S PRIEST'S PROLOGUE AND TALE /

Talk about The Nun's Priest's Tale, helping the students to understand the tale. Help them discover why it has been called, "the greatest chicken joke in the language." Discuss Chanticleer's problem and solution. Talk about the Nun's Priest — what does the reader know about him?

TWENTY-THIRD DAY /

Role-playing. Ask students to think up a problem, then attempt to get out of it by telling one story after another. For example: A boy wishes to convince his parents that he needs a car; have him role-play and try to convince his parents by telling one story after another. Ask two other students to role-play parents and do the same thing. Talk about what all this has to do with The Nun's Priest's Tale.

TWENTY-FOURTH DAY /

There is a game called "Bomb Shelter." In this game players role-play ten different character types who are confined to a bomb shelter. They are told that they must get rid of three people in order to survive. They must decide whom they can do without.

Adapting this game to *The Canterbury Tales,* have students get into the three social class groups — the high status class, the middle class, the lower class — with each student choosing a particular Canterbury character to be. Tell each group that they must get rid of two people. (Don't tell them this until after they have chosen their group and character.) After each group has chosen two, the choices should be discussed by the entire class. Then, of the ones that are allowed to remain in the bomb shelter, tell them three more must be asked to leave. Ask the students to keep throwing characters out until only one remains.

In the discussion following the game, ask them if the first person to be asked to leave is any lesser a person than the last person to be asked to leave. What qualities make a person desirable in a survival situation? What qualities in general make a good person?

Assignment: Read The Wife of Bath's Prologue.

TWENTY-FIFTH DAY — THE WIFE OF BATH'S PROLOGUE /

Before any discussion of the Wife of Bath's Prologue ask the students to sit on the floor in groups of ten and each draw a picture of the Wife of Bath's problem. When they are finished, ask them to exchange papers, interpret the problem, and decide on a solution. The interpretations and solutions should be given orally to the small groups, followed by discussion. This "drawing of problems" could be used for other characters as well.

TWENTY-SIXTH DAY /

Discuss the Wife of Bath's problem. Discussion and reading of the prologue.

TWENTY-SEVENTH DAY /

1. Have a member of Women's Liberation come to talk to the class. Compare her comments and attitudes with the Wife of Bath's.

2. If the member of Women's Liberation is willing, ask a student to role-play the Wife of Bath and have a conversation with the Women's Liberation member.

Assignment: Read The Wife of Bath's Tale.

TWENTY-EIGHTH DAY /

1. Discuss The Wife of Bath's Tale. How does this tale fit with the Wife of Bath's philosophy? How do the boys, especially, feel about such a philosophy?

2. *Writing Assignment* (a) What kind of president and military

general would the Wife of Bath make? (b) Write an imaginary conversation between the Wife of Bath and her daughter on "life."

TWENTY-NINTH DAY /

1. Ask one student to role-play the Wife of Bath, one to play Emily of The Knight's Tale, and one to play the Prioress. The three ladies have just met at a tea. Have a conversation.

2. Have the men on the pilgrimage (role-played by boys in the class) tell the Wife of Bath (role-played by a girl) what they think of her. She may respond to them, deciding which one she would like for a sixth husband.

Assignment: Read The Clerk's Prologue.

THIRTIETH DAY /

Read and discuss The Clerk's Tale in class. (a) Compare Griselda's, Walter's, and the townspeople's attitudes toward others. Which attitude is the most realistic in your opinion? (b) Compare Griselda with the Wife of Bath. (c) Why might the Clerk tell such a tale?

THIRTY-FIRST DAY /

Role-playing: (a) Have the pilgrims interview Griselda, Walter, and a representative of the townspeople. (b) Have a discussion between the Wife of Bath and Griselda about women. (c) Have a debate on womanhood between the Clerk and the Wife of Bath.

THIRTY-SECOND DAY /

1. Have a Discussion about Abraham and Isaac and Job, and compare the Bible stories with the tale of Walter and Griselda.

2. Open discussion of "testing" people and things. Is it necessary? How about constancy? Does that need to be tested? Is it possible?

3. Writing exercise. Which characters really liked The Clerk's Tale and which characters did not, in your opinion?

Assignment: Read The Pardoner's Prologue.

THIRTY-THIRD DAY — THE PARDONER'S PROLOGUE /

1. Read parts of The Pardoner's Prologue aloud and talk about penance.

2. Ask students to close their eyes and imagine the fear of temporal and eternal punishment. Then have them draw pictures of what it would be like never to buy indulgence and therefore be assured of temporal and eternal punishment.

Assignment: Read The Pardoner's Tale.

THIRTY-FOURTH DAY /

1. Discuss The Pardoner's Tale. Discuss the Pardoner himself. How does he differ from the other pilgrims? How is he the same? How does his tale differ from those of other pilgrims? Why did he tell his tale, in your opinion?

2. Role-playing — (a) Have various pilgrims, such as the Knight, the Prioress, the Miller, and the Host tell how they feel about The Pardoner's Prologue and Tale. How did they react to him and what he said? (b) Have a student role-play the Pardoner and go to confession after the pilgrimage. What is he going to say about what he told the pilgrims? Did he think he was telling the pilgrims what they wanted to hear?

THIRTY-FIFTH DAY /

1. Draw a life map for the Pardoner, or for any other pilgrim or character in a tale. A life map is like a road map, telling what things have happened from birth to the present.

2. Writing exercise. Do you know someone who is a modern counterpart of the Pardoner? Of any other pilgrim?

THIRTY-SIXTH DAY /

Now that the class knows and trusts each other quite well, they should be able to do this exercise. Have them decide to which of the three categories — high status, middle class, low class — each person in the class belongs, according to how they act, not according to how much money they have. If possible, have the class assign each person a particular Canterbury character. Tell each person how many votes he received for each class and particular character.

THIRTY-SEVENTH DAY /

As a concluding activity, have the class take a trip together, riding or walking, and have each person tell a tale. It would be interesting if the tales were autobiographical, but the students could tell tales they have heard from others. After the group returns, have each student write up another student's portrait and tale. You will then have your own Canterbury Tales.

THIRTY-EIGHTH DAY OR LATER /

1. After the portraits and tales have been written up, have another discussion about the Middle Ages and Chaucer. How do the Middle Ages compare with today?

2. Role-Playing. (a) Have a man from the thirteenth century have a discussion with a man from the twentieth century about people. (b) Have a student discuss "the class Pilgrimage" with a student role-playing Chaucer.

28

THE PLAY'S THE THING —
A QUARTER-COURSE OUTLINE

— Aaron Hillman

MEMORANDUM FOR STUDENTS

COURSE TITLE /

The Play's the Thing

Description

A course is dramatic communications. It is a look at what has
happened to us (difficulties in the understanding of language and
relationships among people) and what such experiences mean to us
now and for our personal future. We will re-create experiences through
use of drama. Individuals who feel they have specific language or
communications problems are encouraged to enroll.

Insufficient attention is given to developing each individual's communications skills. What results is some ability to absorb knowledge
but insufficient ability to make oneself clear. The lack of clarity in
communications interferes with further educational goals and relationships of the person with other people and life. Work is needed
to understand and use the entire process of organization of thoughts
for transmission, their transmission, and receiving with clarity the
transmission of others. The course is not intended or designed for
theater arts students. Students with communications problems, reading problems, or cognitive skill problems are encouraged to participate in the work.

Primary Texts for Dramatization

Jerome Lawrence and Robert E. Lee   *Inherit the Wind*
Arthur Miller   *The Crucible*
Archibald MacLeish   *J.B.*

Suggested Texts for Enrichment

S. I. Hayakawa   *Language in Thought and Action*
Marshall McLuhan   *Understanding Media*
Viola Spolin   *Improvisation for the Theater*

Goals and Objectives

In the process of your learning in this course, the teacher would like you to consider the following goals and objectives:

1. Studying the many uses of language: language as a "purr," as a "snarl," language used to inform, to express emotion, to check lines of communication.

2. Developing each individual's communications skills so as to make himself clear.

3. Learning the techniques and skills of improvisational theater as they apply to individual communications.

4. Exploring drama and its meaning through dramatic reading and the sense of its affective content.

5. Understanding the techniques of clarity, oral and improvisatory, their necessity, and applications to existence.

6. Organizing thoughts for purposes of transmission, and the transmission of those thoughts.

7. Becoming aware of the differences in sense perceptions, and the problems in meaning or understanding that are created.

8. Identifying breakdowns in modern communications and the role of general semantics in people's lives.

9. Acquiring a sense of taste for the reading and acting out of drama, as well as the knowledge inherent in drama.

10. Improving reading, speaking, thinking, and the use of language by verbal and nonverbal means.

Activities

The primary focus of the course will be the reading of dramatic works and the use of the techniques of improvisational theater. It will not be a theater arts course, but is designed to assist any individual in learning and establishing communication skills while enjoying drama. The course is primarily one of personal involvement. Through drama, problems will be explored and experienced. Exploration will be covered through a merging of cognitive and affective educational experiences. A goal will be to feel what is happening as well as to know what is happening. The class will use drama not only to identify problems but to ascertain how they were handled, how they might be handled, and how they pertain to each individual involved in the class and to his own life. There are no mandatory writing assignments in this class. The primary focus will be on reading aloud and on acting and moving in various verbal and nonverbal ways.

Learning Processes

What follows in this memorandum is a list of learning processes. They will be of value to your understanding of the course and its contents. They will be of special value to you in your own learning and as you contribute to the learning of the class. Responsibility for your own cognitive and affective learning experiences, and sharing with the class, is inherent in the educational process.

Required Work

Each student will be expected to read aloud in the class and to participate in the various activities.

Optional and Enrichment Work Suggestions

There is no written work of any type assigned for this course. The following are suggestions for work that will enhance your learning and understanding of the course and will assist you in understanding yourself.

1. Research paper — Write an original research paper applicable to drama and based on a topic of your choice.

2. Term paper — Peruse at least twelve plays. Synthesize them, document them, and include a bibliography.

3. Discussion — Prepare discussion topics and questions and arrange for presentation to the class.

4. Debates — Arrange formal or semiformal debates and present them to the group.

5. Oral reports — Read articles of your choice to the class or make an oral report on any subject. Allow time for the class to ask questions.

6. Drama — Prepare a play or television script and arrange to have it acted out in class.

7. Improvisation — Prepare an improvisation series and arrange to have it acted out in class. The series must have a theme that follows from one act to another.

8. Art — Use an art medium — painting, ceramics, drawing — to express something about you and this course.

9. Poetry — Poetry may take any form from free verse to the most disciplined, but its content must be directed from you toward the characters in our plays.

10. Homestudy — The teacher will suggest appropriate work for additional enrichment in drama and communications.

Grading

There is no curve. Evaluation will be decided by the two of us in consultation. It will be based on where you were when you entered the course and where you are when you leave.

Testing

Tests are more in the realm of assimilation and integration exercises. These exercises are designed for your evaluation and thought. They are all participatory exercises that are either verbal or nonverbal.

MEMORANDUM FOR TEACHERS

Subject: Implementing the Course of Study

This course is designed to introduce the study of drama and the active reading of drama, and to assist students in working out their feelings about being "on stage." It is *not* designed as a vehicle for theater arts students, but rather to emphasize the element of the English discipline that calls for language instruction. It is designed for any ability level and for individualized instruction. The course is deductive rather than inductive. It is hoped that any teacher using the course will have had extensive training in group process as well as training in English, drama, or improvisational theater. The teacher acts as a guide and consultant and trusts the students to carry the major responsibility for their own learning. However, the teacher must be constantly aware of what is happening to and with each student. The affective goals are given equal status with the cognitive goals in this course. Such teaching and learning are merged in the process of education. The course consists of verbal and nonverbal activity only and there is no required writing or reading inside or outside of class. The teacher encourages and suggests and practices the idea that no one has to do anything he does not want to do as far as affective or experiential classroom activities are concerned. The emphasis of the course is on self-responsibility; that is, learning to respond intellectually and emotionally to any situation in a spontaneous, creative, and healthy manner.

1. *Memorandum for students* — Give each student a copy for his reading and continuing information.
2. *Course title* — Review with the students the meaning and implications of the course title.
3. *Background texts* — The background texts are used for open and oral reading in the classroom. They are not required reading outside.
4. *Suggested readings* — Interesting and provocative materials are suggested to students for their added understanding and enrichment.

5. *Unit title* — A general title is given for the proposed events of the unit.

6. *Thesis* — The thesis is a general statement about the goals of the course as well as a particular unit of study — a guide for exploration.

7. *Homestudy* — Homestudy assignments are recommended work that the student may do outside of class hours.

8. *Roman number divisions* — Each Roman numeral division represents one period of instruction; five represent a typical school week.

9. *Responsibility* — Responsibility is the recurrent theme throughout the course. It is not meant as a proscriptive term, or that someone "owes" something. It is rather an indication of the general purpose of the course: teaching responsibility (ability to respond) to oneself, one's learning, and one's life. In order to be responseable an individual must have space in which to practice it.

10. *Testing* — The "tests" are not intended to find out what the student knows as a result of exposure to this course. They are meant to tie concepts together, to enhance the ongoing learning situation, and to provoke further thought and questions. Grading is accomplished on an individual basis in consultation with the student. It is based on the *total* experience of the student — as his experiences relate to where the student was and where the student is now. In this sense, attendance, participation, tests, and other factors are of equal value in arriving at a decision.

Assimilation and integration do not happen instantaneously. Another learning factor for the teacher is to practice patience and to observe *how* the student is learning. *What* has been learned comes later.

COURSE OUTLINE /

Title: The Play's the Thing

This Unit

Text: Jerome Lawrence and Robert E. Lee, *Inherit the Wind*

Thesis: An idea is always on trial somewhere.

Homestudy: Search out from newspapers, periodicals, or other sources, instances in which people's ideas are on trial or being attacked. With another person or persons improvise scenes about the incident.

Suggested reading: George Bernard Shaw, *Saint Joan*

I. *Inherit the Wind* by Lawrence and Lee
   A. Roll call: ask each student to yell his name as you check off the roll.
   B. Distribute texts and ask the students to look over the play and select roles they might like to read.
   C. Discuss and share the purposes of the course, the goals and objectives, and teaching method. Ask for and work with students' fears, expectations, and desires for the course.
   D. Closure: Think for five minutes in silence about the course.

II. *Inherit the Wind* Act I
   A. Theme: Where did we come from? Where are we going? (Write each day's theme on the chalkboard so students can keep it in mind during the work.)
   B. Roll call: As you call the names, ask the students to respond by stating their place of birth and their goal in life. (The purpose of the roll call is to get a response from everyone and to relax them for the work to come.)
   C. Improvisation: Each student comes to the center and acts out, nonverbally, an occupation. The other students keep guessing aloud until they identify the occupation.
   D. Reading: Act I, Scene I. Ask for volunteers to read the different roles. Read the scene setting and then ask the students to read the play. As they read their parts, the remaining students follow along. They fill in, especially when a stage direction calls for crowd murmur or reaction or expression. The readers are to read in their natural way and not consciously become actors and actresses. They are, however, to express how they are feeling through their voices and bodies as they are reading.
   E. Sharing: End the reading at an appropriate point and ask the students for any reactions to the class today and to the reading. Discuss the question: What does it do for man to establish his past and speculate about his future?
   F. Closure: Students leave by walking backward out of the room.

III. Act I cont.

   A. Theme: Lose your power to laugh and lose your power to think clearly.

   B. Roll call: As you call their names, each student responds by shouting either, "I hear!" or "I believe!" or "Right on!"

   C. Improvisation: Turn to the part of the play that contains the words for the song "Gimme That Old-Time Religion." Lead the group in a spirited singing of the fine old hymn. (Note: If there is a student who can do the leading, have him do it.)

   D. Reading: Pick up the reading from the point where the class left off yesterday. Note: Do not interrupt the reading to correct a pronunciation *until* the person has first tried to speak it. Do not make it a habit but do this only on occasion. (Too much correction can be detrimental.)

   E. Sharing: discussion, and evaluation. Review the theme.

   F. Closure: Everyone leaves the room laughing uproariously.

IV. Act I cont.

   A. Theme: There are few words that everybody understands.

   B. Roll call: As you call names each person responds with a word he thinks few people interpret the same. All words must be different.

   C. Improvisation: Volunteers come to the center and act out a word nonverbally. Audience calls out the word until it is guessed. (Note: Keep a record of volunteers so that all persons of the class get an equal chance to participate in improvisations.)

   D. Reading: Continue reading from previous day's ending.

   E. Sharing: Discuss and evaluate the class. Review the theme.

   F. Closure: Everyone leaves the room after naming a new word they discovered this day in class.

V. Act I cont.

   A. Theme: It's the loneliest feeling in the world to be standing up when everybody else is sitting down.

   B. Roll call: As you call the names each student stands up, looks around at the class, and sits down.

   C. Improvisation: *Pressure.* Have each student experience (non-verbally) as much pressure as he can on his body — the weight of the universe is on him. As the weight comes down his whole body becomes compressed and he almost assumes a prenatal position. Stretch out a little at the end.

D. Reading continues.

E. Sharing: Review, discussion, and evaluation.

F. Closure: All sit down. One by one slip out of the room in silence as the remainder watch.

VI. Act I cont.

A. Theme: The man who has everything figured out is probably a fool.

B. Roll call: As the roll is called each student answers by repeating and filling in the statement, "I feel most foolish when. . . ."

C. Improvisation: Everyone gathers in the center. Everyone greets everyone by looking each other in the eyes, shaking hands, and stating their names. Then they shake hands and make eye contact only. Now they find a new way of saying hello (non-verbally).

D. Reading: Continue reading from the previous day to the end of Act I.

E. Sharing: Review, discussion, and evaluation. Do a critique of Act I.

F. Closure: One person in front, the other in back with his arms in front, making gestures as the other one talks.

VII. *Inherit the Wind* Act II

A. Theme: By knowledge we abandon faith.

B. Roll call: When each student's name is called, they respond by repeating the following statement and filling in the blanks, "I believe in . . . and I believe in. . . ." (Should be said with real fervor.)

C. Improvisation: *Balance*. Stand up and close eyes. Assume a stiff body position and by leaning as far forward and as far backward without falling — a maximum rocking angle, using the body as a pivot — find your own balance point.

D. Reading: Begin reading Act II. This time assign roles to be read on the basis of what you see as the personality of the role and an *opposite* personality type in the reader.

E. Sharing: Review, discussion, and evaluation.

F. Closure: Each one leaves by walking very stately, head high.

VIII. Act II cont.

 A. Theme: An idea is a greater monument than a cathedral.
 B. Roll call: As you call the roll ask the students to respond by shaking a fist and shouting "Yes!" or "No!" according to whether they believe the theme or not.
 C. Improvisation: Walking on a cliff. Draw a line on the floor. One at a time the students pretend they are on the edge of a cliff and each one walks delicately along the cliff edge.
 D. Reading: Continue from previous ending.
 E. Sharing: Review, discussion, and evaluation.
 F. Closure: Each one goes to the door, shouts an idea at the group, and leaves.

 IX. Act II cont.

 A. Theme: Perhaps it is you who have moved away by standing still.
 B. Roll call: As you call the role the students respond by saying what is on their minds *at that moment* (stream of consciousness).
 C. Improvisation: *Mirror.* Two people. One mirrors the other (combing hair, brushing teeth, etc.) One is a mirror and the other is looking in. The mirror must respond to whatever the viewer does.
 D. Reading: Continue from previous ending.
 E. Sharing: Review, discussion, and evaluation.
 F. Closure: Each one leaves by moving arms and legs forward furiously but making little progress.

 X. Act II cont.

 A. Theme: He that troubleth his own house shall inherit the wind.
 B. Roll call: As you call the roll the students respond by each one making the sound of wind.
 C. Improvisation: Walking on rocks. Imagining rocks in a river, cross from one side to the other by stepping on the rocks so as not to fall into the river.
 D. Reading: Finish reading Act II.
 E. Sharing: Review, discussion, and evaluation. Do a critique of Act II.
 F. Closure: The entire group makes the sound of wind in the trees as they are blown out of the room.

XI. *Inherit the Wind* Act III
   A. Theme: Everyone has the right to be wrong.
   B. Roll call: Students respond by an emphatic "Yes!" or "No!" when their names are called, according to whether or not they believe the theme. But, they shake their heads *yes* when they mean *no* and vice versa.
   C. Improvisation: *Warm-up*. Everyone finds space for themselves away from the others and warms up by bending, twisting, and squatting and doing arm circles and bicycle kicks on their backs.
   D. Reading: Begin reading Act III. This time assign male roles to females and female roles to males.
   E. Sharing: Review, discussion, and evaluation.
   F. Closure: Men walk out first, followed at a distance by the women.

XII. Act III cont.
   A. Theme: A thought is like a child. It has to be born. If it dies inside you, part of you dies too!
   B. Roll call: As you call the roll the students respond by *singing* some idea and/or their own names. When calling the roll, the teacher *sings* each name.
   C. Improvisation: Walking on rocks. Imagining rocks in a river, cross from one side to the other by stepping on the rocks so as to not fall into the river. Use the large center of the room for the river and have the students walk from one side to the other.
   D. Reading: Continue from previous ending.
   E. Sharing: Review, discussion, and evaluation.
   F. Closure: As they leave, the students launch into impromptu singing about the day's events.

XIII. ASSIMILATION AND INTEGRATION
   A. Assimilation and Integration: Exercise 1 (see Appendix 1).
   B. Sharing: Review, discussion, and evaluation.

XIV. Act III cont.
   A. Theme: Tomorrow it'll be something else — and another fella will have to stand up.
   B. Roll call: As you call the roll each student stands up and makes a statement beginning with the words "I resent. . . ."
   C. Improvisation: *Judo*. Use hands to push out and slice the air

and use judo chops. Then, imagining a rock in front, push the rock over a mountain, becoming stiff and strained, and again become relaxed by using judo chops.

D. Reading: Continue from previous ending.

E. Sharing: Review, discuss, and evaluate.

F. Closure: Each one leaves imagining he is pushing a heavy rock out the door.

XV. Act III cont.

A. Theme: Which side won?

B. Roll call: As you call the roll each student responds by stating whether he believes the evolutionists or anti-evolutionists won in the trial. (Note: The teacher should be alert to avoid any attacks on individuals, implicit or explicit, from other members of the class for the position an individual takes on the question of evolution.)

C. Improvisation: Play a recording of the *Swan Lake* ballet. As they listen to the music the students are to move to the music but in *slow motion*, very slow and deliberate.

D. Reading: Finish reading Act III.

E. Sharing: Review, discussion, and evaluation. Do a critique of Act III and the play as a whole.

F. Closure: Leave the room in extreme slow motion. Take at least two minutes to do it.

This Unit

Text: Arthur Miller, *The Crucible*

Thesis: The most important questions in life can never be answered by anyone except oneself.

Homestudy: Search out historical incidents in which persons choose death rather than sacrifice a principle. Improvise scenes about the incident.

Suggested reading: Sophocles, *Antigone*

XVI. *The Crucible* by Arthur Miller

A. Roll call: As the roll is called each student responds by saying one word that illustrates how he feels.

B. Improvisation: Volunteers come to the center and act out whatever comes to them as they read these sentences: (1) I won't do it again! (2) Everyone says what I do is bad! (3) Everyone wants everyone to be the same!

C. Distribute copies of *The Crucible*. Ask the students to look over the play and select roles they might like to read.

D. Sharing: Review, discuss, and evaluate.

E. Closure: Each one leaves acting furtive, skulking about. Some unseen something is near and they are aware of its presence.

XVII. *The Crucible* Act I

A. Theme: Look to unnatural things for the cause of it.

B. Roll call: As the roll is called each student responds by finishing the statement, "I am a mirror when I. . . ."

C. Improvisation: *Mirror*. One is the mirror, the other person the one looking in the mirror. The mirror must mirror the initiator. Partners reverse roles.

D. Reading: Ask for volunteers to read the different roles. Read the scene setting and then ask the students to read their roles. Designate a portion of class space as a "stage;" all reading is done there, with chairs as props and regular entrances and exits. Students not reading roles follow along by reading silently. They fill in, especially whenever a stage direction calls for crowd murmur, reaction or expression, or off-stage activity. The readers are to read in their natural way and not consciously become actors or actresses. They are, however, to express how they are feeling through their voices and bodies as they are reading. When directions call for shouting, singing, or screaming, they are expected to "get into it." If they cannot, work for a possible breakthrough but don't force it.

E. Sharing: End the reading at an appropriate point and ask the students for any reactions to the events and experiences. Discuss the theme, share feelings, and evaluate the day.

F. Closure: Leave by twos, one person being the walking mirror of the other.

XVIII. Act I cont.

A. Theme: It is a providence the thing is out now.

B. Roll call: As the roll is called each student responds as if he believes in spirits.

C. Improvisation: Students form partners. One is the sculptor, one is the clay. After the figure is made the group can guess which is which. Reverse roles.

D. Reading: Continue from previous day's ending.

E. Sharing: Review, discuss, and evaluate.

F. Closure: Leave as the statue you would like to be might leave.

XIX. Act I cont.

A. Theme: You have not opened with me.

B. Roll call: As the roll is called each student responds by saying, "The devil you say!" However, each one is to find a different tone, expression, or way of saying it.

C. Improvisation: *Closed circle*. A group forms a circle and excludes one person. That person must break into the circle or break out of the circle.

D. Reading: Continue from previous day's ending.

E. Sharing: Review, discuss, and evaluate.

F. Closure: Leave by alternatingly folding your body up and then unfolding it (as a flower would).

XX. Act I cont.

A. Theme: In his presence a fool felt foolish and thus he made another enemy.

B. Roll call: As the roll is called each student responds by finishing the sentence, "I feel foolish when I. . . ."

C. Improvisation: *Rejection*. Form groups. The groups single one member to be rejected from their activity (which is whatever they wish). This rejected person finds others who have been rejected and starts a group and then rejects someone trying to join them. Share with one another the feelings or rejection.

D. Reading: Continue reading from previous day to the end of Act I.

E. Sharing: Review, discuss, and evaluate. Do a critique of Act I.

F. Closure: Leave by being suspicious of everyone in the group. Imagine you are looking foolish in their eyes.

XXI. *The Crucible* Act II

A. Theme: Look sometimes for the goodness in me, do not judge me.

B. Roll call: As the roll is called each student responds by finishing the sentence, "I judge others by. . . ."

C. Improvisation: *Mirror*. The one person is the mirror, the other looks in the mirror. The mirror must mirror the initiator. Partners change positions. Positions are not designated but must be established nonverbally.

D. Reading: Reading begins by an individual coming "on stage" and reading. No roles are assigned permanently. Readers come and go as they please.

E. Sharing: Review, discuss, and evaluate.

F. Closure: Leave by teaming up and being crazy mirrors (as in an amusement park). One initiates action and the other distorts.

XXII. Act II cont.

A. Theme: The devil's loose in Salem.

B. Roll call: As the roll is called each student responds by stating and finishing the sentence, "A voice within me says. . . ."

C. Improvisation: All students circulate, nonverbally, about the room. Using hands they are to find differing ways to say hello and good-bye.

D. Reading: Continue reading from previous day's ending.

E. Sharing: Review, discuss, and evaluate.

F. Closure: Students leave forming dyads and acting out a telephone conversation as they go.

XXIII. *The Crucible* Act II

A. Theme: No crack in a fortress may be accounted small.

B. Roll call: As the roll is called students respond by rising, moving into a group, facing outward, linking up, and making a solid group.

C. Improvisation: Stay in the groups. Using an imaginary object, go around in a circle and use the object. Each one improvises in his group and the remainder guess what the object is.

D. Reading: Continue from previous day's ending.

E. Sharing: Review, discuss, and evaluate.

F. Closure: Leave by holding hands and arms out stiffly, first to front and then to side; walk deliberately.

XXIV. Act II cont.

A. Theme: We are only what we always were, but naked now.

B. Roll call: As you call the roll students respond by completing the following statement: ". . . is like me because. . . ."

C. Improvisation: Have pairs of students face and study each other. They turn away, remove three objects or change three objects, face one another, and try to name the three changes.

D. Reading: Continue reading from previous day to the end of Act II.

E. Sharing: Review, discuss, and evaluate. Do a critique of Act II.

F. Closure: Leave by wrapping arms tightly about yourself and speaking or looking at no one.

XXV. ASSIMILATION AND INTEGRATION

A. Assimilating and Integration. Exercise 2 (see Appendix 2).

B. Review, discuss, and evaluate.

XXVI. *The Crucible* Act III

A. Theme: We burn a hot fire here, it melts down all concealment.

B. Roll call: As the roll is called each student responds by finishing the statement "I hide myself by. . . ."

C. Improvisation: Act out a scene. Act out either an actual experience or an imaginary one. Examples: student in the principal's office; couple discussing how to ask their parents if they can marry; getting an eviction notice; being accused of a crime you didn't commit; a 25-year old still dominated by parents; being afraid you will be found out; busy, in your mind, trying to conceal something.

D. Reading: Begin reading Act III. This act is to be read loud, fast, furious, and is to be screamed when necessary.

E. Sharing: Review, discuss, and evaluate.

F. Closure: Everyone begins talking loudly in gibberish and flopping their arms about as they leave.

XXVII. Act III cont.

A. Theme: I wish you had some evil in you that you might know me.

B. Roll call: As the roll is called, each student responds by saying something positive about another member of the class. Address that person by name and then make the statement.

C. Improvisation: *Gibberish*. Demonstrate an activity talking in gibberish only. (Gibberish — unintelligible or meaningless language.)

D. Reading: Continue reading from previous day's ending.

E. Sharing: Review, discuss, and evaluate.

F. Closure: Everyone leaves in a group while telling each other how good they were (sincere statements only).

XXVIII. Act III cont.

A. Theme: It was only sport in the beginning.

B. Roll call: As the roll is called each student responds by finishing the statement "I pretend. . . ."

C. Improvisation: *Trapped*. Choose what you are trapped in and have the others guess what it is.

D. Reading: Finish reading Act III.

E. Sharing: Review, discuss, and evaluate. Do a critique of Act III.

F. Closure: Each one leaves and pantomimes playing some sport as they go.

XXIX. *The Crucible* Act IV

A. Theme: "More weight," he says. And died.

B. Roll call: As the roll is called, each student responds by finishing the statement, "I weep for. . . ."

C. Improvisation: *Screaming*. Using the toes, legs, arms, and any other part of the body except the voice, start screaming. Try it several times. Then let loose by screaming vocally.

D. Reading: Begin reading Act IV. Read slowly, deliberately, with agony, yet knowing that passion is spent.

E. Sharing: Review, discuss, and evaluate.

F. Closure: Let the body sag, tired, listless, and slowly drift away.

XXX. Act IV cont.

A. Theme: Show honor now. Show a stony heart and sink them with it!

B. Roll call: Students respond by finishing the statement, "Honor to me is. . . ."

C. Improvisation: *Immobilization*. Slowly and with care, individuals act as a sick or hurt person and are moved from one end of the room to another, gently and firmly, by the group.

D. Reading: Finish reading Act IV.

E. Sharing: Review, discuss, and evaluate. Do a critique of Act IV and the play as a whole. Weep for mankind.

F. Closure: Students leave as they imagine John Proctor walked to the gallows.

This Unit

Text: Archibald MacLeish, *J.B.*

Thesis: Without trials we do not grow.

Homestudy: Observe how people are constantly on trial by life because they are humans. With another person or persons, improvise scenes and incidents that suggest the best ways to cope with life.

Suggested Reading: The Bible, Old Testament, Book of Job.

XXXI. J. B. by Archibald MacLeish
   A. Theme: Life is a circus and not always fun.
   B. Roll call: As the roll is called, each student responds by completing the statement, "I am a. . . ." They finish the statement by citing what part of a circus (what object) they see themselves as.
   C. Improvisation: Who's knocking at the door? Each one knocks on an imaginary door, and from the way he knocks and the way he approaches the door, others guess what type of person he is. The knocker performs nonverbally.
   D. Reading: Distribute texts and ask the students to peruse the play and get the feel of the characters.
   E. Sharing: Review, discuss, and evaluate.
   F. Closure: Students leave by becoming "hawkers" and selling themselves.

XXXII. J. B. Prologue
   A. Theme: Whatsoever is under the whole Heaven is mine!
   B. Roll call: As the roll is called each student steps to the front of the group, strikes an attitude, and declaims the theme (it must be a positive statement).
   C. Improvisation: Changing the environment. Each one acts out working in a forest, being in a cave, prison, or a mountain, indoors, outdoors, in the water, in the jungle, or in the woods, etc.
   D. Reading: Males only read today. Students pair up, and on each page a new duo begins reading (all parts).
   E. Sharing: Review, discuss, and evaluate.
   F. Closure: Students leave by selecting as a partner someone they do not know and walking out hand in hand.

XXXIII. Prologue cont.
   A. Theme: Job knows justice when it's over.

B. Roll call: As you call the roll the first student starts a story about Job and each one elaborates on the story with his own addition.

C. Improvisation: Express a feeling. First, using facial expressions, express sadness, anger, joy, surprise, etc., then express these emotions using other parts of the body.

D. Reading: Females only read today. Students pair up, and on each page a new duo begins reading. Continue reading from previous day's ending.

E. Sharing: Review, discuss, and evaluate.

F. Closure: As you leave, using your face and body, assume the mood that makes you most vulnerable.

XXXIV. *J. B.* Scene One

A. Theme: Everywhere I look I see you.

B. Roll call: As the roll is called each student responds by greeting the group in a different tone or feeling (i.e., sad, angry, pleading, joyous, bitter, etc.).

C. Improvisation: Students stand and move about the room non-verbally. Then they greet by shaking hands, making eye contact, and stating their names—then by shaking elbows, then by shaking ankles, then by whatever.

D. Reading: Roles are read according to sex of characters. The rest read (in unison) the role of the maids.

E. Sharing: Review, discuss, and evaluate.

F. Closure: Find someone in the class who has paid little attention to you. Walk out together.

XXXV. Scene Two

A. Theme: Poisoning their little minds with love of life! At that age!

B. Roll call: As the roll is called each student responds by finishing the statement "It takes courage for me to. . . ."

C. Improvisation: *Imaginary tug-o-war.* Divide into teams of six members. Teams pull on an imaginary rope. Exercise continues until one team remains.

D. Reading: Today anyone reads any role. However, only one person may read one speech. When all have read, the sequence begins again. The first speech is read, someone immediately picks it up, and so on.

E. Sharing: Review, discuss, and evaluate.

F. Closure: Make sentences. As they leave each student states a word that adds to the previous word, etc., all of which makes sense and a sentence.

XXXVI. Scene Three

A. Theme: You think we never knew him?

B. Roll call: As the roll is called each student responds by stating the name of something he has lost and how he feels about that.

C. Improvisation: Sit in a large group, preferably on the floor. Rock back and forth. Close eyes. Now imagine you are in deep grief and allow yourself to weep and wail, to cry aloud.

D. Reading: Today's reading is done by those who feel they most hate war or who are, at present, feeling a sense of loss.

E. Sharing: Review, discuss, and evaluate.

F. Closure: In silence, each member leaves and while leaving, keeps looking for something he has lost.

XXXVII. Scene Four

A. Theme: There's always someone has to tell them, isn't there?

B. Roll call: As the roll is called each student responds by crossing the room, meeting someone, greeting them nonverbally, and let follow what will.

C. Improvisation: Guess the activity. One or two people pantomime an activity and each one in the group who is watching joins in.

D. Reading: In today's reading all parts are read by females only.

E. Sharing: Review, discuss, and evaluate.

F. Closure: One student writes out a rumor and hands it to the teacher. That student whispers the rumor into another student's ear, then leaves. The second student does the same, etc. until all are gone. The next day compare the final rumor with the original one.

XXXVIII. ASSIMILATION AND INTEGRATION

A. Assimilation and Integration. Exercise 3 (see Appendix 3).

B. Sharing: Review, discuss, and evaluate.

XXXIX. Scene Five

A. Theme: Mankind is always ready for anything that hurts.

B. Roll call: As the roll is called each student closes his eyes and responds by saying, "I am most blind when. . . ." Eyes remain closed and he listens to other statements.

    C. Improvisation. *Blind Acting.* Students are given movements and scenes to enact but they must do this with eyes closed. Examples: Meet a person for the first time; know someone is in a room but you are not able to see or hear him.

    D. Reading: All parts in today's reading are read by the males only.

    E. Sharing: Review, discuss, and evaluate.

    F. Closure: With eyes closed, students feel their way out of the room.

XL. Scenes Six and Seven

    A. Theme: Even desperate we can't despair.

    B. Roll call: As the roll is called each person responds by finishing the statement, "I can. . . ."

    C. Improvisation: Form dyads. In silence partners look at one another. Now, with just their hands, they explore each other's faces.

    D. Reading: In today's reading students form male-female partnerships for man-woman conversations. Each one reads to the other. (All couples read to one another aloud at the same time.)

    E. Sharing: Stay in dyads. Review, discuss, and evaluate with one another.

    F. Closure: Students leave the room reading aloud, each one reading his favorite part.

XLI. Scene Eight

    A. Theme: Out of sleep something of our own comes back to us.

    B. Roll call: As the roll is called each student responds by finishing the statement "I reflect. . . ."

    C. Improvisation: *Three-way mirror.* Form triads. One person initiates the action. Two others act as reflections. Switch roles twice.

    D. Reading: In today's reading ask the readers to place themselves on the outside of a circle formed by the other students, and to read inward. One exception is that the student reading the role of J. B. sits in the center of the circle (preferably on the floor).

    E. Sharing: Review, discuss, and evaluate.

    F. Closure: The students are asked to leave in silence, heads bowed, and shuffling.

XLII. Scene Nine

A. Theme: One man's suffering won't count, no matter what his suffering.

B. Roll call: As the roll is called each student responds by finishing the statement, "I blame myself. . . ."

C. Improvisation: *Puppeteer.* Form dyads. One is the puppet, the other the puppeteer. Act out a scene for the group.

D. Reading: Students choose the roles they want to read and move into the center. The remainder of the group forms a circle outside.

E. Sharing: Review, discuss, and evaluate.

F. Closure: Students are asked to leave by walking backward out of the room — very slowly.

XLIII. Scene Ten

A. Theme: In spite of all, *he* understood and *he* forgave.

B. Roll call: As the roll is called each student responds by finishing the statement, "The mask I wear most often is. . . ."

C. Improvisation: *Magic box.* Pass around an imaginary box. Choose an imaginary object from it and by your actions see if the audience can guess what object you have picked.

D. Reading: Readers today are picked for their loud voices.

E. Sharing: Review, discuss, and evaluate.

XLIV. Scene Eleven

A. Theme: I found it growing in the ashes.

B. Roll call: As the roll is called each student responds by rising and stretching his arms far above his head until his heels are barely resting on the floor. The position is held until the roll is completed.

C. Improvisation: Adding a part. A volunteer comes to the center and assumes a stance and attitude that illustrates an object. One at a time each student comes and attaches himself to whoever is already there until the entire group is an intermeshed object. This is done in silence.

D. Reading: Readers today are picked for their soft voices.

E. Sharing: Review, discuss, and evaluate.

F. Closure: In silence, students straighten up the room together and leave soberly.

XLV. *The Play's the Thing*
   A. Theme: Who knows what the end is, ever?
   B. Roll call: The roll is called by each one rising, stating his name, and telling what has been most meaningful for him in the class.
   C. Sharing: Review, discuss, and evaluate the class, the teacher, the students, and the subject, spending periods of time in the following discussion groups (5 to 10 minutes per group):
      1. Group according to whether you liked the play
         (a) *Inherit the Wind*
         (b) *The Crucible*
         (c) *J. B.*
      2. Group according to who is your ideal or favorite:
         (a) John Proctor
         (b) Henry Drummond
         (c) J. B.
      3. Group according to who is your ideal or favorite:
         (a) Elizabeth Proctor
         (b) Miss Brown
         (c) Sarah
      4. Group according to whether you now find yourselves:
         (a) Better readers
         (b) Less inhibited
         (c) Better at being in front of groups
         (d) None of the above
   D. Closure: Move freely among the group making eye contact with each person, shaking hands, and expressing whatever it is you feel. Resolve into a single friendship circle with all hands linked. Say any last things you wish. Arm in arm, leave together.

APPENDIX 1

THE PLAY'S THE THING /

Assimilation and Integration: Exercise 1

Instructions: All of the following action is done in silence unless the instructions are specific about what you are to say.

First Step: Look for accomplishment, achievement, some sort of change in our actors and actresses. Your first task is to sensitize yourself, to train yourself to become more aware of others. You will draw a person's name from the box. Locate that person in the room and think about how well, and in what ways, they have achieved. You will have five minutes for this.

Interlude: Turn off lights. Listen to the recording of Simon and Garfunkel's "Sounds of Silence." Think about the person whose name you drew. Turn lights on.

Second Step: Acknowledge that person's achievement. Go to that person and tell him what you feel about his accomplishment, achievement, and/or change. You will have five minutes.

Interlude: Listen to the "No Thank You" speech in Edmond Rostand's play *Cyrano de Bergerac* as it is read to you.

Third Step: Give recognition to yourself. Give yourself a reward and say to yourself, "I did well." (It doesn't matter whether you are a spectator or an actor, you *did* participate.) For any accomplishment or work brought to a conclusion, you may wish to reward yourself. Give yourself an award, a symbolic award, for something which has value and meaning to you. You will have five minutes.

Interlude: Turn off lights. Listen to the music of Ravel's "Bolero" and think about your reward. Turn lights on.

Fourth Step: As your name is called, walk calmly erect to the center of the room and stand with the M.C. He will present you with the award. The audience will applaud. You will give a bow and return to your seat.

Finale: Gather in a circle at center stage. Join hands. Walk toward one another. Lift hands (still joined) and walk closer together. Back away. Drop hands and look at one another.

Reprise: Sit in the circle and share with one another.

NOTE TO TEACHER: Reproduce these and the following instructions and give a copy to each student before play begins. Have all material available but *do not* lead or direct. Leadership will come out of the group and everyone goes at their own pace. In the reprise, refer to the plays as well as to what happened in class.

APPENDIX 2

THE PLAY'S THE THING /

Assimilation and Integration: Exercise 2

Instructions: All of the following action is done in silence unless the instructions are specific about what you are to say.

First Step: In silence find someone for a partner who is about your size. One of you take the other for a walk while the other keeps his eyes closed. After five minutes stop. Then the "blind" person opens his eyes and the other person closes his eyes. The second person now leads the first back to the room.

Interlude: Everyone does an interpretive dance that reflects how they feel. Form groups of six and sway together.

Second Step: Each group singles out one member to be rejected from an activity (i.e., playing marbles, building sand castles, etc.). This rejected person finds himself with others who have been rejected also and starts a group and then rejects someone trying to join them.

Interlude: Groups break. Walk slowly around the room. Now half the group become (singly) half an object (an incomplete thing). They walk around the room (in slow motion) as that incomplete object. The rest of the group watches from the side. Then they choose someone and join them, physically, to make a complete object out of the incomplete one. Hold the attitude.

Third Step: Three objects move together to form a group of six. Focusing on one person at a time, the group is to bombard each other with all the strengths they see in the person. The person being bombarded should remain silent.

Interlude: Groups break and walk in silence. Half of the group now makes angles with arms, body, or legs and stand in different parts of the room. Rest of the group walks around the room in slow motion and looks at the angle-people from many different directions. Now they become an angle and fit their angle to the one already formed.

Finale: Gather into a friendship circle. Join hands. Break the circle at one point and serpentine in until you can't go any farther. Drop hands and look at one another. Hum as loud as you can.

Reprise: Sit in a circle and share with one another.

APPENDIX 3

THE PLAY'S THE THING /

Assimilation and Integration: Exercise 3

Instructions: All of the following action is done in silence unless the instructions are specific about what you say.

First Step: In silence find a partner you do not know well. Sit back to back. Talk to one another. Turn around and look into each other's eyes — no touching or talking. Now discuss our plays. Now look at one another again and touch (i.e., hold hands) but without talking. Now touch witih your eyes closed and without talking. Now, open your eyes and talk about our plays, but without touching. Then, talk, touch, look at one another, and try to argue.

Interlude: Listen to the music of the *Swan Lake* ballet. Rise and move in very slow motion to the music.

Second Step: Move into groups of six. A volunteer sits outside the group with his back to it. Preferably he should be sitting in such a way that he cannot see the members of the group. However, he must be sitting within hearing distance. Another volunteer states how he feels about the person outside the group. There is no progression and a person may speak anytime about that person sitting outside the group. It is to be an open and frank discussion. As many persons as possible, preferably all in their turn, sit outside the circle and are evaluated by their fellow group members.

Interlude: The groups of six move together until they are connected. Look at one another without talking. Rise and turn your backs on one another. Separate and go as far away from your group as you wish. Stop. Turn and look at your group members. Let happen what will.

Third Step: The whole group divides into smaller groups according to the position each student holds in own family — oldest, youngest, middle, or only child. All groups discuss our plays. Groups divide again according to whether family is (or was) controlled by the mother, father, or neither. Continue discussion. Form dyads. Each person speaks about himself by imagining how his father and mother might discuss him now. Dyads now consider this question and discuss it. What statements that your "mother" or "father" made can you own for yourself?

Finale: Gather into a friendship circle. Join hands and experience one another. Now, with hands across shoulders, listen to the recording of "The Impossible Dream" from *Man of La Mancha*.

Reprise: Sit in a circle and share with one another.

A CAUTIONARY CONCLUSION
— George Isaac Brown

Our first caution, especially related to the last two sections of the book, is that the reader who is a teacher not be seduced into using any of the techniques or approaches without somehow making them a part of his own total teaching approach and philosophy. Unless he does this he will simply be using a gimmick and today's gimmick disappears tomorrow. In all our work with teachers and others, we have found that there are essentially three stages of training and professional development. We begin the initial stage by introducing techniques experientially in the training and then having them utilized by the participants themselves. The next stage seems to be when these techniques become an integral part of a person's philosophy and behavior, through an emphasis not just on the techniques themselves but also on an appreciation of the philosophy and understanding underlying the techniques. This has been described in some of the articles as moving from a teacher who uses confluent techniques to one who becomes a confluent teacher. Finally, being a confluent teacher incorporates a third stage wherein the teacher takes the techniques or approaches learned in stage one and uses them to create new approaches or techniques himself for his own classroom situation. This is analogous to translating a theory from a basic science into a practical engineering principle; the teacher creates his own innovations or modifications in his teaching. This does not preclude further development of basic techniques on his own, for this, too, can be a manifestation of the third stage, that of educational innovator.

To continue our cautionary considerations — there are indeed arguments against confluent education. For example, a point might well be made that confluent education is as value-free as electricity and thus can be dangerous and destructive or, in the least, misused. Electricity can be used to make toast in the morning, but simultaneously switched on in a prison for juicing an electric chair. As we have said earlier, the same principle may apply to the uses of confluent education as a teaching approach for changing people. While we would like to believe confluent education is only used for good, Hitler, in a sense, used psychological principles of confluent education during the Nuremberg rallies. His objective was to manipulate his followers toward his own ends, and he successfully used strong emotional components to accomplish his objective. Advertising is saturated with similar examples. Of course, proper training in confluent education can prepare one for a more perceptive, rational, and intelligent response to such manipulation. An awareness of value decisions — a focus of confluent education — will help counteract the effects of such manipulation.

Another salient issue could be raised as follows: The philosophical position permeating this book is based on an assumption that the growth and development of all human potential is good. We have implied that the more freedom and responsibility an individual has the better, the more open the system the better, etc. On the other hand, one could easily construct an argument that such growth, freedom, and openness could instead actually be counterproductive; that, in fact, right now mankind as a totality does not essentially desire these; that individual man is more comfortable as a member of some larger collective consciousness which we may ascribe to mankind as a whole; that there is some kind of predestination in which the rate and quality of the growth of this larger organism, mankind, is fairly well determined; that to hold back this growth, as in the case of repressive societies, eventually produces violent revolution, or if the growth is too swiftly accelerated, a counterreaction is created which results in a return to more repressive social organizations and stronger conservatism; that, for example, the whole basis for statistics and probability is evidence that mankind operates as this larger organism, and that predictability which is based on statistics is, in fact, a description of the existence of this larger organism. Consequently, innovators who try to hasten the seemingly slow rate of change of the whole organism risk taking on a function similar to that of cancer cells, and become pathological to the welfare of mankind as a whole.

The above is a simple model, which is just arguable enough to be sobering. Hopefully, such questions, issues, and considerations will add to the health of our own skepticisms without at the same time immobilizing us. Certainly we should listen well to critics of our work and examine carefully the Roshamon of responses available to us. The fact remains that in our work we are dealing with the most precious component of humanity — humanness itself. Let us not forget that.

Certainly one of the waking nightmares we have, as editors and contributors to this book, comes from the agony of imagining how our material could well be misused, abused, and seized upon as a rationalization for all sorts of teaching malpractice. In *Human Teaching for Human Learning* there is a chapter entitled "Proceed with Caution." I recommend that chapter to the readers of this book. One of the points made in the chapter is that the teacher or professional person who is using confluent approaches ought to be aware of what this does for *him*, what goodies are in it for him. Hopefully, out of this awareness will come more intelligent use of the approaches, "more intelligent" meaning more appropriate in terms of focusing on student needs in contrast to teacher needs. Until I, as a teacher, am aware of what it does for me to do whatever I am doing as a teacher, of how such actions provide gratification for my ego, meet my private needs, etc. — until I am aware of these conditions, I have no choice in the matter. Once I am aware of this, then I also become aware that I do have a choice and can seek alternatives that might be available, if I choose to do so. The option always remains, of course, that I might choose to continue using my students for my own needs. However, the more my sense of existential presence, of awareness of what is happening with me now as I relate to the world outside of me — which includes my students — then the more my decisions and choices can be made on the basis of a less limited reality. Thus this awareness will lower the probability of my using my students for my own needs, for I will see them more as they really are and less as some part of a projected need of mine.

A question that is raised constantly with regard to affective teaching or affective components in learning is that of the psychic or emotional harm that could be done to students. We know of no students who have been harmed by our work. It has been our experience, working with large numbers of teachers at all levels of instruction, that teachers who are going to abuse their teaching role will do so whether or not they have affective techniques available. If a teacher relates in a toxic or pathological way to his classroom context, whatever the source of his pathology or toxicity, this poison will out, no matter what the vehicle. Many of us have known toxic teachers and administrators who hold all manner of philosophical positions along the educational continuum. But we can hope that those using affective or humanistic or confluent approaches to teaching will have more chances to learn more about themselves through the process, through such exposures and experiences, and will, as a consequence, grow somewhat out of negative and destructive behavior. Such a probability would seem to exist more as a consequence of these innovative approaches than would be likely within a more rigid, highly structured, inflexible, and traditional approach, based on a closed system of punitive, repressive, and authoritarian values.

However, this does not answer the question of how the work in this book could be misused or abused. An example of the lack of awareness with which this book could be misued is illustrated by statements made by a teacher during a workshop conducted by me. In an introductory experiential part of the workshop, I had the members of a group move about in a circle with their eyes closed, experiencing one another through handclasps. After the exercise this teacher made the comment that he felt strange knowing that while his eyes were closed he was being observed by the leader of the exercise, and that now he knew how his own students must have felt when he was doing similar exercises with them in the classroom (he had presented himself as a confluent teacher). What this person had missed was that if he were truly a confluent teacher he would have known at the time how his students were responding to the exercise that he was leading, either by observing how they were acting or by seeking feedback after the exercise through some sort of processing, and that this was precisely a reason for doing the exercise in the first place. The integration of emotion and thinking is a continually ongoing process. When a teacher introduces an experience for his students and ignores the affective consequences, he is missing a major basis for confluence in education. It is like buying new clothes and carrying them around on a clotheshanger without ever putting them on.

We would like to reiterate a fundamental ground rule for all work utilizing confluent education. *No one has to do anything he does not want to do as far as affective experiences go.* Not only should the confluent teacher reiterate this ground rule, but he should also be continually alert to any pressure, no matter how subtle, from himself or members of his class, to explicitly or implicitly push an individual. If the teacher maintains an awareness of student affective response, through both observation and frequent occasions for feedback, such pressure will be less likely to occur. If he has some question about what is happening in his class he can always call in a colleague to observe.

At this stage we do feel confident that confluent education is effective for a great many students. It may, however, in its present stage of development not be appropriate for all students. There are students who seem not to want it, or some parts of it, or seem not to be ready for it. Toward this end, as mentioned in our introduction, we see pluralistic approaches as an expeditious structure to provide a place for confluent education within the educational establishment, and not just through the use of the alternative school model. As we have shown, good confluent practices are readily usable in conventional classrooms. Those teachers, students, and parents who want confluent education should be provided confluent education tracks or other structural opportunities for following and building on the approaches to learning and teaching described in this book.

In sum, we state again: Education is a human enterprise!

This is a postulate upon which confluent education, as we interpret it, is built. We use a democratic society as our frame of reference — democratic, that is, within political, social, and economic categories. Realistically, we admit inadequacies in terms of certain present functioning within these categories. However, this is precisely why we hold confluent education to have such promise for a fuller realization of the democratic potential of our society. More independent, fully functioning individuals, who can perceive clearly and act rationally; who can make choices instead of having choices made for them; who can take responsibility for their private existence and their social milieu — these are the goals which we as writers of this book hold for confluent education.

We have much, very much, yet to learn. Basic questions still remain — with whom, when, under what conditions, at what level, in what sequence, etc. We have learned some things. We have shared much of this in the preceding pages. At least we have moved beyond the beginning. You are most welcome to continue the journey with us.

SELECTED BIBLIOGRAPHY

GESTALT /

Dennison, George. *The Lives of Children: The Story of the First Street School.* New York: Random House, 1969.

Fagan, Joen and Shepherd, Irma Lee, eds. *Gestalt Therapy Now.* Palo Alto, Calif.: Science and Behavior Books, 1970.

Lederman, Janet. *Anger and the Rocking Chair.* New York: Viking Press, 1973.

Naranjo, Claudio. *The Techniques of Gestalt Therapy.* Berkeley, Calif.: The SAT Press, 1973.

———. "Contributions of Gestalt Therapy," in *Ways of Growth: Approaches to Expanding Awareness,* ed. H. A. Otto and J. Mann. New York: Grossman Publishers, 1968.

Perls, Frederick S. *Ego, Hunger and Aggression.* New York: Random House, 1969.

———. "Gestalt Therapy and Human Potentialities." Esalen Paper No. 1. Big Sur, Calif.: Esalen Institute, 1965.

———. *Gestalt Therapy Verbatim.* Lafayette, Calif.: Real People Press, 1969.

———. *In and Out the Garbage Pail.* Lafayette, Calif.: Real People Press, 1969.

———. *The Gestalt Approach and Eyewitness to Therapy.* Ben Lomond, Calif.: Science and Behavior Books, 1973.

———, Hefferline, R. F., and Goodman, Paul. *Gestalt Therapy: Excitement and Growth in Human Personality.* New York: Dell, 1965.

Polster, Erving and Polster, Miriam. *Gestalt Therapy Integrated.* New York: Brunner-Mazel, 1973.

Pursglove, Paul D., ed. *Recognitions in Gestalt Therapy.* New York: Funk & Wagnalls, 1968.

Schiffman, Muriel. *Gestalt Self Therapy and Further Techniques for Personal Growth.* Menlo Park, Calif.: Self Therapy Press, 1971.

———. *Self Therapy: Techniques for Personal Growth.* 340 Santa Monica Avenue, Menlo Park, Calif.: Author, 1967.

Stevens, Barry. *Don't Push the River.* Lafayette, Calif.: Real People Press, 1970.

Stevens, John O. *Awareness: Exploring, Experimenting, Experiencing.* Lafayette, Calif.: Real People Press, 1971.

CONFLUENT EDUCATION /

Alschuler, Alfred S. *Developing Achievement Motivation in Adolescents.* Englewood Cliffs, N. J.: Educational Technology Publications, 1973.

Assagioli, Roberto. *Psychosynthesis.* New York: Viking Press, 1971.

———. *The Act of Will.* New York: Viking Press, 1973.

Borton, Terry. *Reach, Touch and Teach: Student Concerns and Process Education.* New York: McGraw-Hill, 1970.

Bradford, Leland P., Gibb, J., and Benne, K., eds. *T-Group Theory and Laboratory Method: Innovation in Re-Education.* New York: John Wiley, 1964.

Brown, George I. "Affectivity, Classroom Climate, and Teaching." Washington, D.C.: American Federation of Teachers, 1971. EMS No. 6.

———. *Human Teaching for Human Learning.* New York: Viking Press, 1971.

Bugental, J. F. T. *Challenges of Humanistic Psychology.* New York: McGraw-Hill, 1967.

Burton, Arthur, ed. *Encounter: The Theory and Practice of Encounter Groups.* San Francisco: Jossey-Bass, 1969.

Combs, Arthur. *Perceiving 'Behaving' Becoming.* Washington, D.C.: NEA, 1962.

De Mille, Richard. *Put Your Mother on the Ceiling.* New York: Viking Press, 1972.

Egan, Gerard. *Encounter: Group Processes for Interpersonal Growth.* Belmont, Calif.: Brooks-Cole, 1970.

———. *Encounter Groups: Basic Readings.* Belmont, Calif.: Brooks-Cole, 1971.

Fantini, Mario D. and Weinstein, Gerald. *The Disadvantaged: Challenge to Education.* New York: Harper & Row, 1968.

———. *Making Urban Schools Work: Social Realities and the Urban School.* New York: Holt, 1968.

———. *Toward a Contact Curriculum.* New York: Anti-Defamation League of B'nai B'rith, 1968.

Featherstone, Joseph. *Schools Where Children Learn.* New York: Liveright, 1971.

Feldenkrais, Moshe. *Awareness Through Movement.* New York: Harper & Row, 1972.

Frankl, Viktor E. *Man's Search for Meaning: An Introduction to Logotherapy.* Boston: Beacon Press, 1963.

Fromm, Erich. *The Forgotten Language: An Introduction to the Understanding of Dreams, Fairy Tales and Myths.* New York: Rinehart, 1951.

Gattegno, Caleb. *The Adolescent and His Will.* New York: Outerbridge & Dienstfrey, 1971.

Getzels, J. W. and Jackson, P. W. *Creativity and Intelligence.* New York: John Wiley, 1962.

Ghiselin, B., ed. *The Creative Process.* Berkeley, Calif.: University of California Press, 1952.

Gordon, Thomas. *Parent Effectiveness Training.* New York: Peter Wyden, 1970.

Gordon, W. J. J. *Synectics: The Development of Creative Capacity.* New York: Harper & Row, 1961.

Greer, Mary and Rubenstein, Bonnie. *Will the Real Teacher Please Stand Up: A Primer in Humanistic Education.* Pacific Palisades, Calif.: Goodyear Publishing Co., 1972.

Gunther, Bernard. *Sense Relaxation: Below Your Mind.* New York: Macmillan, 1968.

————. *What To Do Till the Messiah Comes.* New York: Macmillan, 1971.

Hentoff, Nat. *Our Children Are Dying.* New York: Viking Press, 1966.

Heath, Douglas H. *Humanizing Schools.* New York: Hayden Book Co., 1971.

Herndon, James. *How to Survive in Your Native Land.* New York: Simon & Schuster, 1971.

Holt, John. *What Do I Do Monday?* New York: Dutton, 1970.

Huxley, Laura. *You Are Not the Target.* New York: Farrar, Strauss & Giroux, 1963.

Jones, Richard M. *Fantasy and Feeling in Education.* New York: New York University Press, 1968.

Koch, Kenneth. *Wishes, Lies and Dreams.* New York: Chelsea House (Random House), 1970.

Kubie, L. S. *Neurotic Distortion of the Creative Process.* Lawrence, Kansas: University of Kansas Press, 1958.

Leonard, George. *Education and Ecstasy.* New York: Delacorte Press, 1968.

————. *The Transformation.* New York: Delacorte Press, 1972.

Luft, Joseph. *Group Processes: An Introduction to Group Dynamics.* Palo Alto, Calif.: The National Press, 1963.

Lyon, Harold C., Jr. *Learning to Feel: Feeling to Learn.* Columbus, Ohio: Charles E. Merrill, 1971.

Marshall, Bernice. *Experiences in Being.* Belmont, Calif.: Brooks-Cole, 1971.

Maslow, A. H. *The Farther Reaches of Human Nature.* New York: Viking Press, 1971.

May, Rollo. *Love and Will.* New York: Norton, 1969.

————. *Power and Innocence.* New York: Norton, 1972.

Murphy, Michael. *Golf in the Kingdom.* New York: Viking Press, 1972.

Naranjo, Claudio. *The One Quest.* New York: Viking Press, 1973.

Otto, H. A. and Mann, J., eds. *Ways of Growth: Approaches to Expanding Human Awareness.* New York: Grossman Publishers, 1968.

Patterson, C. H. *Humanistic Education.* Englewood Cliffs, New Jersey: Prentice-Hall, 1973.

Polanyi, Michael. *The Tacit Dimension.* Garden City, New York: Doubleday, 1966.

Postman, N. and Weingartner, C. *The Soft Revolution.* New York: Dell, 1971.

Raths, L., Harnin, M., and Simon, S. *Values and Teaching: Working with Values in the Classroom.* Columbus, Ohio: Charles E. Merrill, 1966.

Read, Herbert. *Education Through Art.* New York: Pantheon, 1945.

Rogers, C. R. *Carl Rogers on Encounter Groups.* New York: Harper & Row, 1970.

————. *Freedom to Learn.* Columbus, Ohio: Charles E. Merrill, 1969.

Rogers, C. R. and Stevens, B. *Person to Person: The Problem of Being Human.* Walnut Creek, Calif.: Real People Press, 1967.

Rubin, Louis J. *Facts and Feelings in the Classroom.* New York: Viking Press, 1974.

Schmuck, R. A. and Schmuck, Patricia. *Group Processes in the Classroom.* Dubuque, Iowa: William C. Brown, 1971.

Schrank, Jeffrey. *Media in Value Education: A Critical Guide.* Chicago: Argus Communications, 1970.

Silberman, Charles E. *Crisis in the Classroom: The Remaking of American Education.* New York: Random House, 1970.

Simpson, Elizabeth L. *Democracy's Stepchildren.* San Francisco: Jossey-Bass, 1971.

Spolin, Viola. *Improvisation for the Theatre.* Evanston, Ill.: Northwestern University Press, 1963.

Sutich, A. and Vich, Miles, eds. *Readings in Humanistic Psychology.* New York: The Free Press, 1969.

Weinstein, Gerald and Fantini, Mario D. *Toward Humanistic Education: A Curriculum of Affect.* New York: Praeger, 1970.